NATIONAL GEOGRAPHIC

TRAVELER

hong kong

NATIONAL GEOGRAPHIC
TRAVELER

hong kong

by Phil Macdonald

National Geographic
Washington, D.C.

CONTENTS

Pages 2–3: Hiker ascending Victoria Peak, Central District
Left: Tai chi at sunrise on Stanley Beach

TRAVELING WITH EYES OPEN

Alert travelers go with a purpose and leave with a benefit. If you travel responsibly, you can help support wildlife conservation, historic preservation, and cultural enrichment in the places you visit. You can enrich your own travel experience as well.

To be a geo-savvy traveler:

- Recognize that your presence has an impact on the places you visit.

- Spend your time and money in ways that sustain local character. (Besides, it's more interesting that way.)

- Value the destination's natural and cultural heritage.

- Respect the local customs and traditions.

- Express appreciation to local people about things you find interesting and unique to the place: its nature and scenery, music and food, historic villages and buildings.

- Vote with your wallet: Support the people who support the place, patronizing businesses that make an effort to celebrate and protect what's special there. Seek out shops, local restaurants, inns, and tour operators who love their home—who love taking care of it and showing it off. Avoid businesses that detract from the character of the place.

- Enrich yourself, taking home memories and stories to tell, knowing that you have contributed to the preservation and enhancement of the destination.

That is the type of travel now called geotourism, defined as "tourism that sustains or enhances the geographical character of a place—its environment, culture, aesthetics, heritage, and the well-being of its residents." To learn more, visit National Geographic's Center for Sustainable Destinations at *www .nationalgeographic.com/travel/sustainable.*

NATIONAL GEOGRAPHIC

TRAVELER

hong kong

ABOUT THE AUTHORS

Phil Macdonald moved to Hong Kong from Sydney, Australia, in 1989 to continue a career in journalism that had begun eight years earlier in the west coast city of Perth. He worked for the *Hong Kong Standard* and the *South China Morning Post* for a number of years before settling—by way of Laos and Singapore—in Phuket, Thailand, in 1996. He now lives in Bangkok, working as a freelance journalist and writer, and contributing to a number of regional and international publications. His interests include Southeast Asian politics and recent history, and the beaches of Southern Thailand. He is author of the *National Geographic Traveler Taiwan* and co-author of *National Geographic Traveler Thailand* guidebooks.

Ian Lyons helped with research for the Hong Kong Island South and New Territories chapters.

Rory Boland updated and wrote new features for the 2009 edition. He moved to Hong Kong in 2006 and worked as editor at *CityLife* magazine, one of the city's prime tourist publications. He has also contributed articles to the *South China Morning Post* and served as local editor for the first edition of *Zagat Hong Kong*. Boland now lives in Warsaw, Poland, working as a freelance journalist specializing in Central and Eastern Europe.

Charting Your Trip

Like London and New York, Hong Kong is a blockbuster of a town. Touted as Asia's World City and rarely out of the headlines, visitors arrive expecting to be wowed, and Hong Kong doesn't disappoint.

The undoubted star of the show is the city's iconic skyline, a gleaming forest of skyscrapers tightly bound together along the streets of Central. The scene is Futurama meets the Jetsons; webs of overhead walkways wind between buildings, while outdoor escalators whisk frazzled businessmen between bedroom communities halfway up a mountain and their offices below. Hong Kong is where man took on nature and won. Yet the city's strength is in its diversity and, even here at its capitalist core, traditional Hong Kong thrives. Multicolored Buddhist temples with smoke drifting from their doorways, steaming streetside food stalls, and frantic markets packed with bargain hunting locals are all slotted in between the skyscrapers. East and West slide together here like Lego, where self-made millionaires will consult the *Wall Street Journal* and

A coin depicting a dragon, one of the 12 animals in the Chinese astrology

chim fortune sticks before heading for the stock market. Complex and chaotic, the city's energy and enthusiasm is relentless and infectious. And thanks to an excellent metro, bus, and ferry system, plus plentiful and inexpensive taxis, visitors can easily experience it all.

Glitzy, Glamorous Central

The natural starting point for visitors is the Central district on the northern portion of Hong Kong Island, the city's very own temple to capitalism. Here you'll find the designer skyscrapers that have made the city's skyline one of the most impressive in the world. Hidden inside are several of the city's plushest malls, hosting an endless parade of stylish emporiums and swanky boutiques. The area also pulls in Hong Kong's moneyed playthings, splashing their cash in the restaurants and bars of Lan Kwai Fong and SoHo.

The city's passion is, of course, shopping, and Hong Kong's reputation as a haven for hardcore shoppers is well deserved. Perhaps the best area to hunt down a deal is the maze of pedestrianized streets around the Causeway Bay area. Thousands of shops buzz until late into the evening, sating the city's never-ending desire for the next big bargain. Away from the frenzied consumerism, tai chi enthusiasts take advantage of Victoria Park, bending and swaying as the sun stirs over the city.

Airport Express

The best and quickest way to travel between Chek Lap Kok Airport and downtown Hong Kong is on the Airport Express train. The service runs at 12-minute intervals between 5:50 a.m. and 1:13 a.m., taking just 24 minutes to travel the 21-mile (34 km) route between the airport, which is on Lantau Island, and Hong Kong Station in Central, less to Kowloon Station. Tickets cost HK$100 one-way and HK$180 return, and are available inside the terminal.

At both Hong Kong and Kowloon stations there is the option to use free Airport Express buses, which connect to more than 50 Hong Kong hotels; you'll need to present your ticket.

On returning, Airport Express offers in-town check-in, allowing you to check in, including luggage, up to 24 hours in advance (check with your individual airline for specifics).

Crowded, Clamorous Kowloon

Ever the bridesmaid, never the bride, Kowloon, across Victoria Harbour, is Hong Kong Island's scruffier, grittier neighbor. Here, the ever polished mask of modern Hong Kong slips, giving way to more down-to-earth and traditional side.

Immediately on the water's edge is the tourist headquarters of Tsim Sha Tsui, a hopping neighborhood where majestic hotels rub elbows with seedy guesthouses, and a collection of world-class museums brandish Hong Kong's cultural credentials. Along Nathan Road, under glowing neon signs, tailors and touts from every corner of the world jostle tourists looking for their next customer.

Nearby are the implausibly packed streets of Yau Ma Tei and Mong Kok, brimming with street sellers slopping out pots of tasty noodles, fortune-tellers forecasting the future from the bumps in your head, and nighttime markets hawking clothes from across the border. This circus of activity plays to the sounds of clicking mah-jongg tiles and the strains of Cantonese Opera.

NOT TO BE MISSED:

A Beckoning Countryside

Hong Kong's urban jungle is well documented, but few visitors are aware of the city's secret garden, the New Territories. This swath of land north of Kowloon, running right up to the Chinese border, comprises nearly 70 percent of Hong Kong's territory. Luscious, subtropical greenery carpets the area, providing a sanctuary for a safari collection of wildlife, including a number of dedicated reserves. These range from the Mai Po Marshes with their abundant birdlife to the Tai Po Kau Nature Preserve with its pangolins, civet cats, wild boars, and lush flora. Indeed, much of the New Territories is given

Junk cruising Victoria Harbour

Using the Octopus Card

For those planning to use Hong Kong's extensive and efficient public transport system, the simplest and cheapest way to get around is with an Octopus card. This stored value card can be used on nearly all forms of public transport in the city, aside from a few ferry and minibus routes, as well as many shops in Hong Kong, including Park N Shop supermarkets and 7-Eleven.

To use, simply pass the card over an electronic sensor. Cards cost HK$150, of which HK$100 is usable credit and HK$50 a refundable deposit, forfeit if returned within three months. Cards can be bought and recharged at MTR Customer Service Centres inside MTR stations and New World First Bus Customer Service Centres.

over to conserving nature; the Country Parks system is expansive, encompassing mountains and shoreline at the same time offering some superb hiking trails.

Hong Kong's wildlife aren't the only ones to find sanctuary in the New Territories' outback; traditional village life also flourishes in a number of small clan villages spread throughout the territory. These walled villages have been comparatively untouched by Hong Kong's leaping changes and have witnessed the British march in and out of Hong Kong with their culture barely budging.

Islands Worth Exploring

The final part of the Hong Kong jigsaw is its 200 plus islands, spread around the South China Sea. Most are uninhabited and only reached by private sampan, but are ideal beach bolt holes, with endless stretches of empty, golden sands. The largest, Lantau, has its own man-made attractions, including Hong Kong Disneyland, the Po Lin Monastery, and Ngong Ping Cable Car, as well as some popular beaches. Smaller but closer to Hong Kong Island is Lamma Island, one of several that are magnets for artists and dropouts looking to escape the relentless pace of the city. They brought with them bargain-priced pubs and matchless seafood restaurants.

Exotic Excursions

Those with more time certainly shouldn't overlook at least a day trip to Macau, Hong Kong's sister SAR (Special Administrative Region). Frequently in the headlines for its reputation as Asia's sin city, Macau is certainly on a roll when it comes to casinos. The city is booming, attracting in recent years, the likes of the Sands and the Venetian; indeed, Macau is now a larger gambling city than Las Vegas. However, it's not all about roulette; Macau is bristling with the colonial charm of its former owner, Portugal. Buildings here have been far better preserved than in Hong Kong, and, in the city center at least, you'll find an intimate and relaxed slice of sleepy Lisbon.

Mobile Audio Host

Ideal for those who want to explore Hong Kong under their own steam, the Mobile Audio Host system is a city information service accessed through your cell phone. The system already contains commentary on more than 40 of Hong Kong's major sights, as well as restaurant recommendations, shopping tips, and event listings. The easiest way to use the system is to purchase a HK$60 PIN card, which gives you 72 hours of access with no roaming charges. You can purchase a card at any Hong Kong Tourism Board Information and Service Centre (Star Ferry Concourse, Tsim Sha Tsui). A free MP3 version should be available at the time of print (www.discoverhong kong.com).

Another worthy excursion is to Guangzhou, formerly known as Canton. Part of the city has preserved its English colonial past, but its spirit now is the new China, with its highways, bustle, commerce, and skyscrapers.

What to Bring

Hong Kong enjoys a subtropical climate. The coldest weeks are mid-December to February when the temperature can sink to 50° F (10° C). Accordingly, winter clothes are not needed, but cool weather gear is, especially in the winter months after sundown.

May to September is warm and often humid as well as rainy—most of Hong Kong's precipitation occurs during these months. Although summer is warm, the air-conditioning in buildings and on public transportation can be cool enough to warrant a sweater or a light jacket.

From mid-spring to late fall, light-weight, loose, cotton clothing is advisable. T-shirts and neat shorts are acceptable streetwear, especially during the hottest summer months. Some of the higher-end restaurants expect men to wear a jacket, if not a necktie, but most settle for neat, casual attire. Much of your time will be spent on foot, so bring comfortable walking shoes. Sandals—not flip-flops—are acceptable. If you plan on hiking in Hong Kong's country parks, bring a sturdy pair of hiking boots.

No matter what you wear, dress neatly, because people in Hong Kong often measure you by your appearance. And although Hong Kong is a cosmopolitan and fashionable city, women should refrain from wearing revealing clothing.

Final note: It's likely you're going to shop, so leave empty space in your suitcase for purchases.

History & Culture

Chinese New Year decorations

Hong Kong Today

More than a decade after the event, outsiders still frequently ask, "Has Hong Kong changed since its return to China?" Some locals will say "Yes," pointing to political and business deference, even kowtowing, to its new overlord and subtle changes in laws they see as eroding the territory's freedoms. Others will give an emphatic "No." Hong Kong, they say, is still the freewheeling, materialistic, hard-edged, cosmopolitan, exhilarating place it was before the handover.

The doubts that arose among Hong Kong's people during the decade and a half leading up to the handover turned to near panic after June 4, 1989, when troops of the People's Liberation Army violently crushed democracy demonstrations in Beijing's Tiananmen Square. But the dust has long settled. During the ensuing, often painstaking, negotiations that took place between the British and Chinese over the future of Hong Kong, confidence slowly returned.

In the end, the transfer to Chinese sovereignty—although not without more than a few rocky moments—was remarkably smooth. Hong Kong now exists under the Chinese flag as a Special Administrative Region, or SAR. Under the concept of "one country–two systems," coined by China's late leader Deng Xiaoping (1904–1997), it is guaranteed near-full autonomy for 50 years beyond the July 1, 1997, handover.

> When you squeeze more than seven million busy people into just 116 square miles (300 sq km), you get a crowded, bustling, loud, and pushy city in a terrible hurry.

Hong Kong moves with such unbridled dynamism that even these dramatic recent events are brushed aside, if not actually forgotten. It's a new time with a new landlord, but things remain essentially the same. People still go about their business, and pleasure, with a frantic energy rarely found anywhere else. And when you squeeze more than seven million busy people into just 116 square miles (300 sq km), you get a crowded, bustling, loud, and pushy city in a terrible hurry.

Even by the standards of other Asian cities, where frenetic street life is part of the culture, the sheer number of people on Hong Kong's streets is staggering. They are everywhere, both day and night; shopping, working, eating, walking, chatting loudly. But noise and crowds don't faze the gregarious Cantonese—they revel in it, although many visitors have a hard time coping.

Money

What drives this vitality? Money. Hong Kong's economic system embodies the purest form of capitalism found anywhere, a laissez-faire policy of almost total nongovernment interference in business. This suits the hardworking, business-savvy Cantonese, whose obsession with wealth is often regarded as downright obscene by outsiders. But it would be glib to describe this obsession as pure greed. Hong Kong's population was built on successive waves of immigration

The shopping experience at the Temple Street Night Market in Kowloon includes lots of haggling, crowds, street theater, and fortune-tellers.

The third largest of Hong Kong's 230 islands, Lamma is an easy escape from the urban hum.

from neighboring Guangdong Province; poor people escaping famines, wars, and communism arrived in the territory with nothing. Financial security, created through shrewdness and hard work, therefore became the number-one priority.

Wealth is also tied up in the concept of "face," or showing respect. It proffers enormous respect from others who believe those that attain it must carry the admirable qualities of hard work and perseverance. Once this wealth is obtained, it must be displayed in order to earn all-important "face" from others. Hence the ostentatious displays of luxury cars, expensive jewelry and watches, designer-label clothing, and beautiful, immaculately furnished apartments. To the Chinese, showboating is a way of life, and money does indeed buy happiness.

East Meets West

Hong Kong greets East and West with a sleight of hand. Outwardly, it could not appear more Westernized, with its ultramodern airport, the gleaming skyscrapers of Central District, efficient, modern public transportation, clean streets, shady well-kept parks, businesspeople in sharp suits, fashion-conscious women sporting the latest designer brands, and crowded department stores full of everything that is new and desired. But at the core of Hong Kong's vitality lies a culture and traditions that could not be more Chinese.

Ironically, under British rule, Hong Kong became the most Chinese of Chinese cities. While Mao Zedong's Red Guards laid waste to traditions, festivals, customs, and beliefs on the mainland during the Cultural Revolution of the 1960s and 1970s, Hong Kong remained largely unaffected.

Today, in the shabby, winding streets close to Central, row upon row of Chinese herbalists dispense ingredients such as snake musk, pearl powder, lizard skins, and deer antlers. In small shop-house factories Chinese artisans turn out mah-jongg tiles, company chops (seals), decorated chopsticks, and coffins. In other places, shopkeepers use abacuses to tally bills for an astonishing variety of rice and teas. Butchers carve up pigs, and old ladies haggle at fish markets. Inside numerous small, nondescript temples, crushed between high-rise residential towers, devotees burn joss sticks and offer fruit to Taoist gods before seeking counsel with fortune-tellers who read faces and palms. In Victoria Park, Hong Kong Island's largest green space, hundreds of people gather at dawn and dusk to practice the Chinese martial art of tai chi.

Hong Kong's numerous festivals (see p. 50), steeped in centuries-old Chinese traditions, do a lot to define the spirit of the place. Almost always elaborate and colorful, and invariably accompanied by a snaking dragon dance and ear-splitting fireworks, they are approached with an enthusiasm not seen on mainland China.

East does not clash with West in Hong Kong, as happens in other Asian cities, which see Western culture as undermining traditional beliefs. Rather it blends like nowhere else. Here, it is not uncommon for a successful businessman, wise in the ways of Western wheeling and dealing, to hire a *feng shui* master (geomancer) to design his office in such a way that his business will prosper, or for an old lady to make offerings at a temple in the hope her shares on the stock exchange will continue to rise in value.

This successful East–West synergy, and its legacy of a colonial past which is still apparent, are what give Hong Kong much of its appeal. Here, thanks to a tenacious determination to maintain tradition and a ready acceptance of Western culture, discovering the East could not be easier.

Public Holidays

Because most Chinese holidays are based on the lunar calendar, their exact date changes from year to year (visit *www.gov.hk* for a given year's dates). On public holidays, all government offices close, as do some shops. Many public holidays are, however, an excuse for Hong Kongers to go on a shopping spree. The exception is Chinese New Year, when almost all shops close for three to seven days.

January 1	New Year's Day
January/ February	3 days for Chinese New Year
March/April	3 days for Easter; Ching Ming Festival
April/May	Buddha's Birthday
May 1	Labor Day
June	Tuen Ng Dragon Boat Festival
July 1	Hong Kong Special Administrative Region Establishment Day
September/ October	Chinese Mid-Autumn Festival; Chung Yeung Festival
October 1	China National Day
December 25-26	Christmas and Boxing Day

Visitors' Hong Kong

One of your first stops should be Victoria Peak, not only for its magnificent views but also to get some perspective of Hong Kong. From these lofty heights, the territory spreads out at your feet. Remarkable views sweep down steep wooded slopes to the skyscrapers of Central and Wan Chai, across busy Victoria Harbour to the Kowloon Peninsula, and beyond to the hills of the New Territories. Take a walk around the shoulder of the Peak to view the verdant hills, deep valleys, and the convoluted coastline indented with coves and beaches of Hong Kong Island South. Having seen Hong Kong laid out before you, it's time to explore.

Its compactness, along with its excellent public transportation, glut of inexpensive taxis, and streets safe from crime make the territory very visitor friendly. Many areas of Hong Kong can be discovered on foot, especially on Hong Kong Island North and parts of Kowloon.

One of the great delights of the city is to lose yourself in the warren of side streets and alleys that run through Western District and Wan Chai on Hong Kong Island North, and Yau Ma Tai and Mong Kok in Kowloon. This is street life at its best: A barely controlled confusion of thronging crowds spilling off the sidewalks; food vendors selling chicken feet, fish balls, and pieces of cuttlefish on sticks; huge, gaudy neon signs overhead; and street after street of small shops selling all manner of exotic and mysterious goods, from herbal remedies to religious paraphernalia.

Lucky Fish

Goldfish were popularized by emperors of the Tang dynasty (618-907 A.D.), who selectively bred the golden carp (their hue was caused by a genetic mutation) in royal ponds. Since then, carp have had a large presence in Chinese culture.

Linguistically, all fish are considered lucky, as the word for fish, *yu*, is pronounced the same as the word for bounty or surplus. The fish are also mainstays in Chinese art. Interestingly enough, feng shui dictates that having a painting of a goldfish is just as lucky as having an actual fish.

This appears be a world away from sophisticated, glitzy Central District—where modern skyscrapers housing Hong Kong's corporate movers and shakers, opulent hotels, and shopping malls full of designer-label goods cluster on reclaimed land between Victoria Harbour and brooding Victoria Peak. But in some cases, there are only a few blocks separating the bustling grittiness of the side streets and the areas where Hong Kong's material wealth is unashamedly on show.

A wall of high-rise buildings runs almost the full length of Hong Kong Island's northern corridor, but over the peaks that run along the spine of the island and down on its south side, things are decidedly different. Villages nestle in bays lined with tidy beaches and backed by forested hills. Roads climbing over these peaks offer spectacular views of the countryside and the South China Sea beyond. Not surprisingly, Hong Kong Island South is where Hong Kong's wealthy have chosen to build their mansions.

The subway—or Mass Transit Railway (MTR)—burrows under Victoria Harbour in three different places, making access to Kowloon easy. But if you aren't in too much of a hurry, hop on the wonderful Star Ferry for the short trip across the harbor and take in the magnificent panoramas offered by Central's skyline and the

backdrop of Victoria Peak. The Star Ferry takes visitors to the tourist district of Tsim Sha
Tsui, an exuberant place of hotels, bars, restaurants, and an unbelievable number of retail
stores lining the streets, inside arcades, and multilevel shopping centers.

What surprises many first-time visitors is the amount of space set aside for national
parks—or country parks—as they are known in Hong Kong—about 40 percent, mostly
in the New Territories. Characterized by rugged peaks dropping off to wooded valleys
and the sparkling waters of the coastal areas, these country parks are crisscrossed with
miles of well-marked, well-maintained hiking trails. Allow a day for a trip to the New
Territories—if not for the hiking, at least to enjoy the cleaner air, quietude, and less frantic atmosphere. Sai Kung Peninsula in the eastern New Territories is recommended.

Spend a day or two exploring the outlying islands, too; Hong Kong has 234 islands,
the vast majority of them uninhabited. The main ones are easily reached by ferry from
Central and the ferry trip itself is a delight. The two most easily accessible islands are
Lantau—Hong Kong's biggest—and the smaller, more rural Lamma.

Crowds jostle at Hennessy Road in Causeway Bay, one of the city's popular shopping areas.

The People

Ninety-five percent of Hong Kong's population of more than seven million people are Chinese, and the vast majority are able to trace their roots back to the neighboring province of Guangdong. Cantonese dialect, food, and culture make up the fabric of society here. Since the British arrived in the 1840s, Hong Kong has been a magnet for immigrants from mainland China who are seeking a better life. Many faced extreme hardships in China, and Hong Kong was the place where they could improve their lives and those of their children. Rags-to-riches stories are commonplace.

A strong will to succeed can be traced back to these hard times, and parents have instilled these values in their children. People in Hong Kong have an incredible work ethic. It's not unusual for them to work 10 to 12 hours a day, six days a week, although in recent years the government has sought to reduce Hong Kong's exhausting work week to a more relaxed five days.

These long hours, teeming streets where you often have to battle just to stay on the sidewalks, and crowded living conditions—with families of five or six sometimes sharing a tiny apartment—have given many Hong Kong people a competitive and strident na-

From exotic to plain, it's on sale in Kowloon.

ture, often manifest, outwardly at least, in a brusqueness that can offend visitors. Don't always expect a smile and an exchange of pleasantries when making a purchase, or an apology when accidentally jostled or bumped. There is no outward display of hospitality shown to visitors as there is in most other parts of Asia, but neither is there hostility, for that matter. Although Hong Kong people will show a generosity of spirit toward their family and friends, if you are outside that circle, don't expect much.

But Hong Kong still remains a cosmopolitan city, made so by the diverse groups of foreigners who have made their home there, contributing to business, commerce, cuisine, culture, and religion, and giving Hong Kong its sophistication and uniqueness. Filipinos, numbering about 110,000, make up the largest group of foreign nationals. They are mainly women who work as domestic helpers for middle- and upper-class Chinese. Many Thais and Indonesians fill the same role. A large, but dwindling number of Americans, Australians, Canadians, British, and Europeans, collectively known as *gweilos* in Cantonese, make up the majority of the foreign business community. *Gweilos* is a derogatory term meaning "ghost people" or "foreign devils," although its meaning has softened somewhat with use.

Hong Kong also has a sizable population from South Asia. This mixture mainly of Indians and Pakistanis, many of whom have been in Hong Kong for generations, speak fluent Cantonese, hold Hong Kong passports, and are generally involved in retailing and trade. In recent years, as the mainland and Hong Kong have fostered ever stronger business links, an increasing number of mainland Chinese have moved to the city, which, combined with the huge number of mainland tourists, has seen Mandarin challenge English as the second language of choice.

Behavior

Constant contact with foreigners for the last 160 years has made the people of Hong Kong pretty much shock-proof when it comes to the strange ways of Westerners. But Asian concepts of "face," or showing respect, and a nonconfrontational approach to life are still strong. Although you are unlikely to encounter tense situations or bumbling bureaucracy, if you do, try to solve the situation calmly. Losing your temper will get you nowhere, and you will probably be regarded as a "stupid gweilo," not worth dealing with.

Hong Kong people dress well and you are expected to do the same. Clean T-shirts, shorts, and sandals are acceptable streetwear, but flip-flops and sleeveless vests are not. Neat casual wear will get you into all but the most exclusive restaurants.

Leisure

People work hard for their money, but they also know how to spend it, so much of their leisure time revolves around eating, drinking, and shopping with friends and family. Brunch at a noisy dim sum restaurant, followed by a shopping expedition, then possibly a movie and a big dinner at another restaurant is a popular way to spend Sunday—the only full day off for many.

Movies are extremely popular, especially the homegrown ones (see pp. 48–49). Movie theaters showing such films are full most nights of the week.

The young and middle-class have taken to the growing number of upscale Western-style bars, where they often spend a few hours in the evening, enjoying themselves and unwinding after a busy day at work. Trendy, expensive nightclubs, where possession of wealth can be displayed with abandon, are also popular. There are hundreds of noisy karaoke bars and dimly lit pubs where the young of Hong Kong spend their evenings

---

EXPERIENCE: Cantopop Karaoke

An integral part of Hong Kong culture, Cantopop swept the city off its feet during the 1980s and '90s with its combination of clean-cut Cantonese lyrics, catchy pop tunes, and well-marketed acts. Undoubtedly the best place to hear Cantopop is in karaoke bars. Try the strip of bars along Minden Avenue in Tsim Sha Tsui. If you're in a group, rent out a KTV (karaoke television) room, also called a karoake box. The ubiquitous Neway chain is popular; see *www.newaykb.com* for locations. A limited selection of English songs is usually offered.

Many of Hong Kong's 600-odd temples combine Buddhism, Taoism, and Confucianism into a spiritual whole; the atmosphere is much more relaxed than in a Christian church.

drinking and playing hand games such as "rock, paper, scissors."

In summer, legions of people head to Hong Kong Island's beaches on weekends, while the hiking trails and picnic areas in the country parks in the New Territories are popular for those wanting to escape the frantic urban areas.

Hong Kong's citizens love to gamble, and horse racing (see pp. 92–93) is especially popular. During the race season, between mid-September and June, betting enthusiasts pack the stands at Happy Valley and Sha Tin racetracks, while those who don't make it to the track bet at one of the hundreds of off-track betting outlets. At each of the twice-weekly race meetings, a staggering six million bets are laid—quite incredible for a place that has a total population amounting to only a little more than seven million.

Religion & Superstition

Cynics may say that the major religion in Hong Kong is money, and there is surely more than the usual amount of adoration for it here. But there are about 600 temples, shrines, and monasteries throughout the territory, many combining the detached view of life offered by Buddhism, the humility and nonassertiveness of Taoism, and the high principles of Confucianism.

The high-mindedness of these philosophies is often eschewed for more temporal needs. Great attention is paid to appeasing the dead—through ancestral worship—and the spirits, with the aim of improving your own lot. The Chinese don't like to leave things to chance. *Joss,* or luck, has to be kept on your side by mollifying a plethora of gods and spirits with gifts and prayers. Keeping the gods and spirits happy (or at bay in the case of the bad ones) makes joss and its natural partner, wealth, come your way.

Similarly, the counsel of fortune-tellers, who are found mostly in or around temples, is often sought as a way to plan one's life and attain wealth. Dates and numbers that are believed to be auspicious in Chinese culture are central to many actions. Weddings are planned, offices and restaurants are opened, foundation stones of buildings are laid, and newly built boats are launched on dates that are seen to guarantee success.

Numbers are hugely symbolic, based on their sounds in multitonal Cantonese. The number eight *(baat),* for example, sounds similar to the word for prosperity *(fat dat),* and to have it in your telephone number or your license plate is indeed fortunate. The number three *(saam)* sounds like the word for lively or flourishing *(saan),* so it is another lucky number. However, four *(say)* is similar in sound to death *(say—* different tone), so it's a number to be avoided.

The sound principle also works with food—for example, *fat choy,* a dark, fibrous vegetable, is often cooked at Chinese New Year to bring wealth *(fat).* *Kung hei fat choi* (good wishes, good fortune) is the standard New Year greeting.

During the race season, between mid-September and June, betting enthusiasts pack the Happy Valley and Sha Tin racetracks.

Hong Kong's British colonial past has left it with a sizable and active Christian community of more than 500,000, with Protestant and Catholic faiths spread evenly. There are numerous denominational churches scattered throughout the territory. The majority of Hong Kong's 100,000 Muslims are Chinese, although there are significant numbers of devotees originally from South Asia, many of whose families came as soldiers attached to the British army and police. Hong Kong's 12,000 Hindus and Sikhs also are mostly from South Asian backgrounds, and there are some 3,000 members of the Jewish faith here. ■

Food & Drink

Along with shopping, eating is one of Hong Kong's great pastimes. It's usually a social occasion—friends and family gather around a large table to eat amid toasting, chattering, and laughter. The territory is Asia's culinary capital, with a cosmopolitan selection befitting an international city and one restaurant for every 700 people. In 2007, a smoking ban was introduced in both bars and restaurants, so the haze of smoke that once hung over most meals has cleared .

Regional Specialties

Hong Kong abounds in China's huge variety of regional specialties, whose ingredients reflect their geographical location. In northern China, noodles, dumplings, and steamed breads predominate. In the south, rice is plentiful, as are tropical fruits. Coastal areas use a lot of seafood, while farther inland pork and chicken abound. In such regions as Sichuan where spices grow, they are used liberally in the cooking.

Street Food: Hong Kong has countless open-air food stands, from which vendors dispense such specialties as fish balls, cuttlefish-on-a-stick, sausages, noodles, chicken feet, fermented fried tofu, roasted chestnuts (in winter), and grilled, steamed, and deep-fried tidbits. Tiny *dai pai dongs* (see p. 27) can be found all over Hong Kong. Some serve excellent noodle soup, although the entrails and stomach linings hanging from hooks in the exposed kitchens of some of these places can be a turnoff.

Cantonese: This distinctive style from Hong Kong's neighboring province of Guangdong is the most popular and the most varied of all Chinese cuisines. It emphasizes fresh food, using vegetables, chicken, and seafood as its main ingredients. Meals are prepared either by steaming or stir-frying in a wok on a high flame to enhance the taste. Though spices are rarely, if ever, used, sauces are common.

Favorite Cantonese dishes include shrimp with chili sauce, crab in black bean sauce, whole steamed fish, roast pigeon, fried noodles with beef and green bell peppers, barbecue pork, and drunken shrimp —that is to say, shrimp steamed in rice wine.

Beijing: Noodles and dumplings are more prevalent in Beijing's regional cuisine. Restaurant chefs often put on an entertaining show of noodlemaking to the delight of their diners.

They twist and twirl the dough while also peeling off thinner and thinner strands.

The most famous Beijing dish is Peking duck, served on pancakes with plum sauce. Also delicious is beggar's chicken—the bird is stuffed with a mixture of black mushrooms, pickled cabbage, herbs, and onions, then wrapped in lotus leaves, coated in wine-soaked clay, and baked. Mongolian hotpot, usually eaten in the winter, is another favorite. Meat and a variety of vegetables are cooked in a pot on a burner at the diner's table.

Chiu Chow: Chiu Chow cuisine originated in a coastal region in Guangdong Province. Similar to Cantonese, it stresses seafood, and the sauces tend to be sweeter. Westerners may find some dishes unpalatable, such as coagulated pig blood stir-fried with green onions. Duck and goose are popular; baked lobster in pepper sauce is a delight. Chiu Chow's signature foods are shark's fin soup and bird's nest soup.

Sichuan: Lots of herbs and spices—among them chili, peppercorns, fennel, anise, coriander, and garlic—go into making one of China's most fiery cuisines. Time is taken to soak and simmer the dishes so the chilies can leave their mark on the diner. Most dishes come accompanied either by a chili sauce or a spicy sauce. Because Sichuan Province is located so far from the coast, seafood is rare; chicken and pork are usually featured.

A typical Hong Kong meal incorporates many flavorful dishes shared among family and friends.

Cantonese cuisine puts snake to a variety of imaginative—and delicious—uses.

Hunan: Hunan cuisine is similar to the fiery dishes of Sichuan with liberal use of chilies and garlic, and an emphasis on freshness and fragrance. Rice is used as a staple, but northern-style side dishes such as bean curd rolls, dumplings, and savory buns are often served. Fish, shrimp, lotus root, and turtle are some of the main ingredients. Dishes include Dong'an chicken, shark's fin in red sauce, hot and spicy chicken, and lotus seeds in sugar candy.

Dim Sum: A Sunday-morning trip to a dim sum restaurant is a must, if only to see the gregarious Cantonese at their clamorous best. People shout their way through a meal of delicious steamed dumplings, buns, spring rolls, and delicate rice-flour wrappings encasing a glorious array of fillings. In more traditional restaurants, you simply choose what you want from a cart, although this system is in decline. It's now more common to fill in a paper card listing what you want. English is usually available.

Other Specialties: There is more to the food scene than Chinese restaurants; people also enjoy dishes from around the world. Many restaurants serve Indian, Japanese, Vietnamese, Thai, Korean, Indonesian, Singaporean, and Filipino food. Hong Kong also excels at fusion cuisine, combining Eastern and Western ingredients.

Where to Eat

Here you'll find some of Hong Kong's and Asia's best restaurants, with excellent cuisine and impeccable service.

Causeway Bay: Along Tang Lung, Matheson, and Percival Streets, and Sunning Road are plenty of quality regional Chinese restaurants, plus sushi bars and restaurants specializing in shark's fin soup.

Kowloon City: Clustered around Nga Tsin and Nam Kok Roads, dozens of Cantonese, Chiu Chow, Vietnamese, Korean, and Thai eateries offer tasty food and good value.

Lan Kwai Fong & SoHo: These two areas above Central District are full of trendy bars and restaurants offering a wide selection of international cuisine, including French, Italian, Middle Eastern, Spanish, Australian, American, and Mexican.

Sai Kung, Lamma Island & Lei Yue Mun: These seaside locations specialize in fresh seafood, which you can buy from tanks and take to a nearby restaurant to be cooked.

Stanley Village: The bistros lining the waterfront have a laid-back atmosphere.

Chungking Mansions: The city's most authentic Indian and Pakistani food.

Drink

Tea: There is a huge variety of Chinese tea (see pp. 68–69) as befits a country that invented the art of tea drinking. The three basic types are green, black, and oolong. Green tea is usually served free with meals; sugar, lemon, or milk are never added.

Coffee: While coffee is unlikely to displace tea, numerous coffee shops in the more cosmopolitan areas dispense an array of brews and feature stools, benches, tables, and comfy sofas in an airy atmosphere. Ample reading material encourages lingering.

Alcohol: Hong Kong's native beer is San Miguel. Blue Girl and Tsingtao from mainland China are very good. A local microbrewery produces hearty ales, including the wonderfully named and tasty Dragon's Back. Carlsberg is produced locally and Heineken is widely available. European beers are on tap in many pubs and bars.

Many people are partial to cognac and expensive brandies, often mixed with cola, lemonade, or soda and drunk in large quantities. An expensive bottle of cognac on one's table is a status symbol. Though wine is expensive in restaurants, supermarkets sell bottles from Europe, California, Australia, New Zealand, South Africa, and Chile at marked-down prices.

Dining Etiquette

Dishes are brought to the table as soon as they're cooked, and served communally, although diners get their own bowl for rice. It's polite to wait for someone else to start eating or to be invited to do so. In some cases, the host will place a small portion of food in your bowl to initiate proceedings.

You use chopsticks to take the food from your plate and dip it into the dishes of sauce—don't pour sauce onto your plate or into your rice bowl. It's acceptable to hold the rice bowl up and shovel rice into your mouth with the chopsticks. (If you can't handle chopsticks, most restaurants can provide a fork.) Chewed bones are often placed in a pile next to the diner on the tablecloth. Don't expect any fortune cookies; they are an American invention.

Tea accompanies most meals and is drunk throughout (people use it to clean their chopsticks, too). Spontaneous toasts are common during a repast involving alcohol. A diner will raise his or her glass, say a cheery *"Yum seng!"* ("Down the hatch!"), and others will follow suit. Expect your glass to be refilled continually.

EXPERIENCE: Eat at a *Dai Pai Dong*

Many Hong Kongers still swear by the food stalls that line the city's backstreets. At lunchtime, the stalls heave with office workers filling up on cheap, tasty food.

Fewer than 20 of the licensed *dai pai dongs* that once clogged Hong Kong's streets remain. In the 1980s, the government cracked down on the ramshackle stalls or carts with a wok and a wooden bench for customers. However, unofficial dai pai dongs abound. While cleaner than they once were, don't expect gleaming white surfaces and regular hand washing. Dai pai dongs are rough and ready dining; you'll probably share a table with strangers and lunch will be crowded and loud.

With just three or four offerings here, language isn't much of a barrier; simply pick and point. Favorite dishes include congee, noodles, and fish, plus pork and beef balls, deliciously dipped in chili sauce.

Try the **Graham Street market** at the foot of Stanley Street in Central for traditional dai pai dongs. Slightly more formal are the evening-only spots around **Temple Street Market,** which have menus and, because they serve seafood, are more expensive. They buzz from 8 p.m. on.

History of Hong Kong

When Hong Kong became part of Queen Victoria's dominions in 1841, the monarch was amused by the notion that her daughter Princess Victoria Adelaide Mary Louise might become the "Princess of Hong Kong." On the other hand, the foreign secretary, Lord Palmerston, was "greatly mortified and disappointed." He sacked the man responsible for Hong Kong's acquisition, Capt. Charles Elliot, representative of the British crown in China.

Palmerston was interested in greater spoils along China's prosperous coast, not "some barren island with hardly a house on it." The Chinese, for their part, were bemused by the whole affair. Qing dynasty emperor Daoguang (r. 1821–1850), acceding to the loss of this speck of inconsequential land by the compelling argument of Royal Navy guns leveled at the walls of Nanjing (Nanking), treated the affair casually. But his dismissive tone masked shame and anger (it was the first part of China to be taken by force by a Western power), which was not fully appeased for another 156 years until Hong Kong was handed back. The Union Jack was unfurled on January 26, 1841, at Possession Point in the now teeming Western District of Hong Kong Island.

Two years later, the cession of Hong Kong to the British was ratified in the Treaty of Nanking.

When the British arrived, Hong Kong Island had a population of about 3,650 scattered around 20 or so villages and hamlets, while another 2,000 lived on their boats in the harbor. The place was hardly conducive to a large population, given its barren, mountainous terrain and lack of fresh water.

But evidence has been unearthed of habitation dating back some 6,000 years. Artifacts discovered along the coast indicate Hong Kong's neolithic citizens fished, panned for salt, and carved geometrical images on rocks. Arrowheads, knives, fishhooks, socketed axes, and weapons dating from 2000 B.C. have been excavated. On the islands of Lantau and Lamma, stone molds indicate metal was worked locally. In 1999, archaeologists unearthed a neolithic workshop in Sai Kung in the New Territories, revealing hundreds of stone cores, flakes, and tools such as oyster picks and carving tools, as well as polished adzes and rings.

Increasing numbers of people settled in Hong Kong during the Qin (221–206 B.C.) and Han (206 B.C.–A.D. 220) dynasties. Coins from the Han period have been found, and Han relics were also unearthed in a brick tomb discovered in 1955 in the Lei Cheng Uk District of Kowloon. By the time of the Tang dynasty (618–907), China trading ships from India, Arabia, and Persia used Hong Kong's sheltered harbors as anchorage while acquiring silks and porcelain from ports along China's east coast and the Pearl River Delta.

Early Settlers

During the Song dynasty (960–1279), the Cantonese Punti people (Punti means "locals") began moving into the territory of present-day Hong Kong from the

> **When the British arrived, Hong Kong Island had a population of about 3,650.**

A vintage poster depicts the Chinese and British celebrations that occurred on Queen Victoria's Golden Jubilee in January 1888.

southern part of the Chinese mainland. They were followed by the seafaring Hoklo from Fujian, farther north along the coast, and the Hakka who originated from northern China. People tilled the fertile soil of the New Territories and built sturdy walled villages for protection against pirates, robbers, and their neighbors. The area, which fell under the administration of Canton (Guangzhou), was visited by a local administrator, Tang Fu-hip, in 1069. Tang was so taken by the beauty of the countryside and the village of Kam Tin that he later moved his family and ancestral graves there, and his sons became powerful landowners. Over the next two centuries, four other clans—the Hau, the Pang, the Lin, and the Man—arrived, eventually carving out most of Hong Kong between them, although the Tang remained the most powerful.

China's Dynasties

Xia ca 2205–1766 B.C.

Shang ca 1766–1122 B.C.

Zhou
Western ca 1122–771 B.C.
Eastern ca 771–256 B.C.

Qin 221–206 B.C.

Han
Western 206 B.C.–A.D. 9
Xin (Wang Mang) A.D. 9–23
Eastern A.D. 25–220

Three Kingdoms period 220–265

Jin
Western 265–316
Eastern 317–420

Northern
Northern Wei 386–534
Eastern Wei 534–550
Western Wei 535–557
Northern Qi 550–577
Northern Zhou 557–581

Southern
Song 420–479
Qi 479–502
Liang 502–557
Chen 557–589

Sui 581–618

Tang 618–907

Five Dynasties
Later Liang 907–923
Later Tang 923–936
Later Jin 936–947
Later Han 947–950
Later Zhou 951–960

Song Northern 960–1127
Southern 1127–1279

Yuan 1279–1368

Ming 1368–1644

Qing 1644–1911

Republic of China 1911–1949
(maintained in Taiwan)

People's Republic of China
1949–present

Europeans

European ships began arriving along China's southern coast in the early 16th century. The Portuguese, driven by the prospect of lucrative trade, were among the first. In 1517, a flotilla sailed up the Pearl River to Canton. Chinese officials were eventually persuaded to hand over Macau, a small piece of land on the Pearl River Delta, where the Portuguese established a trading post and settlement in 1557.

China, under extreme pressure from Western maritime powers, gradually and reluctantly allowed foreign shipping into four ports. Canton was opened in 1699 and Britain's East India Company was allowed to build a warehouse or "factory" there. The Europeans followed their example. However, only 13 *hongs* (trading companies) could trade at one time. They built their factories on the outskirts of the city.

A multitude of restrictions were placed on foreigners living in Canton: They were only allowed to remain there during the trading season, dictated by favorable winds between October and January, and could not bring their wives ashore, venture from their factory compounds, or learn Chinese.

Despite this, commerce flourished and huge profits were made. But the trade flowed mainly one way. While European traders could not get enough tea, silk, and porcelain, the Chinese were indifferent to woolens, furs, and spices being brought in by the foreign traders. The only thing that interested them was the vast amounts of silver paid in exchange for their exotic goods.

Opium Trade

All this changed. In 1773, the East India Company secured a monopoly on opium, which it sold to British merchants at auction in Calcutta. That year the first shipment arrived in Canton—200 chests, each containing 160 pounds of Bengal opium—where it found a ready market. Opium had been banned in China since 1729, except for medicinal use, and was forbidden outright in 1800. The ban was easily circumvented with the connivance of a never-ending stream of corrupt Chinese officials. Clippers arriving in Canton simply unloaded the contraband onto floating stores before heading into port for customs inspection. The drug was later smuggled ashore.

The use of opium became widespread in China; between 1810 and 1830, yearly shipments increased from 5,000 to 23,000 chests. At its height, there were an estimated one million opium addicts in China, from coolies, ordinary Chinese, traders, and rich merchants to government officials. William Jardine (1784–1843), of the preeminent hong Jardine, Matheson & Company, glibly commented that since "opium is the only real money article sold in China," it had to be smuggled in.

By the 1830s, a huge outflow of silver was being used to pay for the drug, and a major economic crisis loomed. In March 1839, Lin Zexu (1785–1850), a high-ranking official, was appointed by Emperor Daoguang to deal with the problem. With his soldiers, he lay siege to the hongs' factories, refused entry, and stopped food supplies until the opium was surrendered and traders signed pledges to discontinue the trade. The British, under the command of Capt. Charles Elliot, held out for six weeks before handing over more than 20,000 chests of opium. The drug was dumped into trenches by a river, mixed with lime, and flushed out to sea. The British merchants halted all trade with China and headed for Macau.

> **The British, under the command of Capt. Charles Elliot, held out against Lin Zexu's siege for six weeks before handing over more than 20,000 chests of opium. The drug was dumped into trenches by a river, mixed with lime, and flushed out to sea.**

First Opium War

Opium traders began lobbying the sympathetic foreign secretary, Lord Palmerston, for help in solving the trade problem. Palmerston ordered the mobilization of an expeditionary force from India to blockade Canton and demanded a commercial treaty that would swing trade in Britain's favor or the cession of Chinese land where the British could live free from threats. Meanwhile, a Chinese was accidentally killed in a brawl with British seamen on Kowloon Peninsula opposite Hong Kong Island, and Captain Elliot refused to hand over those responsible for trial in a Chinese court. Enraged, authorities in Canton ordered the British off Macau. By August 1839, about 200 merchants and their families found themselves crammed into boats on Hong Kong harbor within gunshot of Chinese war junks.

An expeditionary force of 4,000 arrived in June 1840 and blockaded Canton. The First Opium War (1840–1842) had begun. When treaty negotiations failed, the British began a show of military force, killing 600 Chinese soldiers at a garrison island in the mouth of the Pearl River. Under increasing threat by Britain's naval might, China agreed to a draft treaty at the Convention of Chuenpi in January 1841, which ceded Hong Kong to the British. Captain Elliot, who negotiated the treaty, wasted no time in dispatching Captain Belcher to Hong Kong Island to plant the flag on its western shore. A few days later he proclaimed:

"Full security and protection for all British subjects and foreigners residing in and resorting to the island, so long as they shall continue to conform to the authority of Her Majesty's government."

Both sides were unhappy with the treaty. Palmerston blasted Captain Elliot for failing to extract sufficient concessions from the Chinese. He was recalled in disgrace and replaced by Henry Pottinger (1801–1875), Hong Kong's first governor, who forced more concessions. After further shows of strength by the British—in which Dinghai, Xiamen, and Ningo fell to British gunboats, Shanghai and Zhenjiang were occupied, and Nanking was threatened—the Chinese gave in to demands. The Treaty of Nanking was signed on August 29, 1842, and ratified ten months later. It forced China to pay compensation, open the five ports of Canton, Xiamen, Fuzhou, Ningbo, and Shanghai (the first of the Treaty Ports) to foreigners, and cede Hong Kong to Britain in perpetuity so that the British might have "some Port whereat they may careen and refit their Ships, when required, and keep Stores for that purpose."

New Colony

Building in Hong Kong started soon after the flag was planted. Fifty lots along the northern frontage of the island, later to become Queen's Road, were snapped up, many by the hongs who had shifted their businesses from Canton and Macau. By the end of 1841, 28 foreign merchants had settled in Hong Kong, including Jardine, Matheson & Company, which bought the first plot for £565 and found a safe haven for its opium stores. The navy acquired a plot of land on the seafront, and the army moved in behind, on the lower slopes of what became Victoria Peak. The settlement was called Queen's Town, later renamed Victoria. Unexpectedly, some 12,000 Chinese workers and tradesmen settled to its immediate east and west.

The settlement was called Queen's Town, later renamed Victoria. Unexpectedly, some 12,000 Chinese workers and tradesmen settled to its immediate east and west.

By 1845 the population reached about 25,000, and it continued to swell as people fled China's Taiping Rebellion (1851–1864). The rebellion was led by Hung Xiu-quan (1814–1864), an aspiring bureaucrat. Influenced by Christian missionaries in Guangzhou in the 1830s, Hung believed he was the brother of Jesus and son of God, sent to Earth to destroy the "demons" of the Qing dynasty. He gathered a force of fanatical believers and led a revolt, taking control of large areas of south and central China, including the capital Nanking, where he set up a theocratic-military government. His strict moral laws and political infighting led to divisions. In 1864 the Qing retook the capital; Hung's army of 100,000 committed suicide rather than surrender.

Hong Kong's early failure to live up to expectations irked the hongs, who incurred great expense moving their operations from Canton and Macau. Ships were bypassing Hong Kong, heading straight for the Treaty Ports, and frustration was compounded by the obstinacy of Chinese officials, who paid little heed to the Treaty of Nanking.

Hong Kong's busy harbor soon after British settlement. Some ships bypassed the colony in favor of the Treaty Ports.

Second Opium War

Goading by the hongs to revise the treaty led to the Second Opium War (1856–1858), which was sparked by the arrest of the Chinese crew of the *Arrow*, a Hong Kong ship flying the British flag and anchored off Canton. In August 1856, the Chinese seized the ship, searching for a notorious pirate they believed to be on board. The British were suitably outraged, claiming it was an insult to Queen and country.

Britain, this time in league with France, again flexed its naval muscle along the China coast. Skirmishes ended in 1858 with the signing of the Treaty of Tientsin, which won the British a lease on Kowloon and diplomatic representation in Beijing. But when the first British envoy, Sir Frederick Bruce, was fired at on his way to Beijing to present his credentials, China had effectively reneged and hostilities resumed.

British and French troops occupied Beijing in October 1860. The Chinese succumbed and the Convention of Peking was signed, allowing the cession of Kowloon Peninsula up to what is now Boundary Road, and Stonecutter's Island, in perpetuity. Critically, the convention treaty allowed the British to import opium—for a modest tax—into China. Hong Kong's future suddenly looked very rosy.

Growth

By 1865, the population had risen to 122,000 and Hong Kong had attained a distinctly colonial profile. Government buildings, a police station, jail, post office, and a hospital had been constructed. The spires of handsome churches poked above the large compounds of the hongs, the lawns of rambling Government House swept down toward the harbor, and a grand gentlemen's club was built on the shoreline. A cricket ground, polo club, and horse racetrack were laid.

In true British colonial style, snobbery and class distinction took hold. The elite chose to build mansions in the cool confines near the summit of Victoria Peak, while the less affluent Europeans and wealthy Chinese settled at the Mid-Levels. The Portuguese, Jews, Armenians, and Parsis built their homes at the foot of the Peak, and the vast majority of Chinese continued to live in squalor in the slums of Western and Wan Chai Districts.

Sedan chairs and rickshaws were a popular mode of transportation for the colonialists.

The 1890s was a turbulent decade. Turmoil in China depressed trade. In the face of worldwide economic depression, the Colonial Office demanded more money from Hong Kong for its military defense. The price of silver against sterling was falling. In 1894, the colony was struck by bubonic plague and half of the Chinese population of about 200,000 fled to China. Five hundred people died; Hong Kong was declared an infected port and ships were turned away. Over the next 12 years, the plague took 13,000 lives.

Other European nations began demanding concessions from China, and the British grew increasingly worried that their precious harbor would become vulnerable. Through the Second Opium War, they had received land north beyond Kowloon Peninsula to the Shum Chum (Shenzhen) River, and the surrounding 234 islands. The land, later known as the New Territories, was given over on July 1, 1898, for a 99-year lease.

At the turn of the 20th century, Hong Kong busied itself with public works as it tried to match the needs of 325,000 residents. A tramline along Hong Kong's foreshore was built, land reclamation was completed, reservoirs were planned, power utilities were set up, and port facilities were improved. By 1910, the colony had become the world's third biggest port, and the railroad line from Kowloon to the border with China was completed.

Meanwhile China was being wrenched apart by political upheaval, economic chaos, rebellion, and civil war. Waves of immigrants continued to make their way to Hong Kong. In 1911, Sun Yat-sen, recognized as modern China's founder, led a nationalist revolt that eventually toppled the Qing government and established the Republic of China in 1912.

Born to a farming family in Guangdong Province, Sun had studied in Hawaii, and practiced medicine and fomented revolution in Hong Kong. In 1913, his Nationalist Party (Kuomintang) won the most seats in China's first national elections, but later that year he was forced into exile by the military and his party was expelled from Parliament. Backed by Russia, Sun regained momentum and was on the verge of success when he took ill and died in Beijing in March 1925.

Between World Wars I and II, the Chinese in Hong Kong began to make their mark in business. Chinese companies moved away from insurance, shipbuilding, shipping, and real estate and into enterprises such as banking, finance, and transportation. A Chinese elite prospered and accumulated vast sums of money, although their acceptance among the upper echelons of British society in Hong Kong was guarded. All the money in the world could not buy a mansion on the Peak if you were Chinese. This was to be forever a part of England unsoiled by "foreigners." The Peak Ordinance of 1904, which was not repealed until 1945, banned Chinese, except the servants of Europeans, from living on the Peak.

Japanese Occupation

In 1937, the Japanese—who had occupied Manchuria in northeastern China since 1931—took Beijing and Shanghai and by 1938 controlled major cities in China's coastal regions, including Canton. Refugees poured over the China–Hong Kong border, and by late 1939, Hong Kong's population had surged to 1.6 million, with 500,000 people sleeping in the streets. On December 8, 1941, the day after Pearl Harbor was bombed, Japanese forces swept into Hong Kong. (Though the British earlier realized they had no hope of holding the colony and re-fused to send reinforcements to bolster its poor defenses, Prime Minister Winston Churchill demanded the colony hold out as long as it could.) British forces on the China–Hong Kong border were pushed back through the New Territories and Kowloon, the last being evacuated to Hong Kong Island on December 13.

Before attacking Hong Kong Island, a Japanese officer, Lt. Gen. Takashi Sakai, sent a note to Governor Mark Young demanding surrender. It said in part: "It [the surrender] will be honorable. If not, I, repressing my tears, am obliged to take action to overpower your forces."

> **All the money in the world could not buy a mansion on the Peak if you were Chinese. This was to be forever a part of England unsoiled by "foreigners." The Peak Ordinance of 1904 banned Chinese, except the servants.**

After heavy bombing, the Japanese attacked the island on December 19. British, Canadian, and volunteer troops fought bravely; many were killed. On Christmas Day, Governor Young crossed the harbor to Japanese headquarters at the Peninsula Hotel on Kowloon, and signed the surrender document. During more than three years of occupation, most of the Europeans were interned at Stanley and Sham Shui Po, while the occupiers routinely terrorized the local people. Trade virtually disappeared, and the local currency was almost worthless. Power shortages were common and the island lived under the constant threat of starvation. To ease the strain on resources, the Japanese ordered mass deportations. By the end of the war, Hong Kong's population had been reduced to 600,000.

Following the formal Japanese surrender on August 4, 1945, the colonial secretary Frank Grimson, who had been interned at Stanley, set up a provisional government.

Echoing the adventures of Capt. Charles Elliot just over a century earlier, Grimson acted without authority from London, which was considering requests from the United States to return Hong Kong to Chiang Kai-shek's nationalist China. British rule was soon restored.

Postwar Growth

People flooded back into Hong Kong at the rate of 100,000 a month; by the end of 1947, the population had reached 1.8 million. With the imminent defeat of Chiang's nationalists by Mao Zedong's (1893–1976) communists, hundreds of thousands streamed over the border. When Mao took power in 1949, establishing the People's Republic of China, refugees continued to arrive, many fleeing from the commercial center of Shanghai. The flood was eventually stemmed when the communists sealed off the border between the New Territories and China.

In 1952, Hong Kong's future as a center of trade looked shaky because of the trade embargo instituted by the UN against Communist China. Fortunately, many of the new arrivals from China were businessmen with capital. Aided by a willing workforce, the colony turned to manufacturing. It started with textiles, then moved into plastics, electronics, and watches. Through the 1950s and 1960s, economic growth was 10 percent a year and many of Hong Kong's rags-to-riches stories took place during this period.

Cultural Revolution

By the mid-1960s, China's Cultural Revolution was under way, driven by Mao to instill a revolutionary spirit in the young. From it evolved the Red Guards, who, for the next decade, spread chaos throughout the country. Millions of people were persecuted,

After four years of occupation, the British retook Hong Kong in August 1945.

imprisoned, or killed, and China's cultural heritage was all but destroyed. The troubles spilled over into Hong Kong. In 1966, people rioted over a small increase in fares on the Star Ferry. Strikes by unionists and demonstrations by communist sympathizers followed. Curfews were imposed in 1967; over 8,000 suspected bombs were defused that year. Hundreds more exploded, killing 50 people and injuring many more. But the communists had little support from the majority of Hong Kong people, who were tired of this disruption to their daily lives. China offered little support to the leftists, and by year's end, the turmoil had petered out.

By the late 1960s, China began to move away from its isolationist policies. With the backing of the United States, it gained a seat on the UN Security Council. In 1971 the United States lifted trade sanctions and resumed diplomatic relations, setting Hong Kong on a path of unprecedented economic growth and prosperity.

The 1970s & '80s

Increasing amounts of money in Hong Kong's coffers led to a massive improvement in the quality of life. Murray MacLehose, governor between 1971 and 1982, was the architect. He instituted a huge public housing program, moving hundreds of thousands of people from the colony's slums to multistory apartments, and introduced free compulsory education to junior high school level, paving the way for an educated and skilled future workforce. He also created the Independent Commission Against Corruption (ICAC) in 1974 and gave it almost unfettered powers to investigate and prosecute rampant graft among police and other government officials. The ICAC was incredibly effective and pivotal to Hong Kong's success in attracting international businesses.

Hong Kong Triads

With around half a million members in 50 different gangs, the Triads, or "black societies," are major players in Hong Kong. But although there have been several recent crimes committed by Triad members, the gangs won't ruin your vacation, as they are at once ubiquitous and invisible. Started in the 1760s as anti-imperial societies on mainland China, the Triads only began dabbling in the normal organized crimes a hundred years ago. They migrated to Hong Kong after the Cultural Revolution started cracking down on organized crime. There they have prospered to the point that the police do not try to wipe them out, but only attempt to manage them.

By the late 1970s, China was continuing to open its doors. Most of Hong Kong's factories producing cheap manufacturing products were shifted across the border to Guangdong Province. The territory concentrated on building up its finance and service industries, attracting international companies wanting to take advantage of the burgeoning economies of Asia–particularly the new, trade-liberal "Open Door" policy introduced by China's paramount leader Deng Xiaoping (1904–1997) in 1978. Things had never looked better; the economy was booming and gleaming skyscrapers were altering the skyline of Hong Kong's Central District. By the early to mid-1980s, a contemporary, cosmopolitan Hong Kong had earned its stripes as an international city.

Britain's Prime Minister Margaret Thatcher visited China in 1982, setting off two years of often-bitter negotiations leading to a deal that eventually handed Hong Kong back to China. By 1984, the deal had been struck with the Sino-British Joint Declaration. Hong Kong was returning to China on July 1, 1997, the day the 99-year lease on the New Territories expired. It was to become a Special Administrative Region (SAR), with a high degree of autonomy. It could have its own currency, elect its own government, maintain its judiciary, and keep its capitalist economy and its freedoms for 50 years following its return to Chinese sovereignty. All these rights would be enshrined in a mini-constitution called the Basic Law. Deng tagged this arrangement "one country–two systems."

The Joint Declaration aimed to maintain the confidence of the people of Hong Kong, but given that a significant proportion of its population had fled communism on the mainland, more than a little nervousness was to be expected. The Joint Liaison Group, consisting of Chinese and British diplomats, was formed to agree on arrangements for the transitional period. Constant assurances by both sides helped dispel doubts, but unease simmered.

Tiananmen Square

Doubt turned to near panic after June 4, 1989, when troops of the People's Liberation Army crushed democracy demonstrations in Beijing's Tiananmen Square. In the weeks leading up to it, millions of Hong Kong people had taken to the streets to demonstrate their support. The events that followed were extraordinary. At first there were public outpourings of grief never before seen in Hong Kong, as hundreds of thousands of citizens again took to the streets, wearing black armbands and dressed in mourning in honor of those killed in Tiananmen Square. But then fear took hold. Thinking the same thing could happen in Hong Kong, many looked for an escape hatch. Crowds jammed the consulates of the United States, Australia, Canada, and Singapore seeking residency visas. Tiny countries in the Pacific and Caribbean started selling passports for $10,000, and the territory was flooded by "immigration consultants." In the few years following the bloodshed in Tiananmen Square, more than 100,000 people left. But Hong Kong got back to business, and confidence in the future, even under the Chinese flag, gradually returned.

> [Donald] Tsang oversaw the . . . handover's tenth anniversary. . . . The economy is booming and the rule of law remains solid.

The Handover

Chris Patten, Hong Kong's last governor, arrived in 1992 with a political agenda unseen in previous governors. A politician—he was a Conservative member of Parliament in Britain, but lost his seat in the 1992 elections—Patten tried to institute reforms that the British thought would offer safeguards after the handover. At the time, the Hong Kong legislature, the Legislative Council, was made up of appointed members elected by their professional peers in "functional constituencies," though about a third of the council members were directly elected by universal franchise. Patten introduced a package that allowed for the election of all members of the legislature, much to the outrage of China, who saw it as a dismantling of the political processes set in the Basic Law. Elections under these reforms were held in 1995, but China refused to accept the authority of the new Legislative Council, and appointed its own Provisional Legislature.

Although initially very popular among the ordinary people of Hong Kong, not least for his social reforms and his down-to-earth nature, Patten polarized much of the powerful business community, which had been more than eager to please its future masters in Beijing. He was regularly pilloried by the Chinese government for his outspoken stance on political reform. Patten was replaced by the SAR's first chief executive, Tung Chee-hwa, following a somewhat muted handover ceremony on the evening of June 30, 1997.

Beams of light illuminate a Chinese junk as part of the handover celebrations on July 1, 1997.

Tung, a millionaire shipping magnate, was seen as China's pick for the job, although he was chosen by a selection committee appointed by China's National People's Consultative Committee. Tung rode a wave of popularity following the euphoria of the handover, but things gradually turned sour during his first five-year term as the public saw many of his political decisions more likely made at the behest of China's leaders rather than in the interests of Hong Kong's people. But his government did receive plaudits for the way it managed to stifle the worst ravages of the 1997–1999 Asian economic crisis, which severely affected neighbors Taiwan, Korea, and countries in Southeast Asia.

In 2003, at the behest of China, Tung tried to introduce a security law that brought hundreds of thousands of Hong Kong residents onto the streets in protests. The planned law was shelved, but huge street protests against Tung's rule continued on and off, finally forcing him to step down midway through his second five-year term in early 2005. He was replaced by the territory's financial secretary, Donald Tsang, in June 2005.

Ten Years On

Tsang, who had worked for the former colonial government as financial secretary, was in good standing with Beijing and proved popular with Hong Kongers. Tsang oversaw the 2007 celebrations for the handover's tenth anniversary; the city continues to flourish. The economy is booming and the rule of law remains solid. (Even Margaret Thatcher admitted that her concerns for Hong Kong's future "have largely proved groundless.") The same year, Tsang was elected in Hong Kong's first contested election. Pro-democracy candidate Alan Leong would ultimately come in a distant second, as the Chief Executive elections are still decided by an electoral committee, where Beijing largely pulls the strings, but the competition was symbolically important. Hong Kong's hunt for universal suffrage remains elusive, though, with Beijing constantly moving both the goalposts and the time frame. ■

The Land

Geographically, Hong Kong is an extension of China's Guangdong Province. It sits at its tip, just east of the Pearl River Estuary, and south of the Tropic of Cancer on a similar latitude to Hawaii. The territory covers only 424 square miles (1,098 sq km), but manages a remarkable variety of topographical features—from precipitous peaks plunging down to deep valleys laced with streams to rocky, convoluted coastlines and numerous islands.

These peaks, with summits regularly rising above 1,640 feet (500 m), characterize Hong Kong more than any other natural feature. You can hardly look anywhere without some sheer mountain rising into view. Hong Kong's most famous sight, the view across Victoria Harbour to the gleaming skyscrapers of Central District on Hong Kong Island, is made even more stunning by 1,811-foot (552 m) Victoria Peak looming in the background. From the crests and shoulders of these often mist-cloaked peaks, a great surprise awaits the visitor—remarkable vistas of crowded urban areas existing cheek by jowl with lush, green, mountainous countryside.

When the British arrived in the 1840s, the peaks of Hong Kong Island plunged into Victoria Harbour. Subsequent land reclamation projects pushed the island farther into the harbor; Central District's high-rises are built on reclaimed land. Most of the island's 1.5 million people are squeezed along the narrow northern corridor.

> From the crests and shoulders of [Hong Kong's] peaks . . . a great surprise awaits the visitor—remarkable vistas of crowded urban areas existing cheek by jowl with lush, mountainous countryside.

The flat peninsula of Kowloon has also been increased by landfill. Gleaming Tsim Sha Tsui East was part of Victoria Harbour until the 1980s, and a huge landfill project on the peninsula's western side has claimed more of the harbor. This area, along with adjoining New Kowloon, is one of the most densely populated places on Earth.

Though the New Territories region is relatively uncrowded, a series of "new towns," built since the 1970s, has increased the population significantly. This area is dominated by tall peaks—including Hong Kong's highest, Tai Mo Shan at 3,140 feet (957 m)—which fall to isolated wooded valleys and an indented coastline of bays, coves, beaches, and natural harbors. The northwest part of the New Territories has Hong Kong's only extensive flatlands, an alluvial plain spreading from Tai Mo Shan to the South China Sea.

Hong Kong's 234 outlying islands, the vast majority unpopulated, total 67 square miles (175 sq km). The largest, Lantau, is twice the size of Hong Kong Island and is the site of Hong Kong's international airport. These islands, dotted with small towns and villages, are mostly a peaceful escape from Hong Kong's frenetic urban areas.

Country Parks

Hong Kong has 23 country parks covering 40 percent of the territory's land area. Much of this land, originally at least, became country parks through accident rather

Mirror Pool in Plover Cove Country Park is just one of Hong Kong's hidden refuges.

than through any concerted effort to preserve natural heritage. During the 1950s and 1960s, as development spread from the main population centers, steep terrain got in the way. In the 1970s, these areas gradually became incorporated into country parks.

The parks are laced with a network of hiking trails and nature walks passing through beautiful scenery to the top of windswept peaks, down to wooded valleys, and along rocky coasts. The four extended trails within these parks link up with local ones. The longest, at 60 miles (100 km), is the MacLehose Trail, which crosses the New Territories. The 31-mile (50 km) Hong Kong Trail traverses Hong Kong Island, the 44-mile (70 km) Lantau Trail winds over Lantau Island, and the 48-mile (78 km) Wilson Trail begins at Hong Kong Island South and leads north across the territory. All trails are well maintained and signed with distances between points. Entry to the country parks is marked by map boards indicating the trails; some have visitor centers. There are plenty of easy walks along nature paths.

Wildlife

Hong Kong is home to 47 species of native land mammals. Many of these are nocturnal (bats, for example, make up 22 of the total). Among them are barking deer,

Pokfulam Country Park on Hong Kong Island marries urban and bucolic vistas.

Hong Kong Weather

The only constant in Hong Kong's weather is that it is unpredictable—the skies can turn from sunny to thundery in minutes. Yet Hong Kong does have definite seasons. It sits on the South China Sea, just south of the Tropic of Cancer and has a subtropical climate. Winter (Dec.–Feb.) can see temperature fluctuations between 50°F (10°C) and 76°F (25°C). The temperature can drop to zero on some peaks in the New Territories, but rarely sinks below 45°F (7°C) in urban areas. There is little rain, and humidity is relatively low. Early spring is warm and sunny, but later spring is marked by a sharp increase in humidity. Summer (June–Aug.) is hot, with humidity reaching 90 percent and over, and is subject to heavy bouts of rain. The oppressive humidity makes it uncomfortable and tiring to be outside for prolonged periods. The best times to visit are March to April and late September to November, when humidity drops and there's little or no rainfall. Macau's climate is roughly the same as Hong Kong's, although it does benefit from a refreshing sea breeze.

long-tailed macaque monkeys, mongooses, leopards, armadillo-like pangolins, civet cats, squirrels, Chinese quilled porcupines, and wild boars.

The territory is also surprisingly rich in birdlife, with more than 480 species,

accounting for a third of the total species found in China. At Mai Po Nature Reserve, a protected wetland area in the northwestern New Territories, huge numbers of waterbirds shelter, especially during migration and in the winter, when an average of 60,000 birds from 300 species gather.

Much of Hong Kong's waters are either badly polluted or overfished, so they are not particularly conducive to maintaining a healthy and teeming marine life. Hoi Ha Wan Marine Park, set in a sheltered bay at the northern tip of Sai Kung Peninsula, is a relatively pristine exception to this. The water quality here has allowed stony corals to thrive, with 39 of Hong Kong's recorded corals to be found.

Populations of Chinese white dolphins are found in waters off the north of Lantau Island, although they are threatened by pollution, land reclamation, and overfishing. The government has created the Sha Chau and Lung Kwu Chau Marine Park there in an attempt to preserve and increase numbers. Another marine reserve, Tung Ping Chau, surrounding the island of Ping Chau in Mirs Bay off the northeastern point of Hong Kong, is home to more than 124 species of reef fish and several varieties of coral. ■

Arts & Festivals

The devastating Cultural Revolution of the 1960s and 1970s saw the end of the tradition that was once integral to life on mainland China. But Hong Kong has kept alive many of these customs, and continues to celebrate them with all the clamor and color that make for exciting spectacle.

Chinese Opera

For the Western ear, the sounds emanating from the stage of a Chinese opera can take some getting used to. Performers sing in shrill falsetto, accompanied by the sometimes erratic and deafening banging of drums and gongs, and the high-pitched twanging and screaming of traditional string and wind instruments. Amid this cacophony, heroes in elaborate, multicolored costumes battle overwhelming odds, spirits defend the world against evil, and furtive lovers defy disapproving parents.

Singing, speaking, mime, swordplay, and acrobatics are incorporated into performances held during most of Hong Kong's major festivals. Makeshift stages are erected in public squares with seats in front. Traditionally, operas can last as long as six hours, but today most are limited to about three. You don't have to sit through the whole show, however. People come and go as they please, chat, walk around, and eat.

Three types of Chinese opera are regularly held in Hong Kong. **Beijing opera,** performed in the Mandarin language, is said to be the most refined. **Cantonese opera** is the most popular, owing to the use of the local language and the more down-to-earth themes. The most traditional is **Chiu Chow** or **Chaozhou,** which maintains many of the original elements used when it was staged for the courts of the Ming dynasty.

> Chinese opera relies as much on costumes, makeup, and gestures as it does on song to relate its story to the audience.

Chinese opera relies as much on costumes, makeup, and gestures as it does on song to relate its story to the audience. Trembling shows the character is angry; flicking a sleeve indicates disgust; throwing a hand up and flicking the sleeves back means surprise. Embarrassment is shown by covering the face with a sleeve. When worried, the character will rub his hands together for several minutes.

Heavy makeup is worn in place of the masks that were once used. In Beijing opera, a red face suggests a loyal and honest character, white is for cunning, and blue is for courageous and enterprising. A yellow face means intelligence, a black face shows honesty, and brown often indicates a stubborn person. A dab of white on the nose marks a clown. Color also plays a symbolic part in costumes. Barbarians are dressed in purple, emperors in yellow. In addition, the more elaborate the headdress, the more important the character.

Props are minimal, so actors use exaggerated movement or symbolism to describe actions. Holding a whip indicates the person is riding a horse. A few soldiers can represent an entire army. A character circling the stage means he is on a long journey. Opening a door, walking at night, rowing a boat, eating, drinking, and other activities are indicated by stylized movements. Actors also use facial expressions to help convey specific meanings.

Elaborate, colorful costumes and heavy makeup define Chinese opera performers. The productions—cacophonous and exciting affairs—are popular during festivals.

Lion & Dragon Dances

While the lion is not native to China, it is considered a divine animal possessing nobility and dignity, able to protect truth and ward off evil. Pairs of lion statues often guard the entrances to large homes or buildings, keeping evil at bay and encouraging good fortune. Lion dances are performed at festivals and on special occasions, such as weddings and openings of new enterprises. These are highly athletic affairs involving two people draped in cloth and holding the colorful and animated head of a lion. The lion's movements are accompanied by music. The bearded lion's eyes move, its mouth opens and closes, and the head jerks from side to side. Dragon dances, usually held during festivals, involve a larger group of people. The lead performer holds the multicolored head of the smiling dragon aloft with a pole, while others, partially hidden under cloth, flow in a snaking pattern to symbolize the dragon in flight.

Event Tickets

Hong Kong is often labeled a cultural wasteland. Although it does lack some of the vibrancy of rival metropolises, several quality cultural events usually occur each week, plus a decent lineup of international performing artists and groups during the year. For comprehensive listings, try the free Hong Kong magazine (www.aziacity.com/hk), available weekly in Lan Kwai Fong and Soho bars and restaurants, or the Hong Kong Tourism Board's extensive calendar (www.discoverhongkong.com). Tickets are generally available at event venues, or in advance from Urbtix (tel 2111-5999, www.urbtix.hk) and HK Ticketing (tel 3128-8288, www.hkticketing.com). Both offer online, telephone, and in-person ticketing, with outlets around the city.

Music

Hong Kong's music scene is dominated by Cantopop (see sidebar p. 21), catchy arrangements sung in Cantonese. Incredibly popular and invariably good-looking performers sing of unrequited love and loneliness and most of Hong Kong's young people sing along. Concerts at the Hong Kong Coliseum and Queen Elizabeth Stadium nearly always sell out. Many hits are covers of U.S. and British pop songs, translated into Cantonese (Western pop music does not have a big following here). Cantopop stars appear on TV game and variety shows to maintain their exposure; many cross over into the movie industry. Top of the Cantopops include Leon Lai, Jackie Cheung, Andy Lau, and Aaron Kwok, plus more recent arrivals Sammi Cheung and Nicholas Tse.

Film

Though Hong Kong once had the world's third biggest film industry, only outstripped by Hollywood and Bollywood, today it is in what some argue is a terminal decline. Bigger budgets and audiences have drawn many top talents to the mainland; local films struggle to compete with the Beijing blockbusters. While Hong Kong's films have long been caricatured as over-the-top action films, with Chow Yun-fat, Jackie Chan, and director John Woo household names, the city's film history is far more complex. From the thoughtful offerings of Wong-Kar Wai to the comedies of Stephen Chow, it has one of the world's richest industries, as displayed at the annual Hong Kong Film Festival (see p. 50).

Performance Art

Hong Kong has a number of good performance groups. Dance troupes include the Hong Kong Dance Company, which performs both traditional and modern Chinese

A sleek dragon boat crewed by dozens of frenetic rowers hits the water during the annual June Dragon Boat Race.

dance; the City Contemporary Dance Company, which focuses on modern dance; and the Hong Kong Ballet Company. The Hong Kong Chinese Orchestra performs Chinese and modern music on traditional instruments, while the Hong Kong Philharmonic Orchestra is the resident orchestra at the Hong Kong Cultural Center. Theater groups include the Hong Kong Repertory Theater Company, which puts on mainly Chinese works, and the Chung Ying Theater Company, a vehicle for up-and-coming Hong Kong playwrights. Many of these groups perform at the world-class venues of the Hong Kong Cultural Center and Hong Kong Academy for Performing Arts.

Chinese Arts & Crafts

Europeans have hankered after Chinese arts and crafts since the country was widely opened up to trade from about the 16th century. Silks and porcelains were most highly prized. The market's largest sector is undoubtedly embroideries and brocades, recognized for their excellent craftsmanship. The fine silks used in their production come from the southeast and east, as these are the areas most conducive for growing mulberry trees, whose leaves the silkworms feed on.

Blue-and-white porcelains from Jindezhen county in central China's Jiangxi Province are regarded as the country's best because of their smooth texture and intricate designs.

Carvings—jade, ivory, wood, oxhorn, shell, and stone—are much sought after, with jade being the most popular and the most expensive. Jade carvings come in various shapes and themes, from small figurines to sculptures crafted from huge slabs. Ivory is often used in the deft art of miniature carvings and paintings, and again the range of work is large, from trinkets and figurines to elaborate tableaux from a full elephant tusk mounted on timber.

You can find Chinese arts and crafts at the various markets throughout the city, such as the Jade Market (see p. 137).

Hong Kong Movies

Hong Kong once had the world's third biggest film industry, second only to Bollywood and Hollywood, but the industry has declined in recent years. The quantity produced has shrunk from more than 200 films a year to fewer than 50.

The acrobatic kung fu star Jackie Chan is one Hong Kong actor who has succeeded in Hollywood.

Hong Kong still makes movies at a fraction of the price of Hollywood, though. A little more than a million U.S. dollars is average, while five million or more U.S. dollars funds a big production. A film can be completed in a few months (compared the Hollywood minimum of six months to a year).

Lead roles are filled by a few dozen actors, often Cantopop stars, who are idolized by moviegoers in Hong Kong and other parts of Asia. They are in huge demand, since producers know that assembling a cast of hot actors virtually guarantees success—if not necessarily quality. Such easy pickings led to the involvement of the triads (organized crime gangs) in the movie industry, especially during the early to mid-1990s.

Movies' low budgets are offset by amazing stunt work and cartoon-like violence. This violence is often incessant and hard to take. Scenes that would be completely unacceptable even by Hollywood's loose standards are commonplace in mainstream Hong Kong action movies. The gangster film *The Big Heat* (1988) opens with a power drill piercing a man's hand. In *Run and Kill* (1993), a man incinerates his enemy's 12-year-old daughter, and then, with a snarling smile, places the charred corpse at the father's feet.

But there are some notable exceptions to the splattering violence. Art film director Wong Kar-wai's *Happy Together* won the Palme d'Or at the Cannes Film Festival in 1997, while his excellent *Chungking Express* (1994) trades mayhem for intense dialogue and insight into modern Hong Kong. While huge on stunts and kung fu action, Jackie Chan's movies replace more graphic violence with comedy. His *Drunken Master II* (1994) is a classic of Hong Kong cinema.

Hong Kong movies have enjoyed some popularity in the United States and Europe; interest has been spurred by the appearance of Hong Kong actors and filmmakers in Hollywood. Director John Woo, who produced the blood-soaked cult classic *The Killer* (1989), has enjoyed success replicating the stylized violence of his Hong Kong movies. More recently, Stephen Chow's comedies have made a splash, with *Shaolin Soccer* (2001) and *Kung-Fu Hustle* (2004) being the most notable. The masterful crime classic *Infernal Affairs* (2002) was recently given a Hollywood makeover and released with Leonardo DiCaprio as *The Departed* (2006).

Dramatic actor Chow Yun-fat made his first Hollywood appearance in 1998's *The Replacement Killers*. He has since gone on to acclaim in movies such as *Crouching Tiger, Hidden Dragon* (2000), which won four Academy Awards, including best foreign language film. Other Hong Kong actors, including action superstar Jet Li, also have made an impact on Hollywood. High-kicking kung fu expert Michelle Yeoh (also *Crouching Tiger, Hidden Dragon)*, although Malaysian, got her start in Hong Kong movies.

In recent years, Hong Kong's stars have appeared in China's increasingly big budget epics. Although collaboration has benefited both sides, the growth of production on the mainland threatens to swallow Hong Kong's unique cinema in a greater pan-Chinese cinema. While the talent in acting and directing remains, the huge audiences for films north of the border makes mainland projects far more lucrative than local efforts.

EXPERIENCE: Be Like Bruce Lee in Hong Kong

Martial arts has a long, distinguished history in Hong Kong. And with a wealth of world-class masters, schools continue to flourish.

Possibly the most popular form of martial arts in Hong Kong is Wing Chun, as locals look to follow in the footsteps of Bruce Lee, who famously mastered the form. Lee went on to create his Jeet Kune Do (JKD) discipline, which is more a philosophy than a martial art, and not particularly popular in Hong Kong.

Hong Kongers enjoy martial arts in a competitive sense, but also to keep fit; most forms are good for keeping in shape. Whether you want to pick up a few moves or to master the art, try the schools below.

Shaolin Wushu Culture Centre,
Shek Tsai Po, Tai O, Lantau *(www.shaolincc. org.hk)*. A fantastic retreat set up on Lantau Island to promote traditional Chinese martial arts and Shaolin culture. A wide range of courses includes intensive one-day sessions and overnight camps, introducing beginners to the basics of Shaolin martial arts.

Hong Kong Wushu Union *(tel 2504-8226, www.hkwushuu.com.hk)*. Large organization offering instruction in a number of martial arts at various levels.

Jeet Kune Do *(www.jkd.com.hk)*. Offers information and contacts for those interested in learning the discipline.

Wan Kam Leung *(tel 2388-5662, www. wingchun.com.hk)*. Wan Kam Leung is a Wing Chun master who offers individual and group teaching in English.

Calendar of Festivals

January/February—City Fringe Festival: A month-long alternative arts festival highlights off-beat theater, stand-up comedy, performance art, mime, dance, and art from local and international artists *(tel 2521-7251, www.hkfringe.com.hk).*
Chinese New Year: The first day of the first moon in the Chinese lunar year (dates vary). Shops and businesses may extend the official three-day public holiday to a week or more. Victoria Harbour bursts with fireworks and skyscrapers try to outdo each other with colored-light displays.
Spring Lantern Festival (Yuen Siu): Held on the 15th day of the new moon, the festival celebrates the end of Chinese New Year. Hong Kong glows with lanterns in traditional styles.

February/March—Hong Kong Arts Festival: Top international performers gather in Hong Kong for one of Asia's most prestigious arts festivals. Symphony, theater, ballet, Chinese opera, jazz, and traditional Asian orchestra performances last all month *(tel 2824-3555, www.hk.artsfestival.org).*

March—Hong Kong Artwalk: Fifty plus galleries around Hong Kong open their doors until midnight, offering participants beer, wine, and food *(www.hongkongartwalk.com).*

March/April—Ching Ming: Families head to their ancestors' graves to clean the sites, light incense, burn paper "spirit money," and make offerings of fruit and wine. Traditionally held at the beginning of the third moon of the Chinese lunar calendar, usually in early April.
Hong Kong Rugby Sevens: Three days of rugby usher in the city's biggest sporting event and party. Tickets usually sell out well in advance; the overflow of international spectators soaks up the atmosphere in the bars of Wan Chai *(www.hksevens.com.hk).*

April—Birthday of Tin Hau: Hong Kong's most popular deity—Tin Hau, Goddess of the Sea–is celebrated with decorated boats and colorful street parades. The festival's focus is mainly in the New Territories and outlying islands.
Hong Kong International Film Festival: Hundreds of movies from around the world are screened during this two-week-long celebration of cinema, including films from independent filmmakers. One of the best festivals for those interested in Asian filmmaking *(www.hkiff.org.hk).*
Cheung Chau Bun Festival: Lion dances, parades, and the unique bun scrambling competition on Cheung Chau Island all honor the god Pak Tai *(www.cheungchau.org).*

May—Le French May Festival of Arts: Asia's biggest French festival, when top talent from France performs theater, song, and dance. Art exhibitions also promote French art and culture *(tel 3196-6209, www.frenchmay.com).*

June—Dragon Boat Race Month: 50-foot-long (15 m) boats are rowed by crews of 20 or more to a drummer's beat. The event celebrates Qu Yuan, a third-century B.C. Chinese hero.

July—The first day of the month is a holiday to mark Britain's return of the former colony to China in 1997. There are fireworks in abundance over the harbor.

August/September—Hungry Ghost Festival: People burn wads of paper "money" on little roadside bonfires, usually at sunset, to appease restless spirits—hungry ghosts said to wander the world for a whole lunar month. Some areas stage parades culminating in food offerings to the ghosts.

September/October—Mid-Autumn Festival: This celebrates the bright full harvest moon that invariably shines on the 15th day of the eighth lunar month. Children visit open spaces such as parks, hills, and beaches with their families, waving colorful lanterns lit by candles. It's also when moon cakes, small but heavy and rich round pies, are made. ∎

A teeming and thriving metropolis, capped with a stunning skyline recognizable the world over

Hong Kong Island North

Jade, ivory, and wood seals

Hong Kong Island North

The founding of Hong Kong was an inauspicious affair—a Union Jack casually planted by a Capt. Edward Belcher of the Royal Navy on what is now Possession Street in Western District on January 26, 1841, followed by a quick toast to Her Majesty Queen Victoria. Back home in England, the foreign secretary, Lord Palmerston (1784–1865), could barely contain his contempt for the acquisition of a "barren island with hardly a house upon it. Now it seems obvious that Hong Kong will not be a Mart of Trade."

Dining with a view at Café Deco, atop Victoria Peak

Subsequent generations of residents showed little regard for Palmerston's pessimism and have molded the northern stretch of Hong Kong Island into one of the world's most vibrant places. Today 1.3 million people crowd onto this 30-square-mile (78 sq km) island, 7 percent of the total area of Hong Kong. Most are squeezed along its narrow, flat northern corridor. From its western tip at Kennedy Town to Causeway Bay at its

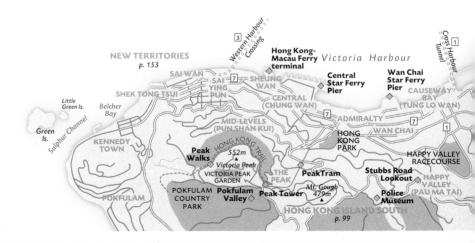

Just beyond the high-rises are the older, bustling, residential and commercial parts of Central, Western, and Wan Chai. Crowds spill from the sidewalks along narrow streets, while at Causeway Bay, shoppers seek the latest fashions in modern department stores. Minutes away, roads and trails wind up steep wooded hills to exclusive residential neighborhoods, the surprising peace of the countryside, and unsurpassed views of urban Hong Kong.

Despite the crowds and the sometimes debilitating heat, this part of Hong Kong is a great place for walking. The area's compactness and the ever changing nature of its streets provide plenty of entertainment. For the foot weary, one of the best ways to take in the northern corridor's sights is to climb aboard a double-decker tram as it trundles from Kennedy Town in the west to Shau Kei Wan near the northeastern tip of the island. ∎

midpoint is a wall of tall skyscrapers. At Central, landfill has pushed the original shoreline more than 200 yards (180 m) into the harbor to accommodate modern high-rise architecture. The view of the skyline across Victoria Harbour from Tsim Sha Tsui, with Victoria Peak as a backdrop, is stunning.

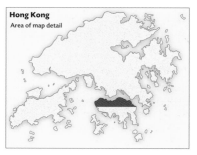

Hong Kong
Area of map detail

NEW TERRITORIES
p. 153

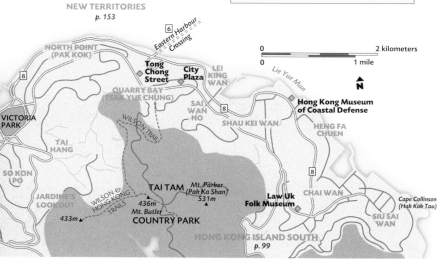

Central to the Peak

Central is the defining image of Hong Kong. It is here where British Hong Kong began in the 1840s and where the dynamism of today's city is at its most evident.

A 26,000-foot escalator rides up the steep incline to the Mid-Levels.

When banker Sir Catchick Paul Chater (1842–1923) arrived in Hong Kong in 1864, the overcrowded Central District edged Victoria Harbour at the foot of Victoria Peak along Queen's Road. The only way to relieve this congestion, Chater reasoned, was to create more land by filling the lapping waters. By 1889, landfill was being poured into Victoria Harbour. Today this reclamation runs for six blocks through some of the world's most expensive real estate. Around the same time, the government decided to forest then-barren Victoria Peak. Trees were hauled up the mountain and planted, eventually creating an area of great natural beauty on the doorstep of a frenetic downtown.

Central is an outstanding spectacle. Dozens of office towers are squeezed onto reclaimed land, and residential blocks climb the lower reaches of Victoria Peak at the Mid-Levels, gradually thinning to luxury apartment blocks and mansions among the mists of the Peak.

SoHo

CAINE

CONDUIT ROBINSON ROAD

Central to Mid-Levels Escalator

MID-LEVELS (PUN SHAN KUI)

LUGARD

ROAD

▲ 552m Victoria Peak (Che Kei Shan)

MOUNT AUSTIN ROAD

HONG KONG ROAD

OLD PEAK ROAD

VICTORIA PEAK GARDEN

HARLECH ROAD

PEAK TRAIL

THE PEAK

Peak Tower

Lion's Pavilion & Lookout

PEAK ROAD

Peak Galleria

FINDLAY

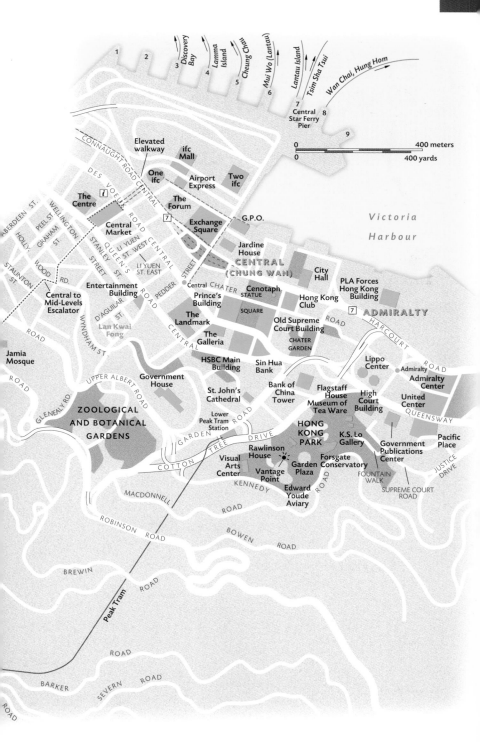

1
2
3 Discovery Bay
4 Lamma Island
5 Cheung Chau
6 Mui Wo (Lantau)
Lantau Island
Tsim Sha Tsui
Wan Chai, Hung Hom
7 Central Star Ferry Pier
8
9

CONNAUGHT ROAD CENTRAL

Elevated walkway

ifc Mall

DES VOEUX ROAD CENTRAL

One ifc

Airport Express

Two ifc

The Centre

The Forum

Central Market

G.P.O.

Exchange Square

Victoria Harbour

0   400 meters
0   400 yards

ABERDEEN ST.
PEEL ST.
WELLINGTON ST.
GRAHAM ST.
HOLLYWOOD RD.
STAUNTON ST.
STANLEY STREET
QUEEN'S ST.
LI YUEN ST. WEST
LI YUEN ST. EAST

Jardine House

CENTRAL
(CHUNG WAN)

City Hall

PLA Forces Hong Kong Building

Entertainment Building

Central to Mid-Levels Escalator

D'AGUILAR ST.
Lan Kwai Fong
WYNDHAM ST.
PEDDER STREET

Central
CHATER

Prince's Building

Cenotaph

CHATER SQUARE

STATUE

Hong Kong Club

Old Supreme Court Building

ADMIRALTY

HARCOURT ROAD

The Landmark

The Galleria

CENTRAL

CHATER GARDEN

Lippo Center

Jamia Mosque

UPPER ALBERT ROAD

Government House

HSBC Main Building

Sin Hua Bank

Flagstaff House Museum of Tea Ware

High Court Building

Admiralty

Admiralty Center

United Center

QUEENSWAY

GLENEALY RD.

St. John's Cathedral

Bank of China Tower

ZOOLOGICAL AND BOTANICAL GARDENS

GARDEN ROAD

Lower Peak Tram Station

HONG KONG PARK

K.S. Lo Gallery

Government Publications Center

Pacific Place

COTTON TREE DRIVE

Visual Arts Center

Rawlinson House

Vantage Point

Garden Plaza

Forsgate Conservatory

FOUNTAIN WALK

JUSTICE DRIVE

MACDONNELL ROAD

KENNEDY ROAD

Edward Youde Aviary

SUPREME COURT ROAD

ROBINSON ROAD

BOWEN ROAD

BREWIN ROAD

Peak Tram

ROAD

BARKER ROAD

SEVERN ROAD

Shopping à la mode at Central's chic Landmark mall

Central District
◣ Map p. 53

Hemmed in by gleaming skyscrapers are pockets of preserved colonial history. Lively markets, noodle stands, restaurants, shophouses, and worn tenement buildings crowd the backstreets. To the east, Victoria Barracks, which once housed the Hong Kong Regiment, has given way to the landscaped beauty of Hong Kong Park.

Just outside the park, the 115-year-old Peak Tram begins its seemingly impossible climb up Victoria Peak. From here, the views are breathtaking. An easy walk around the shoulder of the Peak reveals the green side of Hong Kong Island—lush vegetation, verdant valleys, and vistas of the South China Sea and the outlying islands.

Central District

This small, sometimes absurdly crowded pocket of reclaimed land is the headquarters of hundreds of financial institutions, home to the seat of government, and prestigious address to several upscale shopping centers.

Take the Star Ferry (see p. 122–123) from Tsim Sha Tsui in Kowloon across Victoria Harbour to the ferry's new Central pier for a spectacular introduction to the area. Just south of the ferry concourse, by Connaught Garden and the Henry Moore bronze sculpture "Double Oval," is **Jardine House.** The 600-foot-tall (201 m) building, with its metallic facade and trademark porthole windows, was the highest in Hong Kong when constructed in 1973. Enter the lobby and take the escalator up one floor to a walkway which leads to **Exchange Square,** three semicircular office buildings with gold-bronze polished granite and glass exteriors resembling stacked coins. This is home to the Stock Exchange of Hong Kong, known as the Hang Seng, Asia's largest bourse outside of Japan. The entrance is marked by another Henry Moore bronze, "Oval with Points." More sculptures—"Taichi," a bronze figure representing tai chi exercises from Taiwan's Chu Ming, and Dame Elisabeth Frink's "Water Buffaloes"—sit in pools of cascading water at **The Forum** courtyard, a pleasant plaza with outdoor cafés.

In front of Exchange Square is the **ifc** (International Finance Centre) complex. It comprises the ifc Mall, One ifc at 39 floors, Two ifc, which, at 88 stories, is one of the tallest buildings in the world, and the 55-story Four Seasons Hotel Hong Kong. The **ifc Mall** is a brightly lit chrome and tile collection of cinemas, upscale stores, and restaurants. It encompasses the MTR Hong Kong Station for trains on the Airport Express Line.

Climb D'Aguilar Street, one block east of Li Yuen Street, to the cobbled lanes of lively nightlife center **Lan Kwai Fong.** Dozens of restaurants, bistros, bars, and nightclubs catering to the territory's hip residents cluster in two small lanes.

The pyramid style is echoed at the **Entertainment Building** *(corner of Queen's Rd. Central & Wyndham St.).* Whimsical touches, like the huge balconies on two sides at the penthouse level and an art deco motif in the frieze around the building, lift the beige granite and gray glass facade above the ordinary. Inside is an elegant colonnaded shopping arcade.

Statue Square & East:

Follow Queen's Road Central east and cut through the plaza under the Hongkong and Shanghai Bank Building (see p. 61) to the gardens, pools, and fountains of restful **Statue Square.** It gets its name from British colonial statues, including those of Queen Victoria (r. 1837–1901) and King Edward VII (r. 1901–1910), which once decorated the small park. The Japanese removed them during World War II (Queen Victoria now rests in Victoria Park in Causeway Bay; see pp. 94–96). The lone holdout is frock-coated Sir Thomas Jackson (1841–1915), a onetime chief manager of the Hongkong and Shanghai Bank. The bank's imposing headquarters lies opposite on Queen's Road Central.

Rickshaws

At the Star Ferry concourse, a dwindling number of rickshaw pullers sit ready to take tourists on a short ride or to let them pose (for a modest price) in front of their vehicles.

Invented in Japan, rickshaws were a popular mode of transportation in Hong Kong during the first half of the 20th century. By World War I, some 5,000 carried people around the streets. Their numbers then plummeted, but rickshaws were revived in the difficult days after World War II, when there were an estimated 8,000 on the streets. Numbers fell again as motorized vehicles took over, and by the 1960s they were used mainly as a tourist attraction. Today, only a handful of rickshaws are left.

Bank of China Tower

Map p. 55

1 Garden Rd., Central

City Hall

Map p. 55

51 Edinburgh Pl., Central

2921-2840

Zoological & Botanical Gardens

Map p. 55

Albany Rd., Central

2530-0154

Bus: 3B, 12, 13

Take a look at the two splendid **bronze lion figures** out front—the one at the bank building's eastern end is punctured with a number of bullet holes, a legacy of the Japanese occupation during World War II. On the northern side of Chater Road in Statue Square, a **Cenotaph,** built in 1923 and now a monument to troops who died during the two World Wars, sits amid a lush lawn in front of the Hong Kong Club, the venerable gentleman's establishment.

Just east of Statue Square, on the opposite side of Hong Kong's

INSIDER TIP:

For shopping bargains, visit the Li Yuen Street markets in Central. Nestled among glitzy stores, these tiny alleys are jammed full of bargains, especially cheap clothes.

—JODI ROWLEY
National Geographic field researcher

seat of government, the neoclassical Legislative Council Building (also known as the Old Supreme Court Building; see p. 62), is **Chater Garden.** Designed in similar style to Statue Square, with brick and tiled pathways, gardens, shelters, pools, and lawns, it's a good place to escape the stifling daytime heat. Until 1975, the park was the playing field for the exclusive Hong Kong Cricket Club. Climb the walkway that fringes the eastern end of the garden for excellent views of the towering 1,209-foot (396 m)

Bank of China Tower. Designed by I. M. Pei in 1982, this 70-story building's sharp lines, pristine facade, and intimidating presence dominate Central's skyline. Take the express elevator to the 43rd floor for panoramic views of the city and harbor. Next door, the art deco old Bank of China building is Central's oldest surviving high-rise office tower, completed in 1951.

In the most recent round of reclamation, the waterfront was again pushed back, and the destruction of the iconic 1950s Star Ferry Pier and Queen's Pier, where British governors were traditionally received, caused much popular protest. Sitting just back from the waterfront is **City Hall,** a nondescript building housing a fine concert hall and theater, where you can find information about upcoming performances, and buy tickets.

Zoological & Botanical Gardens: To the south, across Queensway and up Garden Road, you will find the lush tropical vegetation and the Victorian-style gardens, gazebos, and enclosures of the Zoological and Botanical Gardens. Opened in 1864, the gardens are the oldest in Hong Kong and encompass 13 acres (5 ha). The eastern section is known as the Old Gardens; its attractions include a playground, aviaries, a jaguar enclosure, a greenhouse, and a fountain terrace garden. The majority of the zoo's animals are kept in the New Gardens to the west.

Despite the restricted space of some of the animal enclosures, the zoo has a comprehensive selection of Asian wildlife, and is one of

Asia's most important centers for breeding endangered species.

The gardens are bounded by Garden, Robinson, Glenealy, and Upper Albert Roads, and divided into two parts by Albany Road, with a subway linking them.

SoHo & the Mid-Levels Escalator

At Queen's Road Central, Central begins its steep climb toward the residential area of the Mid-Levels. Streets are narrow and winding, with some so steep that steps replace roads. Flashy high-rise buildings give way to more modest stores and restaurants topped by tenements.

Start your journey at **Central Market,** where a first-floor arcade connects you to the Central to the Mid-Levels Escalator *(downhill 6 a.m.–10 a.m.; uphill 10 a.m.– 11 p.m.).* The world's longest covered escalator (2,600 feet/800 m), it was completed in 1993 to ease

the passage of residents getting home via taxi and minibus through the winding streets linking Central to the Mid-Levels. It rides up Cochrane Street past the second-floor windows of apartment buildings and shops to Hollywood Road (see p. 76). It then doglegs west, continuing south up Shelley Street before reaching its final point at Conduit Road in the heart of the Mid-Levels. Passengers can get off at a number or clearly marked exits en route and explore the narrow streets and alleyways.

Stanley Street is worth investigating for its fragrant outdoor noodle and pastry shops. **Graham Street,** one block to the west, is lined with hawkers selling fresh produce. A left turn at **Gage Street** reveals more lively markets. From here, **Peel Street** climbs to Hollywood Road past stores selling religious paraphernalia. East along Hollywood Road for one block brings you to **Lyndhurst Terrace.**

Central to the Mid-Levels Escalator
 Map pp. 54–55

Many of Central's famous skyscrapers tower above the Zoological & Botanical Gardens.

Continue east on Lyndhurst to rejoin the escalator. At Staunton, Elgin, and Shelley Streets, a trendy restaurant and nightclub precinct called **SoHo**—an abbreviation of South of Hollywood Road—has sprung up in the escalator's shadow to rival Lan Kwai Fong (see p. 57). The journey up the escalator takes about 20 minutes, and steps beside it lead back down the hill.

Central's lively back streets harbor noodle shops, small markets, and other vibrant facets of daily life.

Admiralty

Admiralty was the site of the Hong Kong Regiment's Victoria Barracks and, up until the Chinese handover in 1997, the Royal Navy's headquarters at Tamar. After the handover, the site was acquired by the People's Liberation Army and renamed Central Barracks. The barracks are occasionally open to the public. A few of the original buildings remain in Hong Kong Park (see pp. 64–67).

The military vacated Victoria Barracks during the 1970s, freeing the valuable land for redevelopment. Shopping centers, hotels, and office towers replaced them. Admiralty can be reached from Central by taking the elevated walkway at the eastern end of Chater Garden. Along this route are the twin towers of the **Lippo Center,** a brash and dominating office building that features bold "sky windows"—lumpy protrusions hanging from its sides. This building has been nicknamed the "koala tree," as its shape vaguely resembles koalas gripping the trunk of a tree. In the lobby, two dramatic bas-relief murals by one of Hong Kong's best known artists, Gerard D'Henderson, cover the walls.

Next to the Lippo Center, the shopping arcades of the United Center and Admiralty Center join an elevated walkway to glitzy **Pacific Place,** housing department stores, boutiques, bars, cinemas, offices, luxury hotels, and restaurants. When it was completed in the early 1990s, the boldness and enterprise of Pacific Place reflected the optimism and growing affluence of Asia at the time, and it became the prototype for similar developments around the region. The complex is worth a visit for its sheer size and overstatement.

Adjoining Pacific Place, the **High Court Building** is not an example of exceptional architecture, but interesting for its courtrooms where barristers and judges still dress in wigs and flowing robes and proceed through cases with the same due formality of British courts. There are public galleries.

On the ground-floor level between Pacific Place and the High Court is the **Government Publications Center,** a good place to pick up maps and publications on Hong Kong.

HSBC Main Building

When the headquarters of HSBC (formerly the Hongkong & Shanghai Banking Corporation) was completed in 1985, it had cost one billion U.S. dollars, making it the most expensive building ever constructed at the time. But for the bosses of the bank, it was well worth the cost; its innovation and sophistication make it one of the most recognizable buildings in the world.

When architect Sir Norman Foster (b. 1935) took on the challenge of designing the building, his major problem was squeezing it into the space made available at 1 Queen's Road Central after the demolition of the previous headquarters (the current structure is the fourth on this site since the bank's founding in 1865). The bank wanted to fit a huge office tower into an area that would normally preclude such a design.

Foster got around this problem by eliminating a central core; he instead designed a framework that hung from five huge trusses, with eight groups of four-column steel clusters, wrapped in aluminum,

supporting them. The "coat hanger" effect resulted in a building whose floors hang from above, rather than ascend from below. This design also allowed for the inclusion of a giant atrium, opening up a huge amount of space and light. Extra natural light is achieved by the use of computer-controlled mirrors that reflect light into the atrium.

The architect's extensive use of non-reflective glass in the design

---

How to Exchange Business Cards in Hong Kong

Because the city is driven by business, it's hard to overstate the importance of exchanging business cards in Hong Kong. No matter how briefly you interact with someone, you will probably exchange cards. Therefore, it pays to carry an ample supply.

The giving and receiving of business cards is very much tied up with the traditional Chinese idea of face. Be aware that the way in which you receive someone's card will set the tone for your relationship.

A card should be taken by holding its bottom two corners with both hands. The card should always be inspected immediately. Similarly, you should give your card with both hands and be sure that the printing on it faces the recipient. You should also be careful not to write on someone else's business card.

Admiralty

 Map p. 55

High Court Building

✉ 38 Queensway

☎ 2869-0869

Government Publications Center

✉ Room 402, Murray Bldg., Garden Rd., Central

☎ 2537-1910

HSBC Main Building

 Map p. 55

✉ 1 Queen's Rd., Central

☎ 2822-1111

🕐 Closed Sat. 1 p.m. & Sun.

Ⓜ MTR: Central

A Walk Around Central's Colonial Heritage

Hong Kong has few older buildings of architectural merit, but the scattering of historical remnants around Central provides some insight into the territory's colonial past.

The French Mission Building—now housing the Court of Final Appeal—is one of a number of colonial buildings found in Central.

Start in front of the **Old Supreme Court Building ❶** (8 Jackson Rd.), which divides Statue Square and Chater Garden. This fine neoclassical building, with its domed roof, was built in 1912 and became home to the Hong Kong government's legislature in 1985.

From here cross Des Voeux Road Central to the HSBC Building. Walk through its plaza and cross Queen's Road Central to the steps of tree-lined **Battery Path.** A five-minute climb brings you to the redbrick **French Mission Building ❷**. Rebuilt in 1917, it's also neoclassical in design. It now houses the Court of Final Appeal, set up after Hong Kong was handed back to China in 1997. The concrete and slightly mundane buildings across the road are home to the Hong Kong government.

Continue up Battery Path to Garden Road and the 1849 Anglican **St. John's Cathedral ❸** (4–8 Garden Rd., tel 2523-4157). With its

NOT TO BE MISSED:

Old Supreme Court Building • Battery Path • Government House

Gothic-style architecture, cruciform shape, and ornate bell tower above the main entrance, it's the oldest ecclesiastical building in Hong Kong.

Climb Garden Road for five minutes toward the Lower Peak Tram Station at St. John's Building, on the opposite side of Garden Road, to the **Helena May Building ❹** (35 Garden Rd.). It was constructed in 1916 at the request of the wife of Francis Henry May, who governed between 1912 and 1917, as a hostel for young women arriving in the colony, a function it still serves. Stay on the right and keep climbing to

Upper Albert Road and **Government House 5**, official residence for British Hong Kong governors from 1855 to 1997. The building's colonial look was modified during the Japanese occupation with the addition of a rectangular eave tower. It is used now for official functions and open to the public a couple of times a year. There are good views of it from its front gates. The Chief Executive, Donald Tsang, uses it as his official residence, unlike his predecessor. Government House's garden is open to the public six times each year, usually on official holidays. Visitors are also usually allowed to pass by the Drawing Room, Dining Room, and Ballroom on these days.

Backtrack down Upper Albert Road to Lower Albert Road. Follow it to Ice House Street. Opposite is the two-story **Old Dairy Farm Building 6** (Lower Albert Rd.). Built in 1892 and renovated between 1912 and 1917, it is notable for its horizontal striped walls of red brick and white stucco, first-floor porthole windows, ornate shingles, and bull-nose corner. Today it is home to one of

Hong Kong's best known bars at the Foreign Correspondents Club, and The Fringe Club—a vibrant, contemporary arts center.

Opposite, near the intersection of Lower Albert and Glenealy Roads and Wyndham Street, is the home of the Anglican Bishop of Hong Kong at **Bishop's House 7** (1 Lower Albert Rd.). This 1848 building features a circular tower and lookout at one of its corners. Looking south to Glenealy Road, you will notice the Gothic-inspired spire of St. Paul's Church, from the early 20th century.

From the Old Dairy Farm Building, you can make your way down Wyndham Street to Queen's Road Central.

> See area map p. 55
> ▶ Old Supreme Court Building
> ↔ 1.5 miles (2.5 km)
> ⏱ 2 hours
> ▶ Corner of Wyndham St. &
>   Queen's Rd. Central

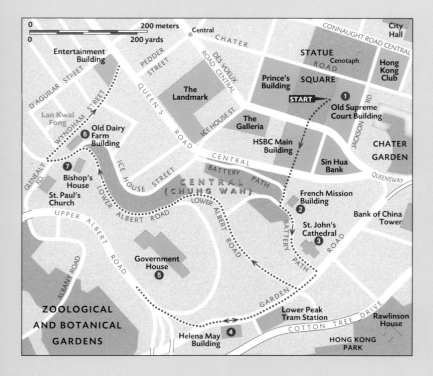

Hong Kong Park

Map p. 52

19 Cotton Tree Dr.

2521-5041

MTR: Admiralty, exit F

reveals the mechanical workings of the building and has earned it the nickname the "robot building." The gears, chains, motors, and

INSIDER TIP:

Hong Kong Park is ignored by most visitors. Stroll it to see flowers, ponds, and people relaxing, as well as the aviary and tea house.

—A. J. TIMOTHY JULL
National Geographic field researcher

other moveable parts of the escalators and elevators are visible.

Although space may have been a problem, money never was. Bank executives stressed to Foster that they wanted the best possible, implying that cost was a secondary matter. The design had to symbolize the power, stability, and technological proficiency of the bank itself. "The world's most expensive building" tag became their proud boast, rather than an embarrassment of excess and a waste of stockholders' money.

The ground floor is public space you can pass through without entering the building. From there, two escalators rise to the main banking hall. They are carefully positioned to take the maximum flow of *qi* or *chi* (energy) into the building, one of the concessions made to the

principles of *feng shui* (see p. 112–113). Two bronze lions, part of the previous bank building, are positioned at each end of the bank, ensuring harmony.

Hong Kong Park

Hong Kong Park is a collection of gardens, greenhouses, museums, galleries, aviaries, playgrounds, and man-made lakes, ponds, and waterfalls sitting between a wall of high-rise buildings and towering mountains. Exploring this 25-acre (10 ha) jumble of artifice, antiquity, and natural beauty makes a delightful respite from Central's crowded streets.

Escalators at Pacific Place (see p. 60) bring you to the park's main entrance at Supreme Court Road (there are two other entrances along Cotton Tree Drive). The **Fountain Walk** takes you to the main gates and inside the park.

Walk to the right of the park's restaurant, past a winding artificial lake to a covered walkway that runs up to **Rawlinson House,** one of a few 19th-century Victoria Barracks buildings in the park, and now the Cotton Tree Drive Marriage Registry. Opposite is **Olympic Square,** a terraced, open-air theater modeled on a Greek amphitheater and built into the hillside. Live music, plays, and puppet theater are performed on Sundays and public holidays.

Steps between the marriage registry and Olympic Square climb to the base of the **Vantage Point,** a circular tower whose spiral staircase leads to an

The unusual skeletal profile of HSBC's headquarters sets it apart from the other skyscraping marvels that fill Central.

observation deck and stunning views of Central, with glimpses of Victoria Harbour. Walk through the walled Tai Chi Court. In the cooler hours of early morning and late afternoon, tai chi practitioners fill its courtyards.

Beyond is the park's most impressive feature, the walkthrough **Edward Youde Aviary.** Named for one of Hong Kong's

3008, closed Tues.), in the restored Cassels Block of Victoria Barracks. One of Hong Kong's more elegant colonial buildings, it has a stepped roof, cool verandas, and a garden setting. A modern gallery annex with a steel and glass spine roof has been added. It houses an exhibition gallery and local artists' studios.

Heading back toward the main entrance past Olympic Square and

Lush vegetation and colonial architecture make Hong Kong Park a refreshing escape from Central's urban melee.

nature-loving colonial governors, it is one of the largest of its type in the world. This huge meshed enclosure, simulating a tropical rain forest, houses 800 birds from 100 species. Beneath the enclosure is the remarkable mock-up of a 1,000-year-old rain forest. You can get close to the birds from the elevated timber walkway, which zigzags through the aviary at tree-canopy level. About 50 feet (15 m) below it, a creek bubbles through the forest.

On the park's southern edge is the **Visual Arts Center** (tel 2521-

the aviary, you will see the impressive **Forsgate Conservatory,** built into a slope. This greenhouse, the largest in East and Southeast Asia, has a number of climate-controlled environments, including a tropical rain forest terraced with dense vegetation and flowering plants, a "dry" plant house replicating a desert, and an exhibition hall.

Flagstaff House Museum of Tea Ware: At the northern perimeter of the park, this museum is housed in one of Hong Kong's oldest surviving colonial buildings. Originally the residence of the commander of British forces in Hong Kong, Flagstaff House has undergone a number of transformations. Today, with its whitewashed, unadorned facade, uncomplicated rectangular shape, columned verandas, huge shuttered windows, and lofty position, it represents one of the finest examples of mid-19th-century colonial architecture in Hong Kong. The interior layout has changed little from the original, though the military commanders' bedrooms, dressing rooms, library, drawing room, and servants quarters are now replaced by galleries.

The fascinating core of the museum's permanent exhibition consists of pieces of tea ware, which date from the Western Zhou period (ca 1122–771 B.C.) up until the present. Song dynasty tea ware includes an elegant teacup on a stand finished in Yingqing glaze, a ewer with a wispy carved peony design, and tea bowls in russet brown glaze and molded designs.

The ground-floor galleries host the "Chinese Tea Drinking" exhibit that shows different methods of tea preparation throughout Chinese history. Exquisite tea ware from the Tang dynasty (618–907) through the Qing dynasty (1644–1911) is displayed here. Temporary exhibits are staged in the upper galleries, and a gift shop just inside its main door sells tea ware, Chinese tea, art books, and exhibition catalogs.

The **K. S. Lo Gallery,** adjacent to the Museum of Tea Ware, contains rare Chinese ceramics from the Song dynasty (960–1279) to the Ming dynasty (1368–1644), as well as seals from the late Ming dynasty to the present.

The Peak

From the Peak's various vantage points spectacular vistas take in most of Hong Kong Island, Kowloon, much of the New Territories, the outlying islands, mainland China, and Macau. A trip to the Peak should be one of

Flagstaff House Museum of Tea Ware

- ✉ 10 Cotton Tree Dr.
- ☎ 2869-0690
- 🕐 Closed Tues.
- 🚇 MTR: Admiralty, exit F

Peak Tram

Taking the Peak Tram from its lower station at Murray House on Garden Road in Central is a memorable way to get to the Peak. Completed in 1888, the tram was the first power-driven form of land transportation in the colony. It was built to satisfy the needs of the colonial elite, who sought a more comfortable way home from Central than a shaky sedan-chair ride up Old Peak Road. Five lateral stations were built en route, enabling passengers to hop off the tram for the trip to their mansions by foot or sedan chair—or, in the case of one resident, by camel.

These days, the modern carriages of the Peak Tram funicular railway carry visitors up from the bustle of Central through the smart apartment blocks of the Mid-Levels at an unbelievable angle. Before the tram glides into its upper station at the Peak Tower, the striking panorama of Central, the harbor, and the Kowloon Peninsula is laid out below as the tram clears the tree line at the mid-reaches of Victoria Peak.

After more than a century of operation, the tram has never had an accident. The 12-minute ride operates daily every 15 minutes from 7 a.m. to midnight.

Chinese Tea

Ancient Chinese texts attribute the discovery of tea to Emperor Shen Nung, who was believed to have ruled about 2737 B.C. According to legend, he was sipping hot, boiled water in his garden when a leaf from a tea bush nearby fell into his cup. He smelled and tasted the infusion and reckoned it was a big improvement over hot water. Tea drinking was born.

Nearly obliterated by the Cultural Revolution, tea drinking is undergoing a mini-revival in Hong Kong. Traditional teahouses, such as this one in Kowloon, are wonderful places to watch a tea master prepare the leaves—then sample the delicious result yourself.

The practice took a while to catch on, however. Though historians can trace the harvesting, manufacture, and drinking of tea back 2,000 years, its cultural significance did not begin until the Tang and Song dynasties. *The Tea Classics,* the bible of tea, written by Lu Yu during the Tang

dynasty, helped to elevate the art of tea drinking throughout China. During the Song dynasty, books, poems, and paintings about tea pushed the act into a cultural experience. During the Ming dynasty scholar Li Ri Hua offered instructions on how and when tea should be consumed:

"One should clean out a room in one's home and place only a tea table and a chair in the room with some boiled water and fragrant tea. Afterwards, sit salutarily and allow one's spirit to become tranquil, light, and natural."

The Chinese believe their view on tea drinking is symbolic of their balanced position toward attitudes and behaviors, and that in the interpretation of the art of tea, you can find the source of their open-mindedness.

Unlike the Japanese, who place heavy emphasis on rigid ceremony, the Chinese concentrate more on preparation, taste, and how to drink tea, with a tea master in charge of proceedings. Traditionally, a red clay pot is used to brew the tea. The tea master rinses the pot and tiny cups—which only hold about two swallows—then places the tea leaves in the pot. Hot spring water from a glass kettle is poured into the pot until the water overflows. The water is quickly drained to enhance the flavor of the tea. More water is poured into the pot and left to steep for under a minute and then poured into the cups ready to drink. Much detail is paid to the amount of tea used, the temperature of the water—different leaves require different temperatures—and how long the tea steeps; too long or too short affects the aroma and taste.

Types of Tea

Of hundreds of varieties of Chinese tea, many of which are sold in merchants' shops in Hong Kong's traditional Western District, there are six major types:

Black tea is a popular type, especially outside of China. The fermentation process turns the tea from green to black, offering a more robust taste.

Compacted tea is black or green tea tightly packed into brick, cake, or ball shapes. Because it's easier to store, it's popular with China's ethnic minorities— especially nomadic herdsmen.

Green tea has the longest history and is most popular, with a freshness and natural fragrance many find appealing. Famous examples include Longjing, Maofeng, Yin-zhen, and Yunwu.

Stores selling innumerable varieties of tea can be found in the Western District.

Scented tea is made by mixing green tea with flower petals using an elaborate process. Sweet osmanthus, jasmine, rose, orchid, and plum flowers are used.

White tea is a silver color and does not cloud when added to water.

Wulong tea mixes the freshness of green tea and the robustness of black tea. It is reputed to be helpful in losing weight and therefore has gained in popularity. Because it grows on cliffs and is difficult to pick, it is one of the more expensive Chinese teas.

Peak Tower

- Map p. 52
- 128 Peak Rd.
- 2849-0668
- Bus: 15; Minibus: 1

www.thepeak.com.hk

the first things visitors do after arriving in Hong Kong, not only for its world-famous views, but to gain a perspective of the city. Pick a cloudless day—increasingly rare with Hong Kong's air pollution problems—and make two journeys, one during daylight and another in the evening to catch a memorable image of Hong Kong illuminated.

The Peak has been the preferred place of residence in Hong Kong since the British arrived in 1841. Top government officials and *taipans* (European merchants) built their mansions there to escape the stifling summer heat—it's cooler than the lower reaches of Hong Kong Island—and were ferried up and down its steep slopes in sedan chairs carried by Chinese coolies. The governor's summer residence was built there and anyone who wished to settle in this rarified atmosphere had to

gain permission from the governor of the day. Up until 1945, Chinese were forbidden to live on the Peak. These days, the area remains a fashionable place, reflected in real estate prices that are among the highest in the world.

Most visitors to Victoria Peak arrive by a funicular railway (see Peak Tram p. 73), which climbs out of Central at an impossible angle to reach the upper station at the **Peak Tower**—a metallic, bowl-shaped landmark. The Peak Tower has had a major renovation and now features a 360-degree viewing terrace on top of the building. The platform offers outstanding views, looking down Victoria Peak to the high-rise residential buildings of Mid-Levels and the gleaming office towers crowded into Central and beyond that to Tsim Sha Tsui fenced in by the jagged mountains of the New Territories. Back down on the ground, the complex is also

The Peak's famous vista over Hong Kong Island and beyond

home to restaurants and shops and the 100-plus waxworks of **Madame Tussauds.**

Across the plaza, the **Peak Galleria** also offers excellent views, restaurants and bars, as well as a supermarket, for those who want to picnic on the Peak. Buses arrive and depart from the Galleria.

Peak Walks: The juxtaposition of Hong Kong Island's countryside and city is at its most evident and dramatic around Victoria Peak. Views from the Peak's northern face look down over green slopes to towering residential and office buildings. From its southern aspect, you can see wooded valleys, cozy waterside communities, and peaceful islands.

All walks start at the confluence of roads next to the Peak Tower and the Galleria. The paths that spread from here are well marked with signs that also provide approximate walking times to different destinations.

The summit of Victoria Peak is another quarter mile (500 m) to the west, up steep Mount Austin Road, opposite the Peak Tower. The Japanese razed the governor's mansion here during World War II, and the area is now a pleasant **garden.** The views, which include the neoclassical mansions of Hong Kong's superwealthy, are magnificent.

One of the most popular walks is a 70-minute amble around the Peak along **Lugard Road** and **Harlech Road.** The 2.2-mile (3.5 km) route encircles Victoria Peak along a smooth, mostly flat pathway. Start at the Peak Tower and head west along Lugard Road

through groves of ferns, stunted Chinese pines, rhododendron, bamboo, and hibiscus. As you head west, views open up to Victoria Harbour, the huge West Kowloon reclamation project, the Yau Ma Tei Typhoon Shelter, and Green and Peng Chau Islands. Lantau, Hong Kong's largest island, comes into view to the west, as does Macau (see pp. 216–227). Farther west you will spot Cheung

INSIDER TIP:

If you take the tram to the top of the Peak, don't go back the same way. Ride a city bus down through interesting neighborhoods.

—A. J. TIMOTHY JULL
National Geographic field researcher

Chau Island and to the southwest, two huge power-plant smokestacks rise from Lamma Island (see pp. 204–205). The pathway rounds to the south side of the island to scenes of lush Pokfulam Valley and the junks and sampans anchored in Aberdeen Typhoon Shelter. The walk ends back at the Peak Tower.

About 1.4 miles (2 km) into the walk, you can take a track that descends into the thickly wooded **Pokfulam Valley** to Pokfulam Reservoir—the entire 1.2-mile (1.9 km) route takes about 40 minutes. From just beyond the reservoir, you can catch a bus back to Central.

For views of the eastern and southeastern sides of Hong Kong

Madame Tussauds

✉ Peak Tower, Level 2

☎ 2849-6966

$ $$

www.madame-tussauds.com.hk

Island, head south down Peak Road about 500 yards (0.5 km) from the Galleria to Plunket Road, which forks to the left and leads to Plantation Road. Follow Plantation Road until it meets **Severn Road,** then turn right and start your first

airport at Chek Lap Kok. Follow Severn Road west as it climbs back toward the Peak to Findlay Road and on to the Galleria. The 3-mile (5 km) walk takes about 90 minutes.

You can also head down to the

Views, views, and yet more views along the Hong Kong Trail

descent as it circles almost halfway around the Peak. From here Aberdeen Typhoon Shelter comes into view. Farther to the left is sprawling Ocean Park (see pp. 114–115), the Deep Water Bay residential area, and Repulse Bay, which is home to Hong Kong's favorite beach.

As Severn Road swings abruptly left, you will see expansive vistas of the eastern section of Hong Kong Island and Victoria Harbour. Causeway Bay Typhoon Shelter and North Point appear on the right, while across the harbor is the skyline of Tsim Sha Tsui and, to its right, the runway of Kai Tak airport, which was replaced in 1998 with the international

Zoological and Botanical Gardens (see p. 58) and on to Central by following the steep and winding **Old Peak Road** down the summit. The road begins between the Peak Tower and Galleria. Stop 100 yards (90 m) down the hill at the Chinese-style **Lion's Pavilion and Lookout** for unhindered views of Central, the harbor, and Tsim Sha Tsui.

Hong Kong Trail

Of Hong Kong Island's 30 square miles (78 sq km), just over a third is given over to country parks. These parks are linked by the 30-mile (48 km) Hong Kong Trail, which traverses the length of Hong Kong Island, taking in four of the island's six country parks (see pp. 40–42), offering a surprising diversity of natural beauty mixed with stunning glimpses of cityscapes from their loftier points.

When the British arrived in 1841, Hong Kong Island was all but barren. A project to reforest the island began in the 1870s, and the results can be appreciated from walks along the Hong Kong Trail.

The trail starts at Victoria Peak (see pp. 67, 70–72) and follows Lugard Road to the west before dropping down to Pokfulam Reservoir. It then heads east over the island's rugged interior to the seaside village of Shek O (see p. 105). The trail runs along the ridges of the peaks dividing the island from east to west. From the upper reaches, grassland descends into scrubland. Farther down, ravines and gullies cut through thick woodlands. Views down the slopes reveal a coastline indented with coves and bays.

Each park has its own characteristics. The peaks of **Pokfulam** command stunning ocean, island, and valley views. Streams crisscross the dense growth in the valleys of **Aberdeen.** Scenic **Tai Tam** (see p. 104) combines forests and Hong Kong's largest (man-made) lake, while the shores of **Shek O** taper off into the South China Sea.

The Hong Kong Trail is split into eight sections, each rated for difficulty. Covering the whole trail in one day would be too strenuous for most; there are no camping facilities. It's better to break up the walk, or choose one section. The trail is well maintained and well marked. You can obtain maps from the Government Publications Center *(Room 402, Murray Bldg., Garden Rd., Central, tel 2537-1910).* ∎

Hong Kong Trail
- Map p. 52
- Starts at Lugard Rd., the Peak
- 1823 (hotline)
- Bus: 15; Minibus: 1
- **www.afcd.gov.hk**

EXPERIENCE: Learn to Cook Chinese Cuisine

If you enjoy the local Chinese food, why not learn how to cook it? All the schools below offer English-language instruction. **Chinese Cuisine Training Institute** *(tel 2538-2371, www.vtc.edu.hk).* A four-hour course at this chef's training college includes a brief introduction to Chinese cooking methods and history, followed by hands-on cooking of two to three dishes. Priced at HK$620.

Chopstick Cooking Centre *(tel 2336-8433).* Chopstick offers two-hour sessions for tourists as well as a weeklong professional, intensive course; both focus on local Cantonese cuisine. Sessions start at HK$780, depending on participation. **Cookery.com.hk** *(tel 2381-0132, www .cookery.com.hk).* Offers intensive one-day courses covering the basics of Cantonese cooking, as well as courses on preparing dim sum and Chinese desserts. Prices are around HK$1,500 for a full day's instruction.

Home Management Centre *(tel 2510-2828, www.heh.com).* By far the best value session offered comes, surprisingly, from the Hong Kong Electric company. Their weekly two-hour session teaches three Chinese dishes, with different dishes each week, for the ridiculously low price of HK$85 per session. The popular class is held Wednesdays at 10:30 a.m; reserve well in advance. The center also offers Pakistani, Indian, and Vietnamese cooking classes.

West of Central

Soon after British settlement, the colonial government set aside the area to the west of Central for the thousands of Chinese emigrants flocking to Hong Kong. Artisans, shopkeepers, traders, and coolies made their homes and set up businesses in this Western District; it became a raucous, industrious place. In storefront workshops, artisans and tradesmen turned out their goods.

Built sometime before the British arrived in 1841, Man Mo Temple in Western is Hong Kong's oldest place of worship.

This is one of the few places left in Hong Kong where you can see Chinese craftsmen working in balconied shop-houses, turning out everything from mah-jongg tiles to company chops (see Name Chops p. 76) and coffins. The shelves and timbered cabinets of Chinese medicine shops are full of bewildering and exotic potions and ingredients such as snake musk, pearl powder, lizard skins, ginseng roots, and deer antlers.

Some people eat meals and snacks on rickety stools and

Meanwhile, the less productive newcomers spent their time in the opium dens, drinking halls, and gambling parlors. Despite modern development spreading west from Central and skyscrapers slowly being slotted in, the Western District has managed to hang on to much of its character. The opium dens, drinking halls, and gambling parlors may be gone, but much of the enterprise of the area remains.

Along the narrow streets and alleyways you will get a glimpse of a more traditional way of life.

INSIDER TIP:

Hollywood Road and Wyndham Street are lined with antiques shops and galleries of contemporary Chinese art that are well worth visiting.

—IAN BAKER
National Geographic field researcher

tables in *dai pai dongs* (sidewalk restaurants); others enjoy *yum cha* (tea drinking) in spartan tea-houses. Abacuses snap and clack into action as wholesalers strike bargains on a startling variety of rice and teas.

Outside the shops on Western's crowded streets, robust

"Flying Pigeon" bicycles weave through traffic delivering wicker baskets full of goods door to door. Wizened old ladies push carts layered with recyclable cardboard and metal, while muscular porters propel their vehicles at a lively pace. Brightly painted trams sound their clanging bells as they trundle along.

In the midst of this lively tone, Western presents good shopping opportunities. Antiques shops selling genuine and fake antiquities line Hollywood Road and its side streets, along with carpet and silk retailers, art galleries, and stores crowded with inexpensive bric-a-brac. It's a good place to pick up a copy of *The Thoughts of Chairman Mao* by Chinese communist leader Mao Zedong (1893–1976), along with other communist paraphernalia.

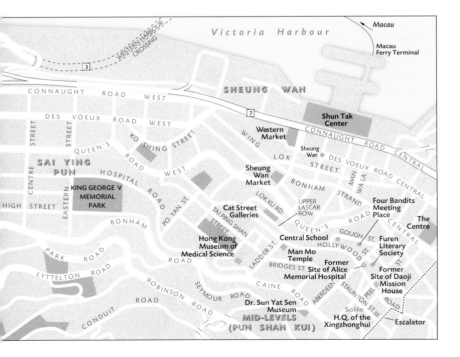

Western District

Western is often referred to as Hong Kong's "Chinatown." Although this may sound absurd in a place where 98 percent of the population is Chinese, it does have a ring of

---

Name Chops

Chops are signature seals which are generally made of wood, although stone and jade models are available, with a name carved in Chinese on the base. They are dipped in ink or pushed onto an inkpad, then impressed on a document to add a signature. Originally used by artists to sign their works on paper or silk, today they are still widely used in Hong Kong by companies and shop owners on receipts, invoices, and other documents. They make great souvenirs or gifts, and Man Wa Lane, also known as Chop Lane, in Sheung Wan is a good place to have one made.

---

truth. The area, with its narrow maze of streets, old buildings, crowds, and constant buzz of shopfront mercantile activity, brims with atmosphere.

Hollywood Road: Carved along the hillside above Western, Hollywood Road was built in 1844 for the British regiment attached there and named after the holly wood trees that used to line the street. It winds its way down from the upper section of Central into the heart of Sheung Wan at Queen's Road West, and makes for a fascinating stroll.

The road and its side streets are lined with dozens of antique stores and other shops selling all manner of merchandise. (Choose with care, however, as not all antiques for sale are genuine.) Here you can buy snuff bottles, carpets, birdcages, name chops, paintings, and teapots.

The stores along the eastern part of Hollywood Road are some of the best in the world for Chinese antiques. As you move farther west, the glass-fronted stores with expensive displays give way to grittier shop-houses selling Chinese knickknacks, or making and selling coffins, funeral wreaths, and antique reproductions.

Beyond Hollywood Road: Cat Street (Upper Lascar Row), an area once notorious for seamen's lodgings and brothels, is opposite Man Mo Temple, one block north from Hollywood Road. It is lined with stalls selling bric-a-brac and fake antiques. At the end of Hollywood Road, keep heading west and lose yourself in the maze of bustling streets and alleys running off Queen's Road West in the **Sai Ying Pun** area, where an enthralling glimpse of old Hong Kong opens up. Here you will find old, worn, four-story buildings with ornate balconies shading footpaths lined with restaurants; stores selling exotic produce such as shark fins, dried fish, rice, tea, and Chinese herbs;

and tiny craftsmen's factories. Cobblers, key-cutters, and barbers work are some of the merchants working from street stands.

To the west of Cat Street, you'll find Des Voeux Road West, which can be smelled before it is seen thanks to the dried seafood shops that line the street. Running parallel to the south are the herbal medicine stalls of Ko Shing Street, which offer an organic cure for every ailment.

Unfortunately, most of these places have been demolished over the years, taking some edge off this short walk. At 7 Castle Road, the **Dr. Sun Yat-sen Museum** has an interesting, if unexciting, exhibition on the leader's life.

Take the Central to Mid-Levels Escalator (see p. 59) to the Stanley Street exit. Head east on Stanley Street until you reach No. 15, the **headquarters of the Xing Zhong Hui** (Revival China Society), a revolutionary organiza-

Dr Sun Yat-sen Museum
- Map p. 75
- 7 Castle Rd.
- 2367-6373
- MTR: Central

www.lcsd.gov.hk

Western's Cat Street harbors a veritable flea market of antiques and bric-a-brac.

Sun Yat-sen Historical Trail:
This trail takes you past sites commemorating Sun Yat-sen (1866–1925), who spent a number of years in Hong Kong fomenting revolution before founding the Chinese republic in 1912 (see p. 34). Each site has a red plaque describing the activities which took place inside.

tion set up by Sun in 1895. On this spot, he and his colleagues plotted the overthrow of the Chinese Qing government.

Farther west at 75 Hollywood Road is **To Tsai Church,** where the Christian Sun attended religious gatherings. At the intersection of Hollywood Road and Aberdeen Street, another

A Walk Around Sheung Wan

Hong Kong's Chinatown, Sheung Wan, reveals an interesting slice of the territory's history. You will encounter some steep hills along the way, so the walk is best tackled in the cool of the early morning—a perfect time to watch one of Hong Kong's most fascinating areas prepare itself for the day.

Curious dried fish and herbs destined for medicinal use fill Sheung Wan shops.

Start your walk at the **Central Police Station ❶** (10 Hollywood Rd.). The imposing, four-story, blue-and-white headquarters block was built in 1919 in neoclassical syle with bold columns at the entrance hall, common in Hong Kong around this time. Once the Central District Headquarters for the Hong Kong Police Force, the police station was decommissioned in 2004, with the historic buildings—declared monuments by Hong Kong—slated to be developed for commercial and tourist use in the near future.

Heading west, the next stop is one of Hong

NOT TO BE MISSED:

Man Mo Temple • Ladder Street • Western Market

Kong's oldest religious sites, the **Man Mo Temple ❷** (see pp. 80–81), at the junction of Hollywood Road and Ladder Street. After exploring the temple, climb the stepped Ladder Street to the intersection with Bridges Street. Many of the buildings along **Ladder Street** are graced with shutters, timber balconies, and

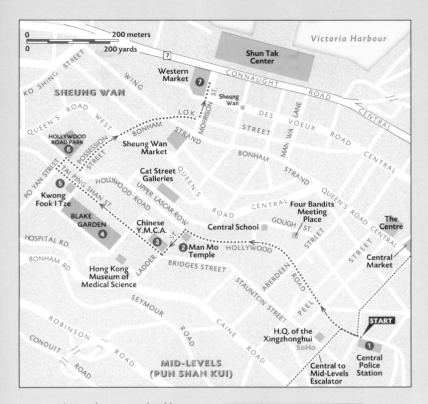

ornate carvings, and are among the oldest remaining homes in Hong Kong. Turn right onto Bridges Street; the **Chinese YMCA ❸**, a large, redbrick hybrid of European and Chinese architecture is at this intersection. At the western end of Bridges Street, follow the lane to Tai Ping Shan Street and **Blake Garden ❹**; next to the entrance gate a plaque commemorates the outbreak of the plague in 1894.

To the west, along ramshackle Tai Ping Shan Street, you will see **Kwong Fook I Tze ❺**, or Tai Ping Shan Temple. Built in the 1850s, its solid red concrete facade is devoid of temple ornateness, but inside at the rear are ancestral tablets, wooden slats in honor of forebears from the mainland who died in Hong Kong. The front hall is dedicated to the Ksitigarbha Buddha, whose blessings allow spirits to rest in peace.

At the western end of Tai Ping Shan Street, turn right into Po Yan Street to Hollywood Road and a shaded patch of green at Hol-

	See area map pp. 74–75
►	Central Police Station
⟷	1 mile (1.6 km)
⏱	1.5 hours
►	Western Market

lywood Road Park ❻. The park is on the site of Possession Point, and a simple information board marks the spot where the British flag was planted for the first time in Hong Kong on January 26, 1841. The park is bordered on the east by Possession Street, which is closed to traffic and filled with hawkers and market stands. Follow Possession Street north over Queen's Road West to curving Bonham Strand, to Morrison Street and **Western Market ❼**, an impressive Edwardian building. The market, which was completed in 1906, was refurbished in 1991 and houses shopping arcades selling fabrics, handicrafts, and souvenirs.

Huge incense coils hang from the ceiling of Man Mo Temple. They can burn for weeks.

A little farther west, at 44 Gough Street, is the building that housed the **Central School,** where Sun was educated.

Man Mo Temple

Man Mo Temple is one of Hong Kong's oldest and, despite its modest size, most important places of worship. Man Mo (literally "civility" and "military") is dedicated to two deities: Man, the god of civil servants and literature, and Mo (also known as Kuanti), the god of war and martial arts. The fierce Mo is also the patron saint of both triads—organized crime gangs—and their natural enemies, the police.

The exact date of the temple's construction remains a mystery, but it is believed that it was well established by the time the British arrived in 1841. The temple underwent major refurbishment in the 1850s.

Outside the entrance to the temple hall are four gilt plaques attached to poles carried during processions. Two of the plaques describe the two gods, while the other two request quiet inside the temple and ask menstruating women to stay away.

Inside, the statue of Man is on the right of the main altar, adorned with red embroidered robes and holding a calligraphy brush. On the left is the red-faced Mo, dressed in green robes and a pearl headdress and wielding a large sword.

The walls are decorated with religious paraphernalia. Huge cone-shaped spirals of smoldering incense hang from

plaque indicates the site of the **Alice Memorial Hospital and Hong Kong College of Medicine** where Sun graduated with a medical degree in 1892. Turn right at Aberdeen Street and take another right down Pak Tze Lane. Stone steps lead to the site of the **Furen Literary Society,** where Sun's comrades hatched revolution.

Back on Aberdeen Street, continue down the hill and turn left at Gough Street. At No. 8 is **Four Bandits Meeting Place,** where one floor of the shop on the site was used by Sun and other leading revolutionaries.

the ceiling, and joss sticks burning in polished brass pots add to the smoky atmosphere. Dull electric bulbs, flickering votive candles, and shafts of sunlight cast an eerie illumination across the hall.

Two brass deer, representing longevity, stand in the temple hall. Near the elaborately decorated main altar are two sedan chairs,

INSIDER TIP:

To get a feel for Hong Kong, go to SoHo. An old book store, a dusty antiques place on Cat Street, and a claypot rice shop below the escalators are some of my favorite spots.

—LYN YIP
travel writer

which are used to parade the divinities during festivals.

The temple has a smaller shrine dedicated to Pao Kung, the god of justice. It also has statues of the Eight Immortals (those who achieved immortality and made their homes in the Sacred Mountains of China), subjects of many legends.

Because of its central location, Man Mo hosts an almost constant stream of tourists and worshippers, but remains tranquil and atmospheric at the same time.

As with most temples in Hong Kong, it is appropriate to leave a small donation after visiting the temple. A shop attached to the temple sells souvenirs.

University of Hong Kong

The University of Hong Kong is the territory's oldest and most prestigious university, with a number of grand buildings on its campus. It is also home to one of Hong Kong's least visited, but nonetheless most intriguing, museums, whose prize exhibit is a collection of Nestorian bronze crosses from northern China.

The 1919 **Hung Hing Ying Building,** which stands opposite the university's main building, is worth a look. A huge white dome

Popular Deities

Chinese religion (a mixture of Buddhist, Taoist, and Confucian beliefs) encompasses more than a hundred deities. Some are more popular than others, and each one is honored by different sections of the community for their redeeming qualities. Students honor certain gods who are seen as scholarly; shopkeepers pray to gods who can bestow riches; fishermen are devotees of deities who protect them from the dangers of the seas; and the sick pray to gods who restore health.

Hong Kong's most popular deities include Tin Hau, the Queen of Heaven and protector of seafarers; Wong Tai Sin, who can bring prosperity; Kwun Yam, the goddess of mercy; Pak Tai, the guardian of peace and order; and Kuanti (or Mo), the protector of soldiers and police.

Man Mo Temple
- Map p. 75
- Corner of Hollywood Rd. & Ladder St., Sheung Wan
- Donation
- Bus: 26

University of Hong Kong
- Map p. 74
- 94 Bonham Rd.
- 2241-5500
- Bus: 3B, 23, 40, 40M, 43, 103; Minibus: 8, 10, 11, 22, 28, 31

www.hku.hk

Chinese Traditional Medicine

Visiting a Chinese pharmacy in Hong Kong is like going inside a miniature museum of natural science. Tucked away in row after row of drawers and glass containers lies a mind-boggling array of dead specimens: coiled snakes, tortoises, grasshoppers, dried fish, stag antlers, rhinoceros horns, testicles and penises from various animals, and a selection of herbs, roots, berries, plants, and mushrooms.

With many people still placing their faith in Chinese traditional medicine, shops such as this one in Central do a brisk trade.

It seems there is hardly an animal, plant, or mineral that is not used as a curative in Chinese traditional medicine. Unfortunately, many endangered species are said to boast curative powers. In fact, often the rarest specimens are considered to have the strongest powers of health promotion.

Although the Hong Kong government strives to regulate the trade, it is important to be aware of what you are buying.

While people in Hong Kong and the rest of China will probably go to a Western-style doctor when serious ailments strike, they may choose Chinese traditional medicine for minor

EXPERIENCE: Acupuncture

Acupuncture is one of Chinese traditional medicine's biggest contributions to the world. It's also been around forever, but the most solid evidence places its rise during the long reign of the Han dynasty (202 B.C.–A.D. 220).

Ever since, acupuncture has been used to treat conditions ranging from hiccups to hypothermia or worse. And, as you've probably guessed by now, Hong Kong is filled with acupuncturists, some more reputable than others. Sites like *www.acufinder.com* and *www.asiaxpat.com* have local listings, or you can ask the man behind the counter at a pharmacy in Sheung Wan, a neighborhood known for its medicinal shops.

To begin an acupuncture session you describe your symptoms to the acupuncturist. He then presses the pins or needles into some of the hundreds of points along your body's meridians, which are pathways on which your chi flows. Then you relax and he readjusts the needles, and you relax some more.

Each session costs between U.S. $60 and $120, and you'll have needles in you for about 20 minutes.

A brief word about the needles: They are thinner than traditional hypodermic needles, so they do not cause pain when inserted, only a brief tingling. And most modern acupuncturalists use disposable stainless steel ones.

---

problems and for preventative and proactive healthcare. After diagnosis, a doctor of traditional Chinese medicine hands the patient a prescription, which is filled by a pharmacist who selects ingredients from the hundreds available in his or her shop. These carefully chosen ingredients are boiled into a soup by the patient, and then consumed.

While Western medicine concentrates on treating the area where symptoms occur, traditional Chinese medicine believes in the need for a balance in the entire body to both regain and maintain good health. It's based around the theory of the negative force of *yin,* the positive force of *yang,* and the five natural elements—metal, wood, water, fire, and earth.

The human body is made up of the competing and complementing forces of yin and yang, and when the balance between the two is disrupted, illness ensues. Also, the theory holds, among the five elements there exists an interdependence and interrestraint that determines their state of constant change. The liver, heart, spleen, lungs, and kidneys correspond with the five elements. The liver, for example, carries the quality of wood, which can be lit up by fire; thus, a person with a liver

disorder can be quick to anger. In this way illness is explained in terms of the developments and changes in nature.

Doctors emphasize the treatment of the whole body, aimed at restoring the balance that was sent askew by illness. Attention is also paid to the season of the year, the environment, and living conditions of the patient. Two people with the same complaint may be prescribed different medicines because of their different internal and external conditions.

Another theory in traditional Chinese medicine is that of the *jing* and *luo,* which is the basis of treatments such as acupuncture and moxibustion (a heat treatment application of "moxa," derived from the ground-up leaves of the herb mugwort, on acupuncture points of the body). The internal organs and the limbs of the body are related and linked by channels through which blood and *chi* (the vital energy or life force) circulate. The main channels are called *jing* while the branches are called *luo.* If there is a blockage in either of these, the blood and vital energy cannot pass through; in time it affects a person's health. To clear the blockage through acupuncture and breathing exercises is the first and fundamental step in curing a disease.

and grand columned portico add character to this redbrick, two-story structure, which currently houses the Music Department. The **Main Building** (1912) is also impressive, with its tiered clock towers crowned with cupolas and its huge Roman columns adding flamboyance to the Edwardian design. The imposing, off-campus **University Hall,** a blend of Gothic and Tudor influences, was built in 1861 and

The University of Hong Kong's Main Building evokes the campus's age-old elegance.

served as a dormitory, chapel, library, and printing house, until the university acquired it in 1954.

University Museum & Art Gallery:

The university's museum is housed in an eye-pleasing, Edwardian-style building, while the smaller art gallery occupies an adjoining building.

Displayed on the museum's first floor are 467 Nestorian bronze crosses, the largest collection of its kind in the world. The crosses belonged to a heretical Christian sect that came to China from Syria during the Tang dynasty (618–907), and date from the time of the Yuan dynasty (1279–1368). They are only about an inch across and vary in shape from crucifix to swastika.

The first floor also holds bronze pieces from the Shang to Tang dynasties, mainly weapons and ritual vessels, along with a series of bronze mirrors from the Early Warring States period (475–221 B.C.).

The museum's second floor is dominated by ceramics spanning 5,000 years. Look for the painted neolithic pottery; Han dynasty (206 B.C.–A.D. 220) clay figures and animals, and lead-glazed burial houses; Song dynasty (960–1279) kiln ware; Sui dynasty (581–618) spittoons; and three-color glazed pottery dating from the Tang dynasty. Recent work exhibited here includes early 20th-century Buddhist monk statuettes and pieces from the Chinese pottery centers of Shiwan and Jingdezhen.

The university's art gallery features works by Ming and Qing dynasty painters, as well as contemporary artists. It also holds temporary exhibitions.

Visitors can relax and enjoy a cup of tea in a replicated traditional teahouse.

Hong Kong Trams

A tram ride is an ideal and fun way to capture the vibrant and colorful street life along Hong Kong Island's northern corridor. These delightful double-decker trams trundle 9 miles (14.5 km) from Kennedy Town in Western District through residential areas, and shopping and commercial precincts, to the old fishing village of Shau Kei Wan at the eastern end of the island.

Hong Kong's trams began operation in 1904, after concerns about them crowding the colony's narrow streets and putting rickshaw pullers out of work were allayed. The colony's newspapers, the most vehement critics of the plan, later praised the tramway when it opened. The *Hong Kong*

Villain Hitting

A somewhat darker side of Hong Kong is the practice of villian hitting, a form of folk sorcery from the Guangdong Province which involves placing a curse on your enemy. The ceremony usually entails a paper representation of the enemy, either a group or an individual, which is then beaten with the cursee's shoe. Although the practice is no longer popular, at Canal Street in Causeway Bay it is still possible to see groups of old women working as villain hitters hunched over plastic stools beating out their client's curses.

Hong Kong Tramways

- Map p. 52
- Whitty St. Tram Depot, Connaught St.
- 2548-7102

www.hktramways .com

INSIDER TIP:

Despite the heat and humidity, be sure to carry a light sweater if taking a long bus ride or hitting the malls— the air-conditioning can be cold.

—RORY BOLAND
National Geographic contributor

Daily Press commented: "The ride was at least three times faster than the best rickshaw, to the blank astonishment of the numbers of Chinese spectators, and the dejected look of rickshaw pullers."

The most interesting section is through the pedestrian-clogged streets of Western to the gleaming high-rises of Central. Hop aboard

at the Kennedy Town terminus, climb upstairs, and sit in the front seat for the best view. The trams run close to the harbor along Connaught Road to Western Market before winding south to bustling Des Voeux Road and on to Central. You can ride the reverse section from Des Voeux Road Central (in front of the HSBC Building) to Kennedy Town or Western Market.

The ride is an incredible bargain—just HK$2. Enter at the rear of the tram and drop the fare in a box when exiting at the front. Hong Kong Tramways is gradually modernizing its fleet, so take the opportunity to ride one of the older versions while they are still around. Private trams, designed in early vintage style with lots of polished teakwood, are available for private charter. ■

East of Central

Districts just east of Central are quintessentially Hong Kong—the modern is often jarringly juxtaposed with the traditional. Steel-and-glass towers lining the harbor give way to the crowded street life of merchants, vendors, and produce markets. Entertainment varies from cultural and performing arts centers to the seediness of hostess bars. People flock to shop in the modern malls and packed discount stores, and to bet at one of the world's most famous racetracks.

Old-time sampans and luxury yachts crowd Causeway Bay Typhoon Shelter.

open space, is a thriving shopping, entertainment, and residential precinct notable for its incessant crowds, huge department stores, restaurants, markets, and shopping bargains. It's a better place to shop than often-aggressive Tsim Sha Tsui (see pp. 124–137).

The relaxed residential district of Happy Valley is home to the Happy Valley Racecourse and, on race days, tens of thousands of passionate bettors come here. A

In Wan Chai, new and old are divided by the tram tracks running along Hennessy Road and Johnston Road. To the north and toward the harbor are the skyscrapers built to offset the high rents of Central. South of the tracks, pedestrians spill from the sidewalks on narrow crowded streets that wind their way past innumerable shophouses and tenements. Be sure to take a tram ride on the top deck to get a bird's-eye view of the action.

Adjacent to Causeway Bay and green and leafy Victoria Park, Hong Kong Island's largest

night at the floodlit races is a must during your visit.

Farther east, the mainly residential areas of North Point, Quarry Bay, and Chai Wan provide few interesting sights for the visitor, but they do give an insight into the living conditions of Hong Kong's people. Here hundreds of residential towers, many with 40 or more floors, rise along the narrow eastern corridor of Hong Kong Island. At the eastern tip of the island is the Hong Kong Museum of Coastal Defense. Thought it's a bit out of the way, it's definitely worth visiting for a glimpse into the territory's lively maritime past.

INSIDER TIP:

Spend an evening at the races in Happy Valley; the location among a forest of sky-scrapers and the roaring crowd make for an electric atmosphere.

—RORY BOLAND
National Geographic contributor

Wan Chai

Wan Chai, one of Hong Kong's most famous districts, earned its less-than-pleasant reputation from its seedy history of bars and

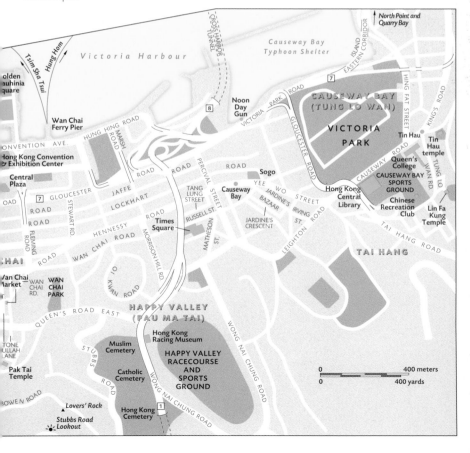

EXPERIENCE: Have a Pint at a British Pub

Outside of Britain itself, Hong Kong has some of the world's most authentic British-style pubs, catering to the city's legion of expats. Here are five of the best:

Bulldogs (17 Lan Kwai Fong, Central, tel 2523-3528). Bulldogs' nearly 50-foot bar is one of the city's most raucous and popular with expats looking to catch sports. They also offer fantastic British and Australian classic meals.

The Chapel (27 Yik Yam St., Happy Valley, tel 2834-6565). Out in the suburbs of Happy Valley, the Chapel offers a relaxed neighborhood feel as well as quality curries and a weekly quiz night.

The Globe (39 Hollywood Rd., Central, tel 2543-1941). Boasting nearly 60 beers and dedicated barflies, the Globe seems like a traditional British local.

Old China Hand (104 Lockhart Rd., Wan Chai, tel 2865-4378). A great place to meet longtime British transplants who've been drinking here since the 1970s, the Old China Hand serves excellent pub grub.

Smugglers Inn (90A Stanley Main St., Stanley, tel 2813-8852). Set on the Stanley seafront, Smugglers is one of Hong Kong's oldest British-styled pubs. Friendly staff ferry pints to both tourists and locals inside an interior lifted from Pirates of the Caribbean.

bordellos. Although this image has been tempered since its rambunctious days as the haunt of U.S. military personnel on "R and R" during the Vietnam conflict in the 1960s and early '70s, the district still has its share of lively nightlife. But it's also a vibrant residential, business, and commercial community, revealing Hong Kong at its bustling best.

Wan Chai North: A good place to begin is at the impressive **Hong Kong Convention and Exhibition Center New Wing** (1 Expo Drive, Wan Chai, tel 2582-2888), covering 16 acres (6.5 ha) of reclaimed land in front of the original convention center building. With its elegant winglike roof and five-story-high glass walls that allow extensive views of the Wan Chai and Central waterfront, it has become a landmark building. Completed in 1997, it was the site for Hong Kong's handover cer-emony, which is commemorated at both the harbor-front **Golden Bauhinia Square,** which holds a flag-raising ceremony at 7:50 a.m. daily, just to the right as you exit the center, and **Reunification Monument,** to the left. Mainland visitors enjoy taking photos at both of these spots. The center has several cafés and restaurants with harbor vistas.

Behind the exhibition center and connected by covered walkways stands one of Hong Kong's tallest buildings, the 1,227-foot (374 m), 78-story **Central Plaza** (18 Harbour Rd.). The silver and gold ceramic-coated sheets on the tower's facade catch the sun's reflection, giving it a glowing aspect. Exaggerated marble colonnades at ground level lead to the vast marble-clad lobby. Head up to the Sky Lobby on the 47th floor for a panoramic sweep across Victoria Harbour to Kowloon.

Follow the walkways south

to **Lockhart Road,** an entertainment strip once frequented by military personnel. The area fell into decline by the 1980s, but was revived during the 1990s with the addition of trendy restaurants, cafés, bars, and nightclubs. Plenty of seedy establishments still exist, however, notably the hostess bars. Rip-offs are common at these overpriced places, so it's wise to avoid them. Members of the U.S. military still stream into the area when in town.

South of Hennessy Road:

South of Hennessey Road and Queen's Road East lies the burgeoning fine-dining district around Star Street, with a host of sophisticated restaurants and bars. On the other side of Queen's Road East, Wan Chai shifts into a more traditional Chinese mode with plenty of intriguing narrow roads and alleys to explore. Sadly, many of the streets that were once home to family-owned shops and market sellers have been earmarked for urban renewal and the residents turned out. Stroll up now empty **Lee Tung Street,** famously known as ing Card Street, once packed with printers of distinctive, red Chinese wedding cards, to see Hong Kong's relentless development in action.

Back across Queen's Road East is the **Hopewell Center** *(183 Queen's Rd. East, tel 2527-7292),* at one time Hong Kong's tallest building. You can ride glass-bubble elevators on the outside of the building to the revolving restaurant and stunning views of the harbor and Victoria Peak at the top.

Another block east is the whitewashed **Old Wanchai Post Office** *(221 Queen's Rd. East, tel 2893-2856, closed Tues.),* built in 1912. It now houses the government's

Central Plaza and the glass-curtained Convention Center dominate the Wan Chai skyline.

Hong Kong Police Museum

- 🅰 Map p. 84
- ✉ 27 Coombe Rd. (intersection of Peak, Stubbs, & Wan Chai Gap Rds.)
- ☎ 2849-7019
- 🕐 Closed Mon., Tues. a.m.
- 🚌 Bus: 1; Minibus: 15

Environmental Resource Center, which dispenses information on efforts to rescue and preserve the territory's environment.

Cross Queen's Road East and wander down to **Tai Yuen Street,** crowded with shops selling goldfish, aquariums, and Chinese herbs, and watch snake vendors prepare their goods for the pot by cracking them on the pavement like whips.

Tai, the Supreme Emperor of the Dark Heaven, cast in Guangzhou in 1604. A second Pak Tai image sports a beard of black horsehair. In the ancestral hall, people burn bamboo and paper offerings expertly folded into airplanes, cars, and homes.

Back at the post office is the start of the **Wan Chai Green Trail,** which climbs through lovely wood-

One of Wan Chai's many herbal medicine shops

Many of the vendors who used to peddle their wares along this street now trade at the sprawling **Wan Chai Market** on the corner of Wan Chai Road and Cross Street.

South of Queen's Road:

One block east of the post office, turn right up Stone Nullah Lane to **Pak Tai Temple,** whose grounds are shaded by luxuriant banyan trees. Built in 1863, this three-chambered temple houses a 10-foot (3 m) copper statue of Pak

lands for about a mile (1.6 km) to **Wan Chai Gap Park.** It gives stunning panoramas at the top but can be tough going. An easier way is to catch bus 7 or minibus 15 from Central to the top of Wan Chai Gap Road, descend by foot to the park at the corner of Bowen Road, and take the trail back to the post office. Before heading down, check out the **Hong Kong Police Museum.** The wonderful collection of exhibits includes the head of the "Sheung Shui tiger," which was shot in 1915 after killing a policeman; weapons, uniforms, and medals; displays of drugs and drug paraphernalia; a mock heroin factory; and a gallery devoted to Hong Kong's infamous triads.

As you head down Wan Chai Gap Road, take a right turn at leafy Bowen Road, originally an aqueduct carrying water from Tai Tam Reservoir (see p. 104) to Central, to the phallic **Lovers' Rock,** in a rocky hillside outcrop. Hundreds of women come on the 6th, 16th, and 26th days of each lunar month to pray for happy marriages for themselves and their children. They burn incense and joss sticks, place paper windmills in sandboxes, hang wine bottles on strings at a nearby tree, and seek the prophecies of fortune-tellers. The spot offers spectacular views of Wan Chai and Happy Valley.

Happy Valley

The residential area of Happy Valley dates from the founding of Hong Kong as a colony in the 1840s. Settlement proved disastrous, as many of the British soldiers billeted there contracted malaria and died. When early settlers headed for higher ground at Central, the mosquito-infested marshlands were drained, and a racetrack was built.

Horse races have been held at Happy Valley since December 1845. **Happy Valley Racecourse** *(tel 2966-7974)* is the best place to witness Hong Kong's obsession

---

EXPERIENCE: Enjoy a Belt-busting Buffet

Although buffets are served throughout the week, Sunday buffets are a Hong Kong institution. The best ones are the breathtaking spread of international dishes in the city's hotels. Most buffets are high quality and good value, depending on how much you can stomach. Prices below are for Sunday; they're considerably cheaper during the week.

Cafe Kool – Kowloon Shangri-La *(64 Mody Rd., Tsim Sha Tsui, tel 2733-8753, 12–3 p.m., Adults HK$268, children HK$198).* Casual but classy, Cafe Kool is perhaps the best value buffet in Hong Kong.
Cafe TOO *(Island Shangri-La, Pacific Place, Supreme Court Rd., Central, tel 2820-8571, 12–3 p.m., Adults HK$328, children HK$208).* Family-friendly and fun, Cafe TOO offers one of Hong Kong's top buffets at a price that won't melt your wallet. As

much theater as restaurant, you can watch your food thrown around at the seven live and energetic cooking stations or catch one of the occasional shows.
Intercontinental– Habourside Restaurant *(18 Salisbury Rd., Tsim Sha Tsui, tel 2313-2323, 11:30 a.m.–3 p.m., Adults HK$638, children HK$318).* Considered one of Hong Kong's premium—and priciest—buffets, the Harbourside Restaurant offers unbeatable views overlooking

Victoria Harbour, and expertly prepared dishes washed down by an endless supply of champagne. Reservations need to be made several weeks, if not months, in advance.
Langham Place–The Place *(555 Shanghai St., Mongkok, tel 3552-3200, 12–2:30 p.m., Adults HK$228, children (4–11) HK$158).* The Place offers high quality at low prices. The real draw is the restaurant's tranquil garden, where you can enjoy their deadly roll call of desserts.

Horse Racing

Hong Kong's residents follow horse racing with a passion not seen in other places. Most Wednesday evenings and Saturdays (and some Sundays) between mid-September and June, tens of thousands make their way to Happy Valley and Sha Tin racetracks. Those who can't be there head to one of the more than 100 off-course betting outlets run by the Hong Kong Jockey Club to lay their bets.

Sha Tin Racecourse opened in 1978 to accommodate Happy Valley's overflow.

In bars, parks, and restaurants people pore over form guides. Catch a taxi and the cabbie's radio will be tuned into the racing. Live race broadcasts on television attract more viewers than any other program. An estimated 70 percent of Hong Kongers have placed a bet, and a staggering six million bets are made per meeting—nearly one bet for every person in Hong Kong.

The reason for this fervor has more to do with the population's love of gambling than its love of equine sport. Horse racing, soccer, and the Mark Six lottery are the only forms of legalized gambling in the territory. The Hong Kong Jockey Club—the controlling organization of horse racing and Hong Kong's largest benevolent body—has devised numerous (and often confusing) betting permutations to help people part with their money and, if lucky, win big. Money lost by punters is poured into charity projects. Certain "exotic" bets, such as double quinellas, tierce, triple tierce, and six-up, can yield hundreds of thousands of dollars for a wager of a few dollars. Every season, the club turns over around HK$100 billion, the highest of any horse racing organization in the world.

The sport is nearly as old as Hong Kong itself. The first race meeting was held in 1845 at Happy Valley after a swamp was drained to allow the construction of a track. During the early years of racing in Hong Kong, the horses were Arabs, hunters, and cavalry mounts. Small but hardy Mongolian ponies were soon introduced and became the sport's mainstay for almost a century. (These days horses come from across the world.)

During the 1850s, a reporter from *The Times* of London visiting Hong Kong wrote: "A Londoner cannot conceive the excitement caused in this island by the race week.... The one mile and a half of road between Happy Valley and the city of Victoria is at the proper time crowded with vehicles and horsemen and pedestrians...."

These words still hold true today. On race nights, up to 40,000 people crowd into the stands at Happy Valley Racecourse (see p. 91). Standard entry is just HK$10, or show your passport at the Badge Office at the main entrance to the Members Enclosure, and get a tourist badge for HK$100. This gives access to restaurants, bars, and boxes. You can also join the Hong Kong Tourism Board's Come Horseracing Tour *(Hong Kong Tourism Board Visitors Hotline, tel 2508-1234)*, which includes transportation, dinner, and seating in the Visitors' Box.

At the larger Sha Tin track (see p. 176), which opened in 1978, the betting crowds can reach as many as 75,000. At both tracks, bettors are pampered with first-class facilities and state-of-the-art technology, including computerized betting windows, a giant video bet indicator screen, and huge 66-by-19-foot (20 x 5.8 m) screens that show races in progress, replays, and form guides.

Studying the racing form is a pre-race ritual.

EXPERIENCE:
Betting on a Winner

The bets in Hong Kong are also called punts. Here is a quick overview:

Win: You pick one horse to win.

Place: Your horse places if it comes in first, second, or third.

Quinella: Betting on two horses to finish first and second. Also known as a reverse forecast.

Quinella Place: Betting on two horses to finish anywhere in the top three.

Tierce: Picking three horses to finish first, second, and third respectively.

Trio: Picking three horses to finish in the top three.

Six Up: For each of the six races, you must pick the horses that win or come in second.

The horses at Hong Kong's racecourses, too, enjoy a lifestyle that is nothing short of enviable. Between races, these sleek, expensive Thoroughbreds pass away their time in air-conditioned stables that feature soothing music and swimming pools.

**Hong Kong
Racing Museum**
🅰 Map p. 87
✉ 2/F Happy
    Valley Stand
☎ 2966-8065
🕐 Closed Mon.
🚋 Happy Valley
    Tram

Causeway Bay
🅰 Map p. 87

Victoria Park
🅰 Map p. 87

with horse racing and gambling. Most Wednesdays during the season (see pp. 92–93), people pack the stands in jostling elation or groaning disappointment as millions of dollars are won or lost.

The **Hong Kong Racing Museum** is ideal for delving into the history of horse racing in Hong

INSIDER TIP:

To experience traditional Chinese medicine or a restorative acupuncture treatment, try Tong Ran Tang in Causeway Bay, or Hui Chun Tang or Eu Yan Sang in Sheung Wan.

—IAN BAKER
National Geographic field researcher

Kong. Its eight galleries and cinema retell the sport's colorful story.

Opposite the main grandstands on Wan Nai Chung Road are several cemeteries *(closed at dusk):* **Catholic, Muslim,** and the largest and most interesting, the **Hong Kong Cemetery,** with the remains of early Protestant settlers, missionaries, soldiers, traders, and civil servants. On the gravestones are tragic tales of malaria, cholera, dysentery, and death in childbirth of Russian, German, American, British, and French settlers.

Causeway Bay

Known in Chinese as Tung Lo Wan ("copper gong bay"), Causeway Bay was one of the

first settlements on Hong Kong Island. Then, it was a deeply indented bay and a haven for fishing boats. *Hongs* (trading companies) built their *godowns* (warehouses) here. Today it is one of Hong Kong's premier shopping districts.

The "Princely Hong," Jardine, Matheson & Company (see p. 31), snapped up land, built godowns, offices, and employee housing, and worked to become the colony's preeminent merchant. Its presence in Causeway Bay is remembered in numerous street names. **Jardine's Bazaar,** formerly a market for the hong's local employees, is lined with old-fashioned Chinese provision stores amd traders, noodle shops,

Tin Hau

Tin Hau, the Queen of Heaven and protector of seafarers, was the daughter of a government official in Fujian Province in the tenth century. She was said to have the ability to heal sickness and to warn seafarers of impending dangers at sea. When she died, a temple was built in her honor and a cult of worship grew as more were built along the Chinese coast.

She is one of Hong Kong's most popular deities, with dozens of temples devoted to her in areas where fisherfolk work. All the temples were built by the sea, but land reclamation projects have left many stranded inland.

Luxury yachts and other boats squeeze into Causeway Bay Typhoon Shelter.

and vegetarian cafés. **Jardine's Crescent** is crowded with stands selling cheap clothing.

Jardine's Crescent leads into Irving Street. Cross the pedestrian bridge to Tung Lo Wan Road, which follows the original shoreline of the bay, past the **Chinese Recreation Club** *(123 Tung Lo Wan Rd., tel 2577-7376)* and, behind it, the **Causeway Bay Sports Ground** *(tel 2890-5127)*.

Tung Lo Wan Road curves and continues east past Shanghainese, Muslim, and vegetarian cafés, churches, and Queen's College before reaching the arterial Causeway Road and Tin Hau Temple Road. From here follow Tin Hau Temple Road a short distance to Dragon Road, where you'll find 200-year-old **Tin Hau Temple,** which honors the Taoist Queen of Heaven and patron of seafarers (see Tin Hau opposite) on an elevated stone platform. This tiny temple once stood at the bay's edge.

From here you can backtrack to Causeway Road and sprawling **Victoria Park** *(tel 2890-5824),* Hong Kong Island's largest public open space. Queen Victoria's stern-faced statue surveys the park from a stone plinth facing Causeway Road. The park has tennis courts, a swimming pool, playgrounds, wooded areas, a café, bowling greens, soccer fields, roller-skating rinks, and, in the morning, legions of tai chi practitioners. It is also one of the few parks in Hong Kong that features an expansive grass lawn that's open to the public—ideal for picnicking.

At the northeastern exit of the park, a pedestrian overpass leads to a waterfront promenade where junks and sampans, and luxury yachts from the nearby Hong Kong Yacht Club, huddle into **Causeway Bay Typhoon Shelter** (an area protected by seawalls of rocks and boulders, where boats berth when

Hong Kong Museum of Coastal Defense

Map p. 53

175 Tung Hei Rd., Shau Kei Wan

2569-1500

Closed Thurs.

$

MTR: Sha Kei Wan, exit B

www.lcsd.gov.hk

typhoon warnings are given). Head west along the promenade to the Jardine Matheson **Noon Day Gun,** made famous by British satirist Noel Coward's 1924 song *Mad Dogs and Englishmen,"* a tale about the foolhardiness of colonists venturing out in the heat of the day.

During the 19th century, Jardine's incurred the wrath of a British naval officer by welcoming ships with unauthorized gun salutes. As punishment, the company was ordered to provide a daily time signal for shipping. The tradition is maintained with the sounding of a bell and the firing of a cannon at noon each day.

Beside the gun, a tunnel takes you under busy Gloucester Road. Head along Paterson Street to the

intersection with Great George Street; follow it onto Russell Street and **Times Square,** notable for its gigantic outdoor video screen, chiming clocks, food halls, restaurants, and upscale retailers.

Causeway Bay's department stores, malls, and electronic and clothing retailers offer better deals and less hassle than the shops in bustling Tsim Sha Tsui. The main shopping area is near Lockhart Road and Yee Wo Street; it includes the huge Japanese department store **Sogo.**

Hong Kong Museum of Coastal Defense

Hong Kong's rich history of coastal defense is illustrated in this museum perched atop a

The coastal defense museum occupies an original naval redoubt, reflecting a long heritage of use.

intersection with Kingston Street, an area known as **Fashion Walk,** to some of Hong Kong's trendiest boutiques and cutting-edge fashion houses. Jutting off from Kingston is Food Street, which, unsurprisingly, has a great selection of restaurants. From Paterson Street, walk to the

headland at the island's northeastern tip. The site was the British Navy's Lei Yue Mun Fort, built in 1887 to defend Victoria Harbour's eastern approaches. The museum was completed in 1999; its main section is housed in the excellently restored redoubt, at Lei Yue Mun's core. A historical trail leads through tunnels to magazines and caponiers (bunkers), past defensive ditches, gun emplacements, and other fortifications.

The redoubt sits prominently at the fort's highest point, at the eastern end. Take an elevator from a lobby near the entrance to the grounds and pass over a narrow bridge, with stunning views of the harbor, to the main entrance. The galleries are housed in the building's casements, former barracks, engine rooms, magazines, and shell and cartridge stores surrounding a large assembly courtyard. From

EXPERIENCE: Dig into Dim Sum

A dim sum lunch is an essential Hong Kong experience, enjoyable as much for the raucous atmosphere as for the food. Based on sharing, dim sum is usually eaten in a group, allowing everybody to taste bite-sized snacks. Dim sum restaurants are noisy, frenetic and fun, especially during the peak lunchtime hours. If no seats are available when you arrive, you'll be added to a waiting list. However, securing a seat can mean using your elbows.

Traditionally dim sum was wheeled around on a cart and you could simply pick and point at what you wanted. Nowadays, most dim sum restaurants provide a menu and you mark your order on a slip; unfortunately, this is often only in Chinese. If no English menu is available, a waiter should be able to explain what dim sum is available. Dishes are served in bamboo baskets and when you've had your fill, the waiter will count your baskets and calculate the bill. Expect to pay around HK$100 per person, more at upscale establishments.

Classic dim sum dishes include barbecue pork buns (char siu so), a uniquely Hong Kong offering of slightly sweet buns stuffed with minced barbecued pork; shrimp dumplings (har gau), finely chopped shrimp inside a steamed dumpling; and water chestnut cake (maa tai gow), a popular dessert. This feast is washed down with lots of tea, said to help digestion.

City Hall Maxim's Palace (2/F Low Block, City Hall, Connaught Rd., Central, tel 2521-1303). One of Hong Kong's most famous dim sum joints, Maxim's offers excellent dishes as well as unbeatable views over the harbor. The opulent interior is often packed with businessmen and wedding parties; expect to wait in line. It's also one of the few places that still brings dishes on a cart or a tray. English menu available

Lin Heung Tea House (160–164 Wellington St., Sheung Wan, tel 2544-4556). This bare-bones cafe offers rough and ready dim sum at its best. What keeps diners coming back are the outstanding dim sum and fair prices. Though an English menu is available, it can be tough to communicate.

Luk Yu Tea House (24–26 Stanley St., Central, tel 2523-5464). A wonderful interior of ceiling fans and wooden booths is the real attraction at this pricey teahouse, operating since 1933. Luk Yu's undeserved reputation for surly service is belied by a host of dedicated regulars and elderly waiters who've often been plying the tables for ten years or more. English menu available.

Tsui Hang Village (Miramar Shopping Centre, 132–134 Nathan Rd., Tsim Sha Tsui, tel 2376-2882). Tsui Hang Village regularly receives positive reviews for fairly priced dim sum. It also has a reputation for its own unique dim sum dishes.

Zen (Pacific Place Shopping Mall, 88 Queensway, Central, tel 2845-4555). For those who don't want to brave the mayhem of traditional dim sum restaurants, Zen offers stylish dining inside a sleek, contemporary interior and masterful, if expensive, dishes. English menus provided.

here, stairs lead to an upper gallery.

You pass in chronological order through 600 years of Hong Kong's coastal defense, with each of the small galleries devoted to particular periods during that time. After the **Orientation Gallery,** you enter the **Ming Period Gallery** (1368–1644), with displays of body armor worn by high-ranking military officers, including blue satin coats, concealed armor vests, and tunics with small metal plates sown into the lining. More of the same is found in the **Qing Period Gallery** (1644–1911), along with crafted bows and decorated spearheads.

....

The British Period Gallery has a detailed model of Murray House, the first military building erected in Hong Kong (1846).

....

The **First Opium War Gallery** (1840–1842) has a collection of opium pipes and paraphernalia, a model of a Chinese war junk and the British warship *Nemesis* opposing each other, and a diorama of the pivotal Battle of Shajio at Humen in the Pearl River Estuary; in this January 1841 clash, the British 37th Madras Native Infantry overran the Chinese garrison. There is also a copy of the Treaty of Nanking—the document allowing cession of Hong Kong

to the British on August 29, 1842—and a short documentary about the war.

The **British Period Gallery** (1841–1860) has many weapons and a detailed model of Murray House (see p. 107), the first military building erected in Hong Kong (1846). The adjoining second and third **British Period Galleries** (1861–1941) contain uniforms, swords, guns, and photographs, plus a full-size diorama of a 19th-century British soldier in a barrack.

The **Battle for Hong Kong Gallery** (December 1941) has a documentary on the Japanese invasion, with footage highlighting the bravery of the vastly undermanned British and Canadian troops, along with weapons and medals. Pick up telephones in the **Japanese Occupation Gallery** (1941–1945) to listen to poignant eyewitness accounts of local people.

The **Volunteers Gallery** traces the history of the Hong Kong Volunteers—also called the Royal Hong Kong Defense Force—from their formation in 1854 as an adjunct to the British military until their disbandment in 1995.

The final gallery, the **Hong Kong Garrison of the PLA,** is a slightly disappointing exhibit of uniforms, a Chinese navy flag of no historical importance, model ships, and self-praising history panels.

Upstairs, the **Coastal Defense Weapons Theater** shows a short documentary on the history of Hong Kong's coastal defense and features the reflective **Cost of War** exhibition. Outside, check out the gun emplacements and tunnels before heading down the hill along the **Historical Trail.** ■

Actors perform a Chinese adaptation of the English drama *The Rivals* at the Acadamy of Performing Arts. The academy is a major venue for drama and dance.

More Places to Visit in Hong Kong North

Hong Kong Academy for Performing Arts

Built by the Hong Kong Jockey Club (see p. 92) in 1985, the academy trains Hong Kong's performing artists and is one of the territory's major venues for drama and dance. It comprises the 1,200-seat **Lyric Theater,** a smaller drama theater, a concert hall for instrumental and choral groups, a recital hall, a studio theater, and an impressive amphitheater in the gardens adjoining the building. The academy has schools of dance, drama, music, technical arts, and television. Public performances are held regularly. www.hkpa.edu Map p. 86 1 Gloucester Rd. 2584-8500 MTR: Wan Chai

Hong Kong Arts Centre

Opposite the Academy for Performing Arts, the center, built in 1977, was the first multipurpose establishment dedicated to supporting local art groups, and fostering and promoting different art disciplines in Hong Kong. The center incorporates visual arts, performing arts, film, video, and media art. It hosts numerous performances, exhibitions, concerts, seminars, and film festivals. It has a number of galleries, including the impressive **Pao Sui Loong** and **Pao Yue Kong Galleries**. These galleries, on the fourth and fifth floors, display contemporary art by local and international artists including paintings, graphic art, sculpture, photography, crafts, and calligraphy. The center's basement **Agnès B. Cinema** is Hong Kong's most active art film theater, while the **Shouson Theater** is used for drama, dance, concerts, and film. www.hkac.org.hk Map p. 86 2 Harbour Rd. 2582-0200 MTR: Wan Chai

Hong Kong Museum of Medical Science

Housed in the Edwardian-style former Pathological Institute, which was founded in 1906 to combat the outbreak of bubonic plague (which had broken out in 1894 in the colony), is a fascinating, but sometimes morbid museum tucked away in the side streets of the Mid-Levels. It chronicles the development of medical science in Hong Kong, with an autopsy room and a laboratory filled with antique equipment, as well as other rooms tracing the development of dentistry and radiology. Most noteworthy, however, is the exhibit comparing traditional Chinese medicine and Western medicine, with displays on acupuncture and Chinese herbs.
www.hkmms.org.hk 🅼 Map p. 75
✉ 2 Caine Lane, Mid-Levels ☎ 2549-5123
🕐 Closed Mon. 🅂 $ 🚌 Bus: 12, 26

Jamia Mosque

Sitting in a tranquil, cool garden and surrounded by high-rises, the Jamia Mosque is reached by a short flight of stone steps and an elaborate wrought-iron gate. The first mosque on this site was built in 1849, then rebuilt and extended in 1915. For decades most of the worshippers were Punjabi Muslims, many of whom served in Hong Kong's pre-World War II police force.
🅼 Map p. 54 ✉ Corner of Shelley & Mosque Sts. (enter from Shelley St.)
🚌 Central to Mid-Levels Escalator

Law UK Folk Museum

The museum is a small and interesting restored Hakka village house. Wax figures in traditional garb, furniture, implements, and farming tools are featured in the museum's living room, bedrooms, cocklofts, kitchen, and storeroom. This particular house, set in peaceful gardens, was the ancestral home of the Law family who settled in the area during the reign of the Emperor Qianlong (1736–1795). The Hakka, still prominent in the New Territories, migrated from northern China from the 18th century. Next to the museum, which nestles in peaceful gardens, is an exhibition gallery with displays and information on traditional Hakka culture and on the restoration of Law UK.
www.lcsd.gov.hk 🅼 Map p. 53 ✉ 14 Kut Shing St., Chai Wan ☎ 2896-7006
🕐 Closed Thurs. 🚇 MTR: Chai Wan, exit B

Quarry Bay

Hong Kong Island's seemingly insatiable desire for more office space has transformed **Tong Chung Street** from a messy side street of car mechanic's shop-houses and *dai pai dongs* (sidewalk restaurants) into a road lined with gleaming office towers, bars, and restaurants. Most nights, especially toward the end of the week, the bars and restaurants fill with office workers, offering a less pretentious atmosphere than Lan Kwai Fong or SoHo.

Nearby is **City Plaza,** which is home to more than 150 stores. Shopping at this huge mall is relatively hassle-free compared to Tsim Sha Tsui and Causeway Bay. Visitors rarely shop here, so prices tend to be lower. The mall also has an ice-skating rink. The high-rise residential buildings surrounding City Plaza are part of the Tai Koo Shing development and are in a style typical of housing for Hong Kong's middle classes.
🅼 Map p. 53 **Quarry Bay** 🚇 MTR: Quarry Bay **City Plaza** 🚇 MTR: Tai Koo Shing

Stubbs Road Lookout

If you want more stunning views, head up to Stubbs Road Lookout. Here you will get uninterrupted panoramas of Victoria Harbour to Kowloon, Happy Valley Racecourse, Causeway Bay, Central, and Wan Chai, equally beguiling at night. The lookout has a handy map board that allows visitors to pinpoint attractions below.
🅼 Map. p. 51 🚌 Bus: 7; Minibus: 15

Distinctly different from Hong Kong Island's urban north, with a slower pace, beaches, and green hills

Hong Kong Island South

Door god at a Tin Hau temple

Hong Kong Island South

Less than 30 minutes by bus or taxi from Central District on Hong Kong Island's northern shore, a completely new aspect of the island opens up. The contrast could not be more staggering. Relentless concrete and steel towers give way to luxuriant countryside, winding roads, spectacular scenery, pretty beaches, and laid-back villages. With a few exceptions, Hong Kong Island South remains remarkably pristine and uncrowded.

The old quay at the southern end of Repulse Bay Beach has been renovated into a modern Chinese temple theme park.

Traveling from the north of the island to the south is an experience in itself, especially when the trip is taken on the upper floor of a double-decker bus. The journey climbs over the green hills that separate the two parts of the island and along snaking roads lined with lush foliage. White-sand beaches curving between rocky headlands come into view, then disappear as the single-lane roads wind their way down to the coast.

Most of the shore on the southern side of the island has not suffered from the huge land reclamation projects carried out in other parts of Hong Kong, and its rugged and convoluted coastline, indented with stunning bays, beaches, and coves, remains intact.

Many of Hong Kong's wealthy have chosen to live on the island's south side, where they can enjoy a peaceful respite from the hectic pace of the downtown areas. The high-rises to

be seen here are not offices; they are almost all residential dwellings. Those who can afford it have built their mansions along the headlands at Shek O, secluded Deep Water Bay, and the Stanley Peninsula.

Because of the startling contrast between north and south, it is almost inevitable that on weekends and during holidays these communities overflow with day-trippers from the north side of the island. The beaches can get packed, the walking trails crowded, and the restaurants

INSIDER TIP:

Visit Hong Kong's nature preserves. You can do so fairly conveniently on public transportation.

—DAVID LEE
National Geographic field researcher

crammed. Come on a weekday if you want to enjoy the slower pace and restful atmosphere found here.

Hong Kong Island South has some of the territory's most popular attractions. Rambling Stanley Market is a hit with both visitors and

locals, and there is a great range of restaurants and a number of historical sights.

Hong Kong's most popular beach at Repulse Bay gets so crowded some days, it's hard to see the sand for all the sunbathers, while the huge floating restaurants at Aberdeen are always busy. On a headland east of Aberdeen, Ocean Park has successfully rejuvenated itself as a first-class theme park and oceanarium, providing an excellent family day out. ∎

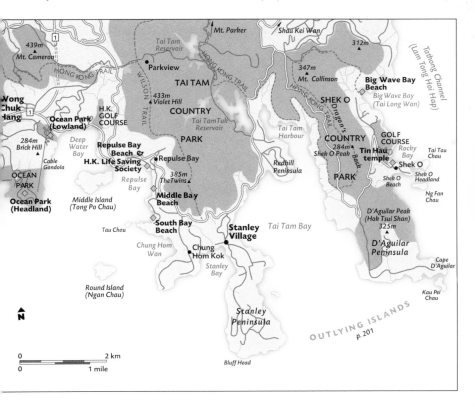

Tai Tam Country Park

Tai Tam Country Park, one of four country parks on Hong Kong Island, is by far the biggest, covering almost a fifth of the island and containing some of its most beautiful countryside. Stretching from Quarry Bay in the north to Repulse Bay and Redhill Peninsula in the south, it straddles the eastern section of the island, offering sweeping scenery and majestic views across Tai Tam Bay.

Tai Tam Reservoir supplies Hong Kong Island with much of its fresh water.

**Tai Tam
Country Park**
Map p. 103
Bus: 6, 61

**Agriculture,
Fisheries, and
Conservation
Department**
1823

www.afcd.gov.hk

Tai Tam's valley is cut by numerous streams, waterfalls, and canopied trees over paths, with fantastic views of the jade green waters of the several reservoirs that give the park its name—Tai Tam means "big pools" in Cantonese. In 1914, Tai Tam Tuk Reservoir displaced Hakka villagers who had farmed the fertile valley for generations.

The park is traversed by sections of the **Hong Kong Trail** (see pp. 72–73) and the rugged **Wilson Trail,** which runs from Stanley, above Repulse Bay and on to Quarry Bay. It is framed on its northern and eastern sides by towering peaks; the tallest is Mount Parker, at 1,663 feet (507 m) the second highest on Hong Kong Island.

An easy 2.2-mile (3.5 km) walk through the park, with a short bus journey at the end, is a delightful way to make your way to Stanley Village (see pp. 106–109). You can descend into the valley at the upscale Hong Kong Parkview, a private residential complex, on Tai Tam Reservoir Road. Just follow the road east a short distance from the Parkview until it narrows into a pedestrian path, which drops down to the Tai Tam Reservoir. A small bridge takes you over the reservoir and along the heavily wooded countryside past Tai Tam Intermediate Reservoir, where the road levels out and skirts Tai Tam Tuk Reservoir eventually to join Tai Tam Road. From here, cross the road and take a bus to Stanley Village. ∎

Shek O

On the southeast coast of Hong Kong Island, the sleepy little seaside village of Shek O is about as remote as it's possible to get on the island. This cluster of houses, separated by narrow alleys, has a population of only about 3,000, although this number swells significantly on weekends when city dwellers seeking a change of scene head for its beach and restaurants.

The town's alleys are worth exploring before heading to the beach or along the headland. Soon after entering the village from the traffic circle near the bus stop, you'll find a tiny **Tin Hau temple** (see sidebar p. 95), with colorful deities painted on its doors. Continue along Shek O Road for a short distance and Shek O's sandy beach comes into view on your right. The ramshackle restaurants at the northern end of the beach are a good place to relax.

Keep walking along the road and up a slight incline to where the road moves out onto **Shek O Headland,** which frames the northern end of Shek O beach. Here the mansions of some of Hong Kong's moneyed line the narrow headland, taking in wonderful panoramas of the South China Sea and the territory's numerous outlying islands.

Walk to the top of the headland for more impressive views of the sea, islands, and the loaf-shaped Cape d'Aguilar, the southeasternmost point on Hong Kong Island. From near the tip of the headland, climb down the steps to a path and onto a small footbridge that crosses over **Tai Tau Chau,** a rocky islet. It takes about ten minutes to climb to a viewing platform at the top. From here you can see northwest to Tung Lung Chau (see p. 214) and Joss House Bay in Clear Water Bay (see pp. 188–189), southwest to the Stanley Peninsula, and south past Cape d'Aguilar to Waglan Island and the Po Toi Islands (see p. 214). ■

Shek O

🗺 Map p. 103

🚇 MTR: Shau Kei Wan, then bus 9

Hiking in Hong Kong

Around 40 percent of Hong Kong is designated as public parks, offering a multitude of trails just outside the city's humming core. Getting outside the city is a must, as the view of the skyscrapers and harbor from the remote hills is wonderful. You will hear talk of the "big four," which mean the four main trails. The longest, yet most rewarding, is the **MacLehose Trail** (60 miles/100 km), but there are also the **Wilson, Hong Kong,** and **Lantau Trails.** Each is well marked in English, but bring a map if you plan on venturing off on your own. Also, as this is Hong Kong, it will be hot, so dress and hydrate accordingly. For information, visit *www. hkwalkers.net.*

Stanley Village

The pretty seaside community of Stanley is another enclave of Hong Kong's wealthy; you can't help but be impressed by the opulent mansions and exclusive apartments lining the only road into the village. It is hard now to imagine that Stanley, known as Chek Chu in Chinese, was the largest settlement on Hong Kong Island when the British arrived in 1841.

Apartment buildings rise along the bay at Stanley, notable also for its copious market.

Stanley Village
- Map p. 103
- Bus: 6, 6A, 6X, 260

During those days Stanley Village was a market town selling produce from the surrounding farms, and a haven for pirates. **Stanley Market** is still here, wedged between a neck of land separating Stanley Bay and Tai Tam Bay, but the goods and the customers have certainly changed. Although not a place to pick up any real bargains, it's still an experience. On weekends, thousands of people pack the market. Among the mad jumble of stands and elbowing crowds, you'll find clothing, souvenirs, paintings, toys, sneakers, brassware, rattan, linens, porcelain, crafts, artifacts, swimwear, and much more.

Immediately in front of the market is the newly constructed **Stanley Promenade,** from

INSIDER TIP:

Don't miss the Stanley Market; shops sell everything from teapots to tailored silk.

—TIFFANY TRENT
National Geographic contributor

which Stanley Main Road runs along the edge of the waterfront, with a string of bars and excellent restaurants. At the end of the road is the colonial era **Murray House** (see p. 108) which was moved here brick by brick from Central. Next door to Murray House is Blake Pier, from which several ferry routes run.

A few minutes' stroll through the village along Stanley Beach Road on the eastern side of the peninsula is **Stanley Main Beach.** On summer weekends, the beach is packed with people and the water is dotted with the colorful sails of windsurfers. The quieter and prettier **St. Stephen's Beach,** south of the village along Wong Ma Kok Road, is a better option for swimming and sunbathing.

The trip to Stanley Village is worth making just for the bus ride from Central District, regarded as the most scenic trip in Hong Kong. It takes 40 minutes to get here from Central, with much of the trip running along Tai Tam Road on the border of Tai Tam Country Park (see p. 104). ∎

EXPERIENCE: Go to a Market

Alongside the city's sleek boutiques and upscale malls, Hong Kong's street markets still flourish. The markets are a great place to rub elbows with the locals and you'll often find them packed. And while these markets are not the bargains they once were, there are still bargains to be found here.

One of Hong Kong's most famous markets is in Stanley. The market primarily targets tourists and offers clothing, toys for the beaches, and Chinese souvenirs at slightly inflated prices. In the city proper, the **Wan Chai Market**, around Cross Street, is a sprawl of stalls popular with locals picking up everything from fresh fruit and vegetables to toys and ties, all at fair prices.

One of the biggest and best markets is **Temple Street Night Market** in Yau Ma Tei, which is between Kowloon Park and Mong Kok. The market operates on Temple Street between 3 p.m. and 11 p.m. and is usually at its bustling best at around 9 p.m. Mostly filled with tourist souvenirs and clothes, the market buzzes with alfresco diners digging in at *dai pai dongs* and the sound of Cantonese opera.

Just up the road on Tung Choi Street in Mong Kok is the **Ladies Market**, which operates from early afternoon until 10:30 p.m. daily. A riot of gaudy colors and raucous bargaining, the market is packed with 10-foot-high (3 m) stalls hawking both men's and women's clothing. You'll also find a great selection of inexpensive Chinese souvenirs and curios here. In most Hong Kong markets, shopping is a contact sport, and this seems to hold especially true at the Ladies Market. Also, don't be surprised if you are tugged on the sleeve by someone whispering, "copy watch," hoping to sell you the imitation of an expensive time piece.

A Walk Around Stanley Village

Stanley is one of Hong Kong Island's most pleasing communities for walking. It has a number of attractions, both man-made and natural, all within easy distance, and a laid-back atmosphere not often found in other parts of Hong Kong.

A monk offers prayers at Stanley's ornate Kwun Yam Temple.

Starting at Stanley Bus Station, cross Stanley Village Road and continue down Stanley New Street, where you will see the start of the famous **Stanley Market ❶** (see p. 106). At the end of the street, turn right onto Stanley Main Road and walk along a line of shops for about 100 yards (90 m) to where the road opens to the water's edge, and a row of brightly painted open-fronted bars and restaurants overlooks Stanley Bay.

Walk a short distance past these along Stanley Main Road to historic **Murray House ❷**, built on reclaimed land at the edge of the bay. This lovely building, now housing the **Hong Kong Maritime Museum** (*www.hkmaritime museum.org, tel 852/2813-2322*) on its first floor and hosting a number of restaurants and shops, is the oldest surviving colonial building in Hong Kong. Built in the early 1840s, it was where the formal surrender of British troops to the Japanese took place in December 1941. It

NOT TO BE MISSED:

Stanley Market • Murray House
• Kwun Yam Temple • Tin Hau
temple • Stanley Military Cemetery

stood on the site of the Bank of China Tower on Queen's Road Central until 1982, when its 4,000 bricks were dismantled, placed in storage, and put back together again on its current site in 1998. On the far side of Murray House, past Blake Pier, is a short track leading up to the **Pak Tai temple,** a tiny, windswept outpost offering views of the South China Sea crashing against the rocks below.

In an open space between Murray House and Stanley Plaza Shopping Center sits one of Hong Kong Island's oldest **Tin Hau temples ❸**, founded in 1767 and dedicated to the protector of seafarers (see Tin Hau p. 94). The present bunker-style structure dates from 1938, but the inside is impressive, with some wonderfully crafted model junks.

Take the path to the west of Murray House and continue up the hill to the **Kwun Yam Temple** ❹. Inside a pavilion above the temple is the 20-foot (6 m) statue of Kwun Yam, the Goddess of Mercy (see Kwun Yam p. 148).

Head back to the bus station via the same route (it takes less than ten minutes). From here, walk east along Stanley Village Road for about 50 yards (45 m); on your right is the 1859 **Old Stanley Police Station** ❺, the oldest surviving police building in Hong Kong, although it now houses a supermarket.

Just beyond the police station, the road forks onto Wong Ma Kok Road. A short walk along and to your left is the entrance to **Stanley Military Cemetery** ❻, whose rows of uniform gravestones set amid neatly

manicured lawns serve as a poignant reminder of the lives that were lost during the Japanese occupation here. The cemetery was opened in the early days of the colony—a few colonists' graves remain—but was closed for 70 years until it reopened in 1942 as the death toll mounted during occupation.

Continue along Wong Ma Kok Road to shaded Wong Ma Kok Path on the right and head down to the pleasant **St. Stephen's Beach** ❼. It's a better alternative for swimming and sunbathing than crowded Stanley Main Beach, which is a short walk northeast from the bus station along Stanley Beach Road.

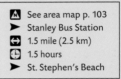

🗺 See area map p. 103
▶ Stanley Bus Station
↔ 1.5 mile (2.5 km)
🕐 1.5 hours
▶ St. Stephen's Beach

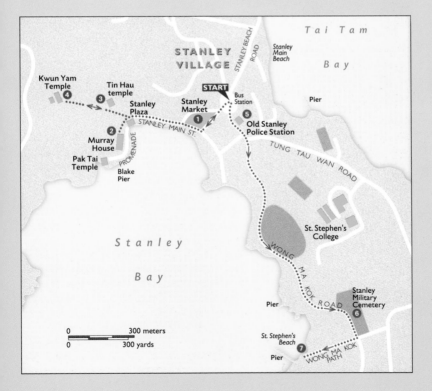

Repulse Bay

Repulse Bay got its name from the actions of H.M.S. *Repulse,* which took part in a campaign by British forces in the 1840s to rid the place of pirates. From the nearby hills, Japanese forces launched an attack in late 1941 on British and Canadian troops based here to keep supply lines opened between Stanley and Aberdeen.

South Bay Beach offers a quieter alternative to crowded Repulse Bay Beach.

Repulse Bay Beach

⚠ Map p. 103

✉ Beach Rd., Repulse Bay

🕐 No lifeguard patrols Dec.–Feb.

🚌 Bus: 6, 6A, 6X, 66, 260

Today Repulse Bay is home to Hong Kong Island's longest and most popular beach, **Repulse Bay Beach.** In the summer, this clean, white stretch of sand is packed with thousands of swimmers escaping the territory's sweltering heat—up to 30,000 people come on Sundays. It's also one of the few beaches that get crowded midweek. Oddly, after the official beach season ends in November, it is near deserted even though temperatures can reach the mid-80s (25°C). The beach has showers and changing rooms, although the murky water doesn't invite a dip. If you need more room, walk along the shoreline for 10 minutes to the less crowded **Middle Bay Beach,** or for another 20 minutes to **South Bay Beach.**

Repulse Bay once served as a playground for Hong Kong's elite. The colonial Repulse Bay Hotel, built in 1920, was regarded as one of the finest beach resort hotels in Asia, the perfect place to take afternoon tea on the veranda and enjoy views across the bay. Despite public outcry, it was demolished in the early 1980s and replaced by one of Hong Kong's oddest buildings, a high-rise apartment building called the **Repulse Bay.**

This long, curving, blue high-rise stands out from the other apartment buildings on the hills behind the beach because of a distinctive pink-framed square hole in its middle. During its planning, a *feng shui* master was consulted, a common practice in Hong Kong. The master informed the architects that the dragon inhabiting the hills behind the building would be unable to come down to drink at the bay if the design went ahead as one long continuous structure.

Lifeguards

Lifeguards perched on lookout towers are a common sight on Hong Kong's beaches. The territory's first lifeguard club was founded in 1956, and today 476 lifeguards, patrol the 41 official beaches between March and November. Although shark attacks in Hong Kong are rare, a spate of fatal incidents around Sai Kung in the 1990s led to shark nets being installed at 32 of the local beaches. For the Leisure and Cultural Department's full list of beaches with shark nets, see *www.lcsd.gov.hk* or call 1823.

The distinctive hole was created to enable the dragon to pass through, thus quenching its thirst.

In a rather sad concession to the demolition of the graceful

INSIDER TIP:

At Repulse Bay, see the beautiful temple dedicated to Kwun Yam (Goddess of Mercy) and Tin Hau (Queen of Heaven).

—TIFFANY TRENT
National Geographic contributor

old Repulse Bay Hotel, a terrace with lawns, palms, fountains, and a replica of the facade of the hotel has been built at the front of the Repulse Bay apartments. It houses a number of good restaurants including the popular **Verandah,** (see page 251) where you can still indulge in afternoon tea, or champagne brunch every Sunday, and shop in its upscale shopping arcade.

At the eastern end of Beach Road, which fronts the bay, the training headquarters of the **Hong Kong Life Saving Society** (see sidebar at left) is flanked by huge statues of Kwun Yam, Goddess of Mercy (see sidebar p. 148), and Tin Hau, Queen of Heaven and protector of seafarers (see sidebar p. 94). The bizarre and garish collection of statues on the grounds draws hordes of worshippers burning joss sticks and offering prayers.

The place is filled with imaginative and colorful depictions of elephants, camels, lions, goats, a four-faced Buddha, and Kwun Yam riding a fish.

Each time you cross the **Bridge of Longevity** at the front of the grounds, legend has it that three days are added to your life. ∎

Feng Shui

The Chinese philosophy of *feng shui* (literally "wind water") has become a worldwide phenomenon in recent years, but it has been a part of the culture of Hong Kong from its earliest days. It aims for harmony, and when this is achieved, good luck, synonymous with health and wealth, will follow.

A square hole cut into the Repulse Bay apartment complex allows the dragon that inhabits the hills behind to drink from the bay.

A feng shui master attempts to align the flows of energy called *chi*, considered to be the breath of nature, in a space or building using a special compass called a *lopan*. This compass helps determine the energy characteristics of a space. Complex mathematical calculations are also involved. Hills, water, and buildings can all affect the flow of chi, because everything in the universe has an energy force.

The first villages built in the New Territories were located in sites that captured the chi, and today feng shui continues to be an accepted part of many aspects of life in the city.

By having buildings—or even items in your home or office—in the optimum position to harmonize the energy in and around them, you are able to create areas that protect you from harm and bring you prosperity, good health, or happiness. For example, the head of a bed should not be directly opposite a door, where an enemy could enter in the night and easily see you. A view over water is said to be good for making you prosperous, as water brings with it abundance. If you don't have a sea view, don't worry, the same effect can be achieved by having an aquarium filled with many goldfish.

Doors are important to feng shui because they are considered to be the channels through which bad spirits can enter. For this reason, several clan halls in the New Territories have spirit screens located behind the main doors to prevent a direct view to the heart of the building.

Also in the New Territories, and sometimes even in urban areas, you may see a small octagonal mirror above the front door. This, again, is for protection against bad spirits; it is believed that on seeing their reflection the demons will turn tail.

Many of the territory's buildings have been the subject of considerable feng shui debate. In the 1980s, newspapers were full of reports on the allegedly bad feng shui of the Bank of China Building in Central. Its structure of interlocking triangles, ending in sharp points, apparently looked too much like knife blades according to some critical feng shui masters, who warned that if left it could cause economic damage. This problematic design was compounded by the fact that the bank was located on part of what is seen as a dragon's back—a line of good fortune that runs past the nearby Cheung Kong Center, the HSBC building, and into the financial heart of the city. To offset criticism, the Bank of China was opened on the eighth day of the eighth month in 1988—eight is a lucky number, and that day was divined to be the luckiest of the 20th century.

Another example is the Government House in Central, believed to have one of the territory's best feng shui locations, with uninterrupted views between mountains and sea. That is, it was once considered one of the best, until the Bank of China building bisected it with an angle. Many suspect this misfortune resulted in a bad fall taken by Britain's visiting Prime Minister Margaret Thatcher; the building now remains empty most of the year.

EXPERIENCE: Learn Feng Shui

Skybird Travel Agency (tel 2369-9628, www.skybird.com.hk). This agency operates an expert tour of Hong Kong's most important feng shui buildings, explaining the principles behind them. The tour, which starts at the Lung Cheung Road lookout, pieces together how the Hong Kong jigsaw of island, harbor, and mountains work in harmony. It then visits Nine Dragons Wall and finishes with the skyscrapers that surround Statue Square, including the HSBC building. Tours depart Tuesdays, Thursdays, and Saturdays, last three and a half hours and cost HK$320.

Hong Kong Tourism Board (tel 2508-1234, www.discoverhongkong.com). Those looking to learn the basics of feng shui can enjoy a free one-hour lesson courtesy of the Hong Kong Tourism Board. The class takes place every Thursday at 10:30 a.m. and is led by one of Hong Kong's most respected feng shui practitioners, Alex Yu. Participants must preregister; places are limited to 30, and you will need your passport.

Feng Shui Master Raymond Lo (tel 2736-9568, www.raymond-lo.com). Those looking for a more in-depth experience can contact expert feng shui master Raymond Lo, who offers intensive three-day courses at various levels, as well as examinations. He also appears in select world cities, meaning you can finish your feng shui degree at home.

Ocean Park

Situated on a hilly peninsula on the south side of Hong Kong Island, this 200-acre (80 ha) park is a world-class combination oceanarium, zoo, and amusement park and one of Hong Kong's most popular tourist attractions. The park had become a little tired in recent years, but thanks to an injection of cash, it has unveiled a host of new and revamped attractions.

Entering the park at the Lowland, you come to a cocoon-shaped **Butterfly House,** aflutter with thousands of Technicolor butterflies. Nearby

An escalator takes visitors past stunning views to the park's Headland section.

is an equally colorful **Goldfish Pagoda,** full of darting, bug-eyed Chinese and Japanese goldfish. Then head to **Amazing Amazon,** an impressive trek through the simulated wilds of South America, with macaws, toucans, and flamingoes. Amazing Amazon also houses the **Caverns of Darkness,** a 3-D mock-up of an ancient South American temple, and the **Amazing Birds Show,** where parrots, hawks, owls, and ibises show off their natural behavior with various tricks.

The **Club Giant Panda Habitat** holds four of the rare animals, An An and Jia Jia, gifts from the People's Republic of China in 1999, and Le Le and Ying Ying, who joined them in 2007. The foursome reside in an indoor, climate-controlled enclosure that replicates their native habitat in the Chinese province of Sichuan.

Unsurprisingly, kids love the adjacent **Kids' World,** where they can have a close encounter with dolphins at Dolphin University.

To reach the **Headland,** take the eight-minute cable-car ride and enjoy stunning views over the South China Sea and Repulse Bay.

At the end of the ride, head for **Atoll Reef,** one of the park's most popular attractions. It succeeds in making you feel as if you have entered an underwater realm. You get to view more

Ocean Park Special Fish

Although there are thousands of animal species at Ocean Park, see the rare Chinese sturgeon (*Acipenser sinensis*). The fish has been threatened by the construction of the Ghezouba Dam, which disrupted its spawning grounds in the Yangtze River; they wouldn't survive at all if it weren't for hatcheries. In addition to being an endangered species, the sturgeon is a living fossil, having plied the waters for 140 million years. In honor of the 2008 Summer Olympics, Chinese officials gave Hong Kong five of these rare animals, one for each of the Olympic rings; they went to Ocean Park.

Unfortunately, the sturgeons were not placed in a separate tank, and within days one was killed by barracudas. Understandably, the Chinese officials were peeved, but Ocean Park pointed out that they had placed the sturgeons in a communal tank on the advice of Chinese scientists. China relented and supplied Ocean Park with a replacement fish.

than 4,000 creatures from 400 species swimming, floating, and bottom-feeding. At the terrific **Shark Aquarium** you come face to face with 250 sharks from 35 species. The park runs a captive breeding program for some of the shark species, including the black tip reef shark and the rare pygmy swellshark. The recently added **Sea Jelly Spectacular** has become one of the park's most popular attractions. The complement of more than 1,000 sea jellies is theatrically enhanced by cutting-edge special effects and mood lighting.

The 3,500-seat **Ocean Theater** has dolphins and sea lions performing the usual ball-balancing, hoop-jumping, synchronized swimming, and audience-splashing tricks. At **Pacific Pier,** modeled after the natural habitat of seals and sea lions off the coast of California, there is an underwater viewing tunnel. You can also feed the animals.

At the southeastern corner of the headland are a number of white-knuckle rides, including **The Dragon** roller coaster. Perched frighteningly on the edge of a cliff, it shoots you through three loops, including one in reverse, at speeds reaching 50 miles an hour (80 kph).

Another roller coaster, the Wild West-themed **Mine Train,** flies alarmingly along a 2,300-foot (700 m) track full of twists, turns, and a gravity-defying 280-foot (85 m) plunge. The pulse-quickening **Raging River** ride swirls through a series of twists and turns down a narrow ravine before lurching into a breathtaking vertical drop at the end of the ride. If that's not enough excitement, thrill-seekers can plummet 20 floors or 200 feet (60 m) in free fall at **The Abyss.**

Ocean Park is currently undergoing a major renovation and expansion, with the number of attractions set to double on completion of the changes in 2012. The park will remain open throughout the process, with major new additions being continually added. Highlights include the **Typhoon Stunt Show,** a frozen **Indoor Ice Palace** and a **Killer Whale Show,** as well as a number of hotels. A connection to the MTR is also promised. ∎

Ocean Park

- Map p. 103
- Ocean Park Rd., Aberdeen
- 2552-0291
- $$$$
- Ocean Park bus 629 from Admiralty MTR, or 6A, 6X from Central

www.oceanpark .com.hk

Aberdeen

Aberdeen was a small fishing village and haven for smugglers and pirates when the British arrived. The colonial navy purged the pirates, and the *hongs* (trading companies) built dry docks for their trading fleets. Fishing, along with boatbuilding, remains the occupation of many families, while visitors flock here to dine at the gigantic floating restaurants anchored in the harbor.

The iconic Jumbo floating restaurant has been refurbished into a complex of fine dining, sightseeing, shopping, and cultural attractions.

Aberdeen

 Map p. 102

Bus: 70 from Central, 70, 37B from Admiralty

Jumbo Kingdom

✉ Shum Wan Pier Drive, Wong Chuk Hang

☎ 2553-9111

www.jumbo.com.hk

Aberdeen is known in Chinese as Heung Kong Tsai ("little fragrant" harbor), a name likely derived from the village's trade in sweet-smelling sandalwood used for incense. This term is now used to describe all of the Special Administrative Region—Hong Kong.

Fishing boats start returning to port at 4 a.m. and continue unloading their catches at the frenetic **Wholesale Fish Market** at the western end of Aberdeen Praya Road until noon. From here, live seafood is loaded onto vans with water tanks and transported to restaurants and markets throughout Hong Kong.

Walking a little farther east along the waterfront brings you to a dock,

where inevitably you will be offered a sampan harbor tour. It's easy to negotiate the original price—usually HK$100—down by half, and the 30-minute tour is worth taking.

The sampans motor past boatyards and lanes of anchored boats, giving a brief glimpse into the lives of the dwindling number of fishing families aboard their vessels (see Boat People opposite). Men repair their nets and hang up fish to dry in the sun, women wash clothes and dishes amid potted plants on deck, chained dogs bark as sampans drift too close, and tethered children play and wander around the decks.

Aberdeen's most famous landmark is the gigantic floating

Jumbo Kingdom, two Chinese-style buildings that once housed cavernous restaurants and since have been transformed into a modern complex of dining, entertainment, and cultural attractions. Perpetually popular with visiting groups of Chinese mainlanders, who arrive to dine on Jumbo's fresh seafood, the complex is also home to the slightly more intimate restaurants Dragon Court and the sleek Top Deck. Jumbo Kingdom runs free ferries from Aberdeen Promenade.

The Jumbo Kingdom faces the exclusive Aberdeen Marina Club, with rows of luxury craft to the front and the crowded island of **Ap Lei Chau** to the rear. The

INSIDER TIP:

Take in one of the floating restaurants in Aberdeen Harbor. Jumbo's is the biggest and the best.

—A. J. TIMOTHY JULL
National Geographic field researcher

a **Tin Hau temple** set pleasantly amid trees, shrubs, and potted plants. Originally constructed in 1851, the temple was rebuilt in 2001 after it was found to be sinking into the ground.

Follow Aberdeen Main Road behind the temple to the steep but shady Peel Rise and the enormous **Chinese Permanent**

Boat People

Many of the high-rise apartments in Aberdeen were built in the 1980s as the government encouraged the town's Hoklo boat people to leave their floating harbor homes and settle for a life on dry land. The Hoklo, who came to Hong Kong from Swatow in Guangdong Province in the 19th century, are distinguished by their wide conical hats. Although the Hoklo are a hardy people, those who remain on their boats in Aberdeen Harbor enjoy plenty of creature comforts, which are very much of the 21st century. Many boats are equipped with refrigerators, washing machines and dryers, satellite television, and air conditioners. Life on the sea can still be dangerous, however. Toddlers are often put on a tether to ensure they can't stray to the edge of the boat and fall in. As the viability of fishing in Hong Kong's waters has waned, though, so has the number of boat people.

island is a major boatbuilding center and huge residential complex. Walk across the bridge connecting it to the mainland for glittering evening views of the harbor and floating restaurants.

Pass through Aberdeen's busy, compact downtown by heading north up Aberdeen Main Road to the junction with Aberdeen Reservoir Road, where you'll find

Cemetery. The terraced hillsides are packed with gravestones overlooking the South China Sea, although Aberdeen's high-rise apartment buildings have blocked some of the graves' views. This is an unfortunate aspect of progress in Hong Kong, as being buried on a hillside, overlooking the water, is the most auspicious resting place in Chinese culture. ■

More Places to Visit on Hong Kong Island South

The seaside village of Shek O, with its sandy beach and ramshackle restaurants, is a favorite spot for a weekend getaway.

Big Wave Bay Beach

North of the village of Shek O, past the coastal Shek O Country Club and Golf Course, is the excellent and almost entirely deserted Big Wave Bay Beach. Get off the bus from Shau Kei Wan where it curves to meet the golf course at Big Wave Bay Road—the intersection is well marked. From here, follow the road for about ten minutes to the beach. Alternatively, rent a bicycle in Shek O village and ride the 1.2 miles (2 km) to the beach, backed by a wooded area, rising to the peaks on Mount Collinson and Shek O, both part of the Shek O Country Park.

Big Wave Bay can mount a sizable swell given the right weather conditions, usually when typhoons are passing close to Hong Kong. It's one of only two beaches that produce good waves for surfing; the other is Tai Long Wan in Sai Kung Country Park (see pp. 186–190). **M** Map p. 103 **MTR:** Shau Kei Wan, then bus 9

Deep Water Bay

Deep Water Bay bites deeply into Hong Kong Island between the headlands separating Repulse Bay and Aberdeen and is fronted by 500 yards (450 m) of clean white sand and shady trees. It's one of the island's best beaches, made even more so by the lack of crowds, especially during the week. This super-exclusive area of mansions, outrageously expensive rental apartments, and the terribly upper crust Hong Kong Golf Club has a barbecue area at the eastern end of the beach and a couple of outlets for food and drink. You can reach Repulse Bay by following the waterfront promenade east around the headland for about a mile (1.6 km). **M** Map p. 103 **Bus:** 6A, 260

Dragon's Back

The undulating, windswept ridge of Dragon's Back, named for its narrow spine, is a favorite launch site for paragliders and one of the best hiking trails in the territory. Get off the bus from Shau Kei Wan to Shek O Village at the well-marked entrance to Shek O Country Park. The 90-minute walk (one way) to the ridge is steep in parts but well worth the effort. From the highest point at **Shek O Peak** (932 feet/284 m), fantastic views spread along the jagged coastline from the cliffs above Big Wave Bay and carry across to the Shek O Golf Course, Shek O Village, and beyond to Cape d'Aguilar at the island's southeasternmost tip. **M** Map p. 103 **MTR:** Shau Kei Wan, then bus 9

Across Victoria Harbour from Hong Kong Island, an area that's crowded, bustling, and endlessly fascinating

Kowloon

Freshwater pearls

Kowloon

Kowloon—ceded to the British "in perpetuity" in 1856—is a corruption of the Cantonese *gau lung* (nine dragons) named for the range of rugged mountain peaks backing the peninsula. Legend holds that when Song dynasty boy-emperor Di Ping arrived here in 1277 fleeing the Mongol hordes, he counted eight peaks and commented there must be eight dragons here. But his consul reminded him that since he was here, and he was also a dragon, there must be nine.

Kowloon's peaks have been mostly ground down to make way for development and fill for Victoria Harbour, and this area of a little more than 19 square miles (47 sq km) is now one of the most crowded spots on Earth. From the tourist district of Tsim Sha Tsui to Boundary Street in chaotic Mong Kok, Kowloon is packed with high-rise tenement buildings, people, and traffic. While Kowloon generally presents a grittier side of Hong Kong, skyscrapers are quickly appearing along the waterfront and the International Commerce Centre, currently under construction, will bring the city's tallest buildings to the shores of Kowloon for the first time.

Most visitors will spend time in Tsim Sha Tsui, Hong Kong's best known tourist and shopping district, which includes the hawker-lined streets of Nathan Road. Next door is the glitzy Tsim Sha Tsui East, which rose from reclaimed land in the 1980s and is now a fashionable hotel and nightclub district. Fronting Tsim Sha Tsui and Tsim Sha Tsui East is the Waterfront Promenade, beginning just to the east of the Star Ferry terminal. A walk along the promenade during the cool of the evening reveals glittering vistas of the high-rise office towers on Central.

Wander farther down the peninsula into the more traditional districts of Yau Ma Tei and Mong Kok, where vibrant street life rubs shoulders with the future, the latter embodied in the Langham Place shopping and hotel complex. Among the thronging crowds in these areas, you'll find street markets specializing in jade, goldfish, flowers, birds, and clothing, and shops selling a wide range of traditional Chinese goods.

Kowloon also has its share of cultural attractions. The Hong Kong Cultural Center on the Tsim Sha Tsui waterfront hosts top international performers, while the nearby Hong Kong Museum of Art is one of the best museums in the region. At the excellent Hong Kong Museum of History in Tsim Sha Tsui East, you can learn about the lively history of the territory.

Most places of interest in Kowloon are reached by hopping on and off the efficient MTR (Mass Transit Railway) that runs down the spine of the peninsula. ■

NOT TO BE MISSED:

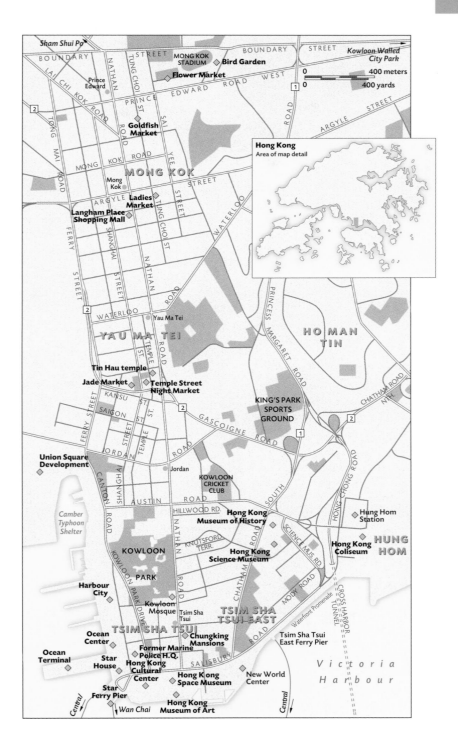

Sham Shui Po

BOUNDARY STREET

MONG KOK STADIUM

◇ Bird Garden

BOUNDARY STREET WEST

Kowloon Walled City Park

Prince Edward

◆ Flower Market

EDWARD ROAD WEST

0 _____ 400 meters

0 _____ 400 yards

◆ Goldfish Market

ARGYLE STREET

MONG KOK ROAD

MONG KOK

Mong Kok

◆ Ladies Market

ARGYLE STREET

◇ Langham Place Shopping Mall

WATERLOO ROAD

NATHAN ROAD

Hong Kong
Area of map detail

WATERLOO ROAD

Yau Ma Tei

YAU MA TEI

HO MAN TIN

Tin Hau temple

Jade Market ◇

◇ Temple Street Night Market

KANSU ST.

SAIGON ST.

PRINCESS MARGARET ROAD

CHATHAM ROAD NTH.

GASCOIGNE ROAD

KING'S PARK SPORTS GROUND

JORDAN ROAD

Union Square Development ◇

Jordan

KOWLOON CRICKET CLUB

AUSTIN ROAD

Camber Typhoon Shelter

HILLWOOD RD.

Hong Kong Museum of History

Hung Hom Station ◇

HONG CHONG ROAD

KOWLOON PARK

KNUTSFORD TERR.

Hong Kong Science Museum

SCIENCE MUS RD.

Hong Kong Coliseum

HUNG HOM

Harbour City ◇

Kowloon Mosque ◇

Tsim Sha Tsui

TSIM SHA TSUI EAST

MODY ROAD

Waterfront Promenade

CROSS HARBOR TUNNEL

Ocean Center ◇

TSIM SHA TSUI

◇ Chungking Mansions

Tsim Sha Tsui East Ferry Pier

Ocean Terminal ◇

Star House ◇

Former Marine Police H.Q. ◇

Hong Kong Cultural Center ◇

SALISBURY ROAD

Hong Kong Space Museum ◇

New World Center ◇

Victoria Harbour

Star Ferry Pier ◇

Central

Wan Chai

Hong Kong Museum of Art ◇

Central

Star Ferry

A trip across Victoria Harbour aboard the Star Ferry is one of the world's great travel bargains at just HK$2.20. These hulking, utilitarian green-and-white vessels shuttle across the harbor 450 times a day carrying thousands of commuters between Tsim Sha Tsui, Central, and Wan Chai. Even the most jaded passenger cannot help but look up now and again to catch the remarkable views on this short voyage.

Star Ferry
- Ⓜ Map p. 121
- ☎ 2367-7065
- 🕐 6.30 a.m.– 11:30 p.m.
- 💲 $
- **www.starferry .com.hk**

The Star Ferry service dates back more than a hundred years and has been plying Victoria Harbour regularly ever since. Riding these ferries, which have whimsical names such as *Celestial Star, Twinkling Star, Morn-* *ing Star,* and *Electric Star,* evokes a satisfying sense of history and timelessness contrary to the dynamism of today's Hong Kong. The demolition of the historical Central Star Ferry Pier in 2006 spurred a rare and passionate burst of public protest in Hong Kong, and has forced the government to take

Hong Kong Heights

Hong Kong's iconic skyline is said to boast more skyscrapers than anywhere else in the world; with many of them standing shoulder to shoulder in Central, the city offers a breathtaking cityscape. Undoubtedly the best way to see the skyline is during the nightly Symphony of Lights show, when a swath of lights and lasers are shone on and from the tallest buildings in town. For the best view, head for the Avenue of Stars on the Tsim Sha Tsui waterfront. Elsewhere, the Hopewell Centre *(183 Queens Rd. East)* has a breathtaking glass elevator that whisks visitors up to the 56th floor, while the 70-story Bank of China Tower *(1 Garden Rd.)* has a viewing platform on the 43rd floor.

INSIDER TIP:

The best ride in Hong Kong is also the cheapest: the ferry from Kowloon (Tsim Sha Tsui) to any of several places on Hong Kong Island. At night, the ride offers a spectacular view of the lights of Hong Kong.

—A. J. TIMOTHY JULL
National Geographic field researcher

a more sensitive approach to future development.

The double-ended ferries can be steered by wheelhouses on either end, which allows for surprisingly speedy berthing and departure. There are two decks: The upper deck is more expensive than the lower. They

The Star Ferry evokes a sense of the past in a modern city.

were originally conceived to allow Europeans to travel apart from the Chinese commuters. Choose the upper deck for your trip as it offers better views; also, the lower decks have a tendency to smell rather unpleasantly of diesel.

Old-fashioned though the Star Ferry may be, it is still hard to beat for efficiency and sheer fun. You rarely have to wait more than seven or eight minutes to catch a ferry. To board the vessel, just drop the fare into a slot at the turnstile, and head down the ramp to the ferry's gate. Clanging bells and a green light signal boarding time. ■

Tsim Sha Tsui

At the tip of Kowloon Peninsula lies the brash and glittering Tsim Sha Tsui district—the tourists' Hong Kong—a tightly packed and frenetic pocket of shops, hotels, bars, restaurants, camera and electronic outlets, fast food stores, neon signs, street hustlers, tourists, and masses of people. Here you will see the consumerism and relentlessness of Hong Kong at its most rampant.

Neon signs on Peking Road

Tsim Sha Tsui
Map p. 121, 127

The southern terminus of the KCR (Kowloon–Canton Railway) was adjacent to the Star Ferry Concourse until it was moved to Hung Hom in 1975; its former location is marked by the station's **clock tower.** Looking distinctly out of place, the 144-foot (44 m) square tower, with a clock on each side, was built in 1915 and is topped with a gracefully colonnaded cupola. Opposite

the concourse is **Star House,** an unremarkable looking building but home to a huge arts and crafts store, a great place to buy Chinese handicrafts (see p. 47).

Beside Star House, a short harborside walkway takes you to escalators up to **Ocean Terminal,** a combined pier for cruise ships and shopping complex that juts out into Victoria Harbour. The four-story pier was the first container terminal in Hong Kong, but these days passengers simply disembark their cruise liners and go shopping. It is part of the sprawling complex of hotels and shopping centers— **Ocean Center and Harbor City**—that runs for nearly a half mile (1 km) between the harbor and Canton Road. Stores here sell designer clothes, electronics, housewares, books, and perfume.

Back at Star House, walk east along Salisbury Road and cross Canton Road to the **Former Marine Police Headquarters.** Built in 1884, it is Hong Kong's fourth oldest surviving building and one of its most impressive colonial relics, with wide, shady colonnaded verandas, arched windows, and bold brickwork. The headquarters includes the main building, stables, and roundhouse. Though the complex has fallen prey to developers, they have, at least, slotted a hotel, restaurants, and shops into the buildings, keeping much of the character intact.

Another colonial gem, the **Peninsula Hotel,** stands a block farther east along Salisbury Road (*tel 2920-2888*). Opened in 1928, it quickly established itself as one of Asia's premier hotels. Although it lost its harborside location to land reclamation, it still has a commanding presence. Look inside the gorgeous lobby with cornices, graceful pillars, and gilded ceiling moldings. The Peninsula still carries on its very British tradition of high tea every afternoon, accompanied by a string quartet (see sidebar this page).

Nathan Road

When Matthew Nathan, who governed from 1904 to 1907,

decided that the Kowloon Peninsula needed a gracious boulevard lined with banyan trees, the local citizens were incredulous at such a grandiose project in this sparsely populated area. The road was quickly dubbed "Nathan's folly." Now the lower sections of Nathan Road and its maze of side streets and arcades are an extravaganza of consumerism. Thousands of shops are crammed along the strip—tailors, jewelers, shoe and

High Tea at the Peninsula

After eight decades, the Peninsula remains one of Asia's finest hotels. The refined interior used to be the hottest spot in town for Hong Kong's British overlords to see and be seen. Today, you can still pretend to be royalty at the Pen's high tea ceremony, a holdover from colonialism. Served inside The Lobby restaurant, you'll find a selection of finger sandwiches, cakes, and English scones served on silver platters. High tea is served from 2 p.m. to 7 p.m. daily, with lines often out the door. Reservations recommended. Flip-flops and shorts are not permitted.

clothing stores, camera and electronic stores, and bars and restaurants. Street hawkers and hustlers offering "copy watches" line the crowded sidewalks. A walk down this section of Nathan Road (see pp. 126–127), dubbed the Golden

A Walk Down Nathan Road

Join the throngs of shoppers and tourists for a wander down Hong Kong's most famous strip. You'll be hustled by touts, bustled by crowds, and dazzled by glittering window displays, but you'll also discover some quiet retreats and get a glimpse into Hong Kong's past.

Nathan Road shops purvey everything from clothing to electronics to jewelry.

Start at the southern end of Nathan Road where it intersects with Salisbury Road near the harborfront, and head north alongside the **Peninsula Hotel ❶** (see p. 125). Take a look at the gracious and opulent lobby, then continue on past Middle Road. On the opposite side of Nathan Road, you'll see **Chungking Mansions ❷** (Nos. 36–44). The crumbling and foreboding exterior is matched by the decrepit interior of the guesthouses, ethnic restaurants and remittance stores, but this icon (see p. 128) is as much a part of Hong Kong as the skyscrapers of Central and the best place to see Hong Kong's multicultural engine at work.

Back on its western side, past Peking and Haiphong Roads, Nathan Road becomes less frenetic. The sidewalk widens at the entrance to **Kowloon Park ❸** (see pp. 132–133) and the crowds thin a little. The park is a pleasant place to escape the noise of Nathan Road. On its edge, on the corner of Haiphong Road, is the elaborate **Kowloon Mosque and Islamic Center ❹,**

NOT TO BE MISSED:

Peninsula Hotel • Kowloon Park
• Hong Kong Observatory

Hong Kong's largest mosque. Built in 1984, it replaced a mosque constructed in 1896 for British Indian troops garrisoned at the since demolished Whitfield Barracks—now Kowloon Park.

A little farther north is the upscale shopping strip of mainly clothing stores called **Park Lane Shoppers' Boulevard ❺,** shaded with what is left of Nathan Road's banyan trees. Cross Nathan Road at the nearby pedestrian crossing and head north one block to Granville Road, lined with inexpensive clothing outlets and fashion overrun shops, a favorite spot for bargain hunters. Don't expect helpful service, refunds, or the chance to try on the clothes before you buy. Similar stores can be found on Kimberley Road (one block north) and

Cameron Road (one block south).

Back on Nathan Road, head north past Kimberley and Observatory Roads to the **Antiquities and Monuments Office Resource Center** ⑥ (*136 Nathan Rd., tel 2208-4400*). Built in 1902 as the Kowloon British School, the building is reminiscent of the Victorian Gothic design of British schools of that era. Inside are displays of the work of the office in maintaining and restoring historic buildings. Next door is another example of late-Victorian Gothic architecture, **St. Andrews Church** ⑦. It was used as a Shinto shrine during the Japanese occupation. After inspecting the church, backtrack to Observatory Road and the 1883 **Hong Kong**

Observatory ⑧ (*tel 2926-8200*), on the top of a small hill, which still serves as a weather-monitoring station. This graceful, colonial Victorian building has plastered brick and wide, shady colonnaded verandas along its length on both of its two floors. Group tours can be taken by prior arrangement with the Antiquities and Monuments Office.

ⓐ	See area map p. 121
►	Peninsula Hotel
↔	0.6 mile (1 km)
⏱	1 hour
►	Hong Kong Observatory

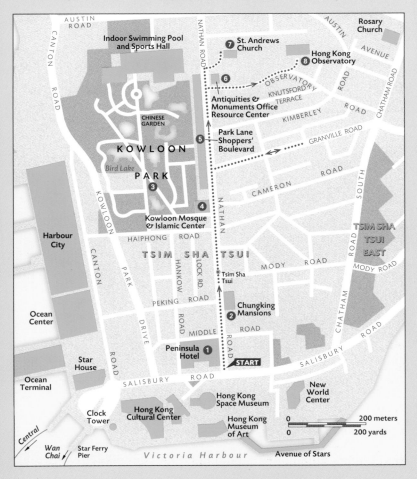

Hong Kong Cultural Center

- Map p. 121
- 10 Salisbury Rd.
- 2734-2009
- Star Ferry

Mile, is certainly worthwhile, but as a place to shop, it's overrated. Prices tend to be higher than other shopping precincts, such as Causeway Bay (see pp. 94–95), and rip-offs are common. At Nos. 36–44 lies **Chungking Mansions**, multicultural Hong Kong at its best (see p. 132).

Take time to explore the web of side streets off Nathan Road with its maze of shops and arcades. The area to the west, including Lock and Hankow Roads, is full of electronics and silk stores, while the area to the east has a lot of clothing stores.

Cultural Center, Museum of Art, & Space Museum

Since the completion of the Hong Kong Cultural Center in 1989, the territory has become the preeminent Asian city for performing arts, able to attract top international performers to a world-class venue. The adjoining Museum of Art is one of the best of its kind in the region, while the Space Museum offers a decent diversion for kids.

INSIDER TIP:

If you want to avoid crowds, it's best to get out and about in the morning, just at the time everything starts to open. Streets, walkways, stores, shops and transportation all get busier as the day goes on.

—DR. JODI ROWLEY
National Geographic field researcher

EXPERIENCE: Chungking Mansions

Time magazine dubbed Chungking Mansions the "best example of globalization in action" in Asia. The building's bustling alleys are filled with a multicultural United Nations of Indians, Pakistanis, and Nigerians, as well as an estimated 120 or so other nationalities.

At the diminutive Nathan Road *(Nos. 36–44)* entrance, visitors are met by a cacophony of catcalls offering everything from hashish to home-cooked Indian food—claiming both are the best in town. Inside, the maze of dingy alleyways lined with secondhand cellphone shops and family-owned food stalls reverberates with the racket of bartering traders and the smells of the subcontinent.

The best way to experience the Mansions' vibrancy is to enjoy the excellent food cooked by its residents. Indian,

Nepalese, and Pakistani food predominate, and on the ground floor you can help yourself to freshly cooked, takeout samosas, *pakoras,* and *dosas* for next to nothing. Upstairs, a warren of sit-down restaurants offers some of the most authentic ethnic cuisine in town. Several of the restaurants, often known as messes or clubs, are less than rigid about hygiene and working air-conditioning can be considered a bonus; however, the food is generally excellent. Most Pakistani restaurants don't allow alcohol, while some of the Indian ones that do are BYOB. Try the canteen-style **Islamabad Club** *(Flat C3, 4/F, Block C)* for quality Halal food or the **Delhi Club** *(Flat B4, 3/F, B Block),* for a more upscale affair. Chungking's addresses can be tough to find; ask a restaurant hawker on the ground floor to guide you through the sprawling complex.

The Cultural Center's promenade capitalizes on its spectacular harborside setting.

Cultural Center: At first glance, the Cultural Center can be viewed uncharitably—all those pink tiles and a magnificent harbor setting but no windows! But it grows on you, especially viewed from different angles. The main feature is its sweeping concave roof, lifting to sharp lines at each end of the building. A plaza set with palm trees, pillars, and ponds enlivens its waterside frontage, and an elevated promenade provides stunning views across the harbor.

Inside, the facilities are world-class. The 2,100-seat, oval-shaped **Concert Hall** has adjustable acoustic curtains and a magnificent 8,000-pipe Rieger Orgelbau organ, one of the largest in the world. Its 1,750-seat **Grand Theater** is equally impressive, with a revolving stage wagon. There is also a 500-seat **Studio Theater,** exhibition room, rehearsal rooms, and a couple of restaurants. There are regular performances by the excellent Hong Kong Chinese Orchestra, the Hong Kong Symphony Orchestra, and a stream of international performers. You can buy tickets at the information counter in the main lobby.

Museum of Art: The museum has six galleries, which do justice to its magnificent collection of artifacts. Five are reserved for fine art, Chinese antiquities, historical photographs, and contemporary Hong Kong art, while the sixth has visiting exhibits.

The fine **Chinese Antiquities Gallery** on the third floor has an extensive collection of ceramics from the neolithic period to the present day. It also displays textiles and costumes, including dragon robes, common clothing, official robes, and Mandarin squares, as well as bronzes, snuff bottles, bamboo carvings, jade, and lacquerware.

Also on the third floor is the fascinating **Historical Pictures Gallery.** More than a thousand oil paintings, watercolors, drawings, and photographs from both Chinese and European artists present a vivid picture of China and the Treaty Ports of Hong Kong and Macau in the 18th and 19th centuries.

On the second floor is the **Contemporary Hong Kong Art**

Hong Kong Museum of Art

- ✉ 10 Salisbury Rd.
- ☎ 2721-0116
- 🕐 Closed Thurs.
- 💲 $
- 🚢 Star Ferry

A Victoria Harbour cruise is vital to any trip to Hong Kong.

Hong Kong Space Museum

- ✉ 10 Salisbury Rd.
- ☎ 2721-0226
- 🕐 Closed Tues.
- 💲 $
- 🚇 Star Ferry

Gallery, Hong Kong's largest collection, mainly from local artists. It presents an interesting fusion of Eastern and Western styles. Here also you will find the works of the **Xubaizhai Gallery of Chinese Painting and Calligraphy,** a gift to the museum by art patron and collector Low Chuck-tiew (1911–1993). Exhibits date from the fifth century to the present, with the emphasis on the Ming and Qing dynasties.

The **Chinese Fine Art Gallery** on the fourth floor majors on the works of masters from the adjoining Guangdong Province.

The museum also offers fine views across the harbor through a glass wall on the southern face of the building.

Space Museum: This museum is housed in an odd-shaped building that looks like one half of a giant golf ball. Inside are two exhibition halls with numerous displays, some of which are interactive.

The **Hall of Space and Science** traces human endeavors in space, including a history of ancient astronomy, science fiction, early rockets, satellites, the space shuttle, and future space programs. There's a lump of moon rock, models of space ships, and videos of space flights and moon walks.

The **Hall of Astronomy** looks at the solar system, solar science, and the stars through a number of displays, and an Omnimax screen in the **Space Theater** shows movies on natural history and space.

Harbor Cruises

A visit to Victoria Harbour while in Hong Kong is inevitable, even if it's just for a short trip on the Star Ferry. If you want to spend more time on the harbor, options range from private charters to lunch and dinner cruises, or you can just hop on a passenger ferry for a leisurely trip to one of the outlying islands.

The eight-minute cruise across Victoria Harbour on the **Star Ferry** (see pp. 122–123) from Central to Tsim Sha Tsui is one of the world's classic ferry trips. The ferry also plies Tsim Sha Tsui to Wan Chai, Hung Hom in Kowloon to Central, and Hung Hom to Wan Chai.

New World First Ferry Services *(tel 2131-8181)* and the **Hong Kong Kowloon Ferry company** *(tel 2815-6063)* have fleets that service the outlying islands. Ferries leave from Outlying Islands Ferry Piers 4, 5, and 6 in front of the ifc building in Central. From here, big, lumbering passenger boats regularly head to Lantau, Cheung Chau, Peng Chau, and Lamma Islands, with most of these trips taking around one hour, although there are some faster vessels. There are two classes, ordinary and deluxe. Buy a deluxe ticket and head to the open-air fantail at the rear of the boat—the air-conditioning in the cabin can be freezing rather than cooling—for a pleasant trip. Snacks and beverages are available from a kiosk on board. Trips to the outlying islands are best taken during the week when it's less crowded.

A fast ferry leaves at roughly 20-minute intervals to the satellite community of Discovery Bay on Lantau from Outlying Islands Ferry Pier 3 in Central.

A plethora of private harbor cruises are available; both the day- and nighttime cruises are recommended. Most tour companies will

Star Ferry

- Map p. 121
- 2367-7065
- Open 6:30 a.m.– 11:30 p.m.
- $
- **www.starferry .com.hk**

EXPERIENCE: Take a Junk Ride

Junks, the bat-winged wooden boats that once choked Victoria Harbour (and were a symbol of the city) are all but gone, replaced by monstrous container ships. However, you can still enjoy this unique Hong Kong experience with the groups and companies below.

Aqua Luna *(tel 2116 8821 www.aqua.com.hk).* The *Aqua Luna* is an exquisite and genuine junk where you can enjoy delicious snacks and killer cocktails while sailing across the harbor. There are about eight trips a day between Central and Tsim Sha Tsui, costing between HK$150 and HK$180, with one drink thrown in.

Duk Ling *(Hong Kong Tourism Board Visitor Centre, Star Ferry Concourse, Tsim Sha Tsui, Peak Piazza, Causeway Bay MTR Station, Hong Kong International*

Airport, tel 2508-1234, www.discoverhongkong. com). This traditional wooden junk once plied Hong Kong's waterways for fish; now it is run in partnership with the Tourism Board and offers one-hour rides in Victoria Harbour. With only eight weekly sailings, four on each Thursday and Saturday, the *Duk Ling* is very popular. Registering ahead of time, in person, is mandatory. You'll need your passport and HK$50.

Saffron Cruises *(tel 2857-1311, www*

.saffron-cruises.com). For Hong Kongers, particularly expats, a junk ride is synonymous with booze cruise. On weekends, a flotilla of chartered boats, laden with beer and food, make for secluded beaches. Unfortunately, if you don't have an invite, you can't come aboard, as these junks are chartered. Luckily, Saffron Cruises hosts a series of monthly events, such as wine tasting and theme nights, open to individuals. They also hire charters.

Kowloon Park

- Map p. 121
- Austin Rd.
- 2724-3344
- $ (swimming pool)
- MTR: Tsim Sha Tsui, exit A1

pick you up from your hotel and deliver you to a pier on Kowloon or Hong Kong Island for boarding.

Hong Kong Ferry Holdings *(tel 2802-2886)* runs the Pearl of the Orient dinner cruise, with dancing and a live band. The largest, **Watertours** *(tel 2926-3868, www.watertours.com.hk),* offers a number of evening cruises on its tourist renditions of traditional Chinese junks. One takes you along the northern shoreline of Hong Kong Island, another to Lei Yue Mun Village in east Kowloon for a seafood dinner. They also offer a 90-minute cruise through Victoria Harbour, taking in the nightly Symphony of Lights, along with music and commentary. Most of these tours include an open bar. Watertours also offers a cruise highlighting some of Hong

Art Market

The recent westernization and influx of wealth that China has experienced has caused an eruption in the art market. Hong Kong, Beijing, and other cities that were once cultural outposts have joined Paris, London, and New York as anchors of the international art market. The Chinese aesthetic, an age-old continuum of ink and wash dragons and waterfalls, has recently shifted towards the western canon. In a spate of capitalist irony, a Hong Kong billionaire spent $17.3 million on a portrait of Chairman Mao by Andy Warhol in 2006.

Kong's ambitious infrastructure projects, such as the harborside Kowloon Expressway, Stonecutter's Island (no longer an island due to landfill) and its Chinese People's Liberation Army (PLA) navy base, and the impressive Tsing Ma Bridge linking the Hong Kong International Airport at Chek Lap Kok.

Jubilee International Tour Center *(tel 2530-0535, www.jubilee .com.hk)* has a Chinese junk available for a four-hour private charter to the pleasant beaches and islands of Sai Kung in the New Territories. Numerous family businesses (see the Hong Kong yellow pages) also charter modern launches for day trips, known locally as "junk trips," although the boats bear only a faint resemblance to traditional junks. They pick up from a pre-arranged spot and take you to Sai Kung.

Hong Kong Dolphinwatch Ltd. *(tel 2984-1414, www.hkdolphinwatch. com)* runs trips every Wednesday, Friday, and Sunday to see the rare Pearl River Delta white dolphins, or pink dolphins (see pp. 206–207). You are picked up from the Kowloon Hotel in Tsim Sha Tsui for a bus ride to Tung Chung, on North Lantau. There you board a boat and head for the dolphins. They claim the chance of seeing a dolphin is +97 percent, and if you don't spot any on your trip, the company will take you another time for free.

Kowloon Park

Kowloon Park offers a welcome respite from the cluttered, crowded streets of Tsim Sha Tsui. Formerly Whitfield Barracks, an encampment for British troops, it combines green spaces, recreational facilities, and a collection of attention-grabbing artifice.

The main entrance is on Austin Road, which runs between Nathan and Canton Roads; you pass a soccer field to an arcade that leads into the park. There are also entrances along Nathan, Canton,

works by local and international artists, and a circular **sculpture garden,** featuring a bronze cast of English scientist Isaac Newton, by British sculptor Eduardo Paolozzi (b. 1924).

At the **Bird Lake,** watch the pink flamingos preening against

Tsim Sha Tsui East

Map p. 121

The Waterfront Promenade offers front-row seats to Hong Kong's incredible skyline.

and Haiphong Roads. The indoor Olympic swimming pool and adjoining outdoor free-form pools are good places to cool off, but are packed on weekends.

Outside the arcade stand the **Landmark,** a 61-foot (18.6 m), imposing skeletal tower in a shallow pool, created by Canadian sculptor Raymond Arnatt. From the tower, a thoroughfare cuts through the park; well-marked paths lead from it to a number of weird and wonderful attractions.

The **Chinese Garden,** with its shrubs and shady trees, snaking covered walkway, and pagoda is worth a visit. On the opposite side of the thoroughfare lies an **aviary** full of colorful parrots and parakeets. Beyond the Chinese Garden is a neatly clipped **maze,** a **sculptured walk** full of

the backdrop of the high-rises on Canton Road. Beyond the lake, a giant **totem pole** rises incongruously. Opposite, get a change of perspective from the 121-foot (37 m) **Viewing Cone.** The **Discovery Playground** is Whitfield Barracks' old gun emplacement.

Tsim Sha Tsui East

Tsim Sha Tsui East sits in stark contrast to its much older neighbor, Tsim Sha Tsui. This area of luxury hotels, modern shopping malls, and nightclubs grew from reclaimed land in the 1980s. It serves mainly as a glitzy entertainment area for those willing to part with large sums of money.

Just to the east of Nathan Road is **Knutsford Terrace,** a strip of alfresco bars offering a better mix

Hong Kong Museum of History

A Map p. 121

✉ 100 Chatham Rd. South, Tsim Sha Tsui East

☎ 2724-9042

🕐 Closed Tues.

$ $

🚇 MTR: Tsim Sha Tsui

www.lcsd.gov.hk

of locals and expats than similar strips on Hong Kong Island. Tsim Sha Tsui East is better known, however, for its luxurious Japanese nightclubs, which offer live bands, floor shows, and hostess services. The extravagant **Club Bboss** *(New Mandarin Plaza, 14 Science Museum Rd., tel 2369-2883)* features a mini Rolls-Royce-styled vehicle that takes patrons to their tables, and a flowing stream full of carp.

The **Waterfront Promenade,** a walkway with some of the best views of Hong Kong, is home to the **Avenue of Stars,** featuring plaques and handprints from some of the city's biggest cinematic names, including Hong Kong's most famous Hollywood export, Jackie Chan. Just beyond the

A diorama at the Hong Kong Museum of History depicts Hong Kong's earliest inhabitants.

promenade's eastern end is the **Hong Kong Coliseum** *(9 Cheong Wan Rd., Hung Hom, tel 2355-7234)*, an odd, inverted pyramid-shaped entertainment center. This 12,500-seat arena is the major venue for Hong Kong's Cantopop performers and fans (see sidebar p. 21).

Hong Kong Museum of History

The Hong Kong Museum of History, one of the territory's most impressive museums, tells the story of Hong Kong. Visitors are guided through 6,000 years of history with imaginative uses of ecological settings, panoramic screens, dioramas, and interactive programs. This museum is essential for those with an interest in Hong Kong's fascinating past.

Start your tour just inside the entrance with an overview in **The Natural Environment.** Descend into the gallery via the escalator to a globe of the Earth held in a cradle of rock, featuring Hong Kong and the South China area. From there you enter a rock-lined tunnel to begin a "Journey to the Center of the Earth," with multiple theater screens explaining Hong Kong's geological and climatic history and marine environments.

Next, you come to an artificial forest with mounted insects, birds, and small mammals, and all the appropriate sound effects. Following on from this is the **Prehistory** area, whose exhibits neatly piece together archaeology and prehistory. Dioramas of archaeological digs and a 140-foot-long (42 m) beach show reconstructions of a stilt-house, a site for making stone tools, a burial site, and a pottery-making site.

Make your way up a ramp, past collections of finds dating from China's predynastic times, to the **Dynasties Gallery,** where artifacts and displays from each of the dynastic periods tell the story of China.

A typical village gateway marks the entrance to the **Folk Culture**

Gallery. This lively area highlights Hong Kong and South China's main ethnic groups, with a full-size copy of a boat dweller's fishing junk, a light-and-sound show illustrating the lifestyle of the Hoklo people, and a diorama showing how they harvested salt. There is also a display of the typical farming life of the Hakka, Hong Kong's largest ethnic group. The territory's reputation as a place without culture is belied by the lion dances, Cantonese opera, and Cheung Chau bun display.

From here an escalator takes you back to the main lobby. Head up the nearby escalator to the second floor and the **Opium Wars and the Cession of Hong Kong.** The first part covers the Opium Wars (1840–1842 and 1856–1858; see pp. 31–33) and contains a facade from the Bocca

Tigris Fort, a key defensive position for the Chinese forces during the First Opium War. Walk through the facade to the Opium War Theater, where this intriguing story is presented in a multimedia show. The display also features the Fountain Arch monument, which once stood proudly at Possession Point.

The **Growth of the City Gallery** portrays a century of history beginning in 1840. Here you will find copies of banks, trading companies, a colonial clubhouse, post office, tea shop, grocery store, herbal medicine shop, tailor shop, and Cantonese teahouse. A typical apartment set in a re-creation of a Chinese settlement from the 1930s shows living conditions.

An alleyway leads upstairs where period rooms, interactive units, and displays re-create prewar government and administration,

---

EXPERIENCE: Visit a Hong Kong Tailor

Hong Kong is famed for its nimble fingered tailors, and while not as cheap as it once was, getting suited and booted in the city is still good value.

Unfortunately, among the hundreds of tailors available, the quality varies wildly, and there are plenty of tourist traps. Generally the ones who try to pull you into their shops from Nathan Road are poor value; you'll often find the suit falling apart before you've reached the airport. Likewise, the legendary 24-hour suit, while possible, is almost always ill-fitting. Real tailors will ask you back for two, if not three, fittings over three to five days. Many high-end

tailors, including those listed below, also undertake international tailoring tours. **Cosmo Circle** (Shop 18, The Elegance at Sheraton Hotel, 20 Nathan Rd., Tsim Sha Tsui, tel 2730-1906, www. cosmocircle.com). Expect superior service inside this vast space, whose bright uncluttered interior is a breed apart from the traditional Hong Kong tailor. **Express Custom Tailor** (Star House, Shop No 18, 3 Salisbury Rd., Tsim Sha Tsui, tel 2199-7965). For both men

and women. Delivery in two or three weeks. **Sam's Tailor** (G/F Burlington Arcade, 94 Nathan Rd., Tsim Sha Tsui, tel 2367-9423, www.samstailor.biz). Sam's is the tailor to the famous; David Bowie and former U.S. President Bill Clinton have been outfitted here. Claims that the hype doesn't live up to the experience abound, although loyal customers vow the family-owned tailor still turns out some of Hong Kong's premium suits.

Hong Kong Science Museum

- Map p. 121
- 2 Science Museum Rd., Tsim Sha Tsui East
- 2732-3232
- Closed Thurs.
- $ (free Wed.)
- MTR: Tsim Sha Tsui

www.lcsd.gov.hk

law enforcement, early industries, and education. There are also sections covering Sun Yat-sen (see pp. 34–35) and the role of Hong Kong in modern Chinese history.

Exiting the teahouse or the alleyway, you come to the street gallery, where a full-scale double-decker tram houses a multimedia show on prewar transportation.

The **Japanese Occupation Gallery** begins with the interior of a bomb shelter. Artifacts and exhibits recount the dark days of occupation, the Japanese surrender, and immediate postwar events.

The **Modern Metropolis and the Return to China** highlights the huge waves of immigration, industrialization, natural disasters, and problems such as water rationing. A 1960s cinema celebrates Hong Kong's movie industry. Further exhibitions cover postwar education, the stock market, and Hong Kong's explosive growth.

The final gallery focuses on the signing of the Sino-British Joint Declaration in 1984, and the 1997 Handover Ceremony. A multimedia production relives the often turbulent development of China–Hong Kong relations.

Hong Kong Science Museum

The Hong Kong Science Museum is the most popular museum in the territory. It is four floors of fun; if you bring children, count on spending a few hours here before you can drag them away.

Of the 500 or so exhibits arranged thematically, nearly two-thirds are interactive. At the entry level (on the first floor), a giant video screen called a **Vidiwall**

plays a short introductory video. At the center of the hall is an **Exhibits and Facilities Directory System** where you can press buttons on a computer screen for layouts of the exhibition halls and location, and a description of each exhibit.

Dominating the museum, beginning on the ground floor, a level below the main entrance, is the **Energy Machine,** a 70-foot-high (22 m) contraption of scaffolding, tubing, spiraling tracks, and bronze drums. When set in motion, a continuous stream of balls roll around the tracks of its two towers like a roller coaster, producing dramatic sound and visual effects. In the **Motion** section, you can lie on a bed of nails or sit in a rotating room and learn how to toss a

INSIDER TIP:

Visit the fascinating Hong Kong Science Museum. It has a place of honor on the harbor, with an even better view than you can get from the Peninsula Hotel behind it.

—JAY PASACHOFF
National Geographic field researcher

curve ball. In the **Life Science** section, you can assess your sight, hearing, and endurance.

The first-floor **Electricity and Magnetism** section lets you check the amount of static electricity in your body at the Hand Battery. In the second-floor **Transportation** section, you can take off from

A mad scientist's dream: The curious Energy Machine spirals up through Hong Kong Science Museum's four levels.

Hong Kong International Airport in the Flight Simulator. On the third floor, the **Energy Efficiency Centre** examines the effect of energy on the environment and the application of renewable energies.

Yau Ma Tei

Yau Ma Tei presents a rougher side of Hong Kong than Tsim Sha Tsui. It's a district of packed sidewalks, crowded tenements, shops, dai pai dongs, street markets, and endless fascination— ideal for exploring on foot.

Start at the grid of streets between Jordan Road and Kansu Street, west of Nathan Road. Shops along **Canton Road** specialize in ivory and mah-jongg sets, while **Reclamation Street** is known for its paper models of houses and cars and notes from "Hell Bank" used for burning at funerals and festivals to aid financial security for relatives in the afterlife. **Saigon Street** has a street market; the shops on other streets do a brisk business selling bronze and plastic deities, brass incense burners, and wooden altars.

At the intersection of Battery and Kansu Streets are the two squat buildings of the **Jade Market,** which is busiest in the morning. Hundreds of stands sell amulets, beads, necklaces, and statues made of the green stone, which the Chinese believe has healing powers. Unless you know a lot about jade, settle for a trinket. Just outside, Temple Street South brims with gold and silver merchants.

Nearby on Public Square Street, off Shanghai Street, stands a **Tin Hau temple,** which stood on the waterfront until a reclamation project.. Immense incense coils hang above the entrance to the largest hall, which is dominated by an image of Tin Hau. Also here are 60 identical figures of Tai Sui, a deity entwined in Chinese astrology, and representing the 60-year lunar calendar. Worshippers slip Hell Bank notes under the deity representing the year of their birth. Fortune-tellers gather nearby to read the *chim* (bamboo fortune sticks).

Along **Shanghai Street,** shops sell traditional red wedding outfits, embroidered pillowcases, and other bridal items. ■

Yau Ma Tei
🅰 Map p. 121

Martial Arts

During the 1970s, the legendary Bruce Lee (1940–1973) introduced Western moviegoers to Chinese martial arts. Though his onscreen exploits projected a confrontational and violent side, that's just part of the picture.

Hong Kong residents traditionally practice tai chi in the city's open spaces, especially parks.

Kung fu has become the generic term to describe any martial art that comes from China. There are, in fact, hundreds of different styles originating centuries ago to relatively recently. Their core is reflected in the name kung fu, which can be used for describing anything that requires a person to invest both time and effort into training to become skillful. Chefs, artists, musicians, and computer programers can all be said to have good "kung fu." The correct name— and literal translation—for martial arts in China is *wushu*.

Wushu is also the name of a particular form of martial art, which experts claim epitomizes the "art" in martial arts. It uses natural movement to exhibit traditional techniques and can be performed by individuals, in pairs, or in groups, either bare-handed or armed with traditional Chinese weaponry (swords, staffs, and spears), in noncontact competition. Wushu proffers an athletic and aesthetic performance rich in detail, style, speed, power, and level of difficulty. Watching exponents dodge flailing swords and staffs with amazing skill is exciting theater.

INSIDER TIP:

In addition to the tai chi morning classes, Kowloon Park on Sundays holds free demonstrations of drumming and lion and dragon dances.

—DIANA BUDIMAN
Hong Kong Tourism Board

Kung fu's slow, steady, fluid movements are based on ancient combat techniques.

At dawn and dusk in Hong Kong's open spaces you will witness the world's most popular martial art as groups of mainly elderly people go through their daily tai chi exercises. Flowing movements are performed slowly, as if the practitioner were moving through very thick air. This slow action allows for deep breathing and concentration, which, in turn, promotes a calm, tranquil, and centered disposition as the body's internal energy or life force—*chi*—comes into play.

Regular tai chi exercise keeps joints flexible, muscles toned, and allows for better circulation and balance. The slow-motion movements help neutralize stress and release the tensions that tend to accrue in daily life. Although it may not seem so, tai chi has its roots in combat. It teaches resistance to force by yielding to it and redirecting it away from the target, hence "the vigorous is subdued by the soft."

Bruce Lee incorporated the martial art *wing chun* into his list of skills before moving on to create his own style, Jeet Kune Do. Wing chun was developed by a Buddhist nun, Ng Mui, from the famous Shaolin temple in Henan Province, who passed it on to a young girl named Wing Chun. The art is ferocious and dynamic and relatively easy to learn.

It eschews the more elaborate and flourishing movements of other martial arts and relies on speed, evasion, and economy of action, characterized by short explosive hand attacks, low kicks, and simultaneous attack and defense. It uses the "centerline theory," which draws an imaginary line down the center of the body, including the eyes, nose, lips, mouth, throat, heart, solar plexus, and groin, and directs all attacks and blocks there. Because it places less emphasis on strength, it is popular among women as an effective method of self-defense, the original intention of its inventor.

EXPERIENCE:
Take a Tai Chi Class

To see tai chi in action simply head to Hong Kong's parks at the break of day—both **Victoria Park** and **Kowloon Park** host large groups. If you'd like to take part, the Hong Kong Tourism Board *(tel 2508-1234, www.discoverhongkong.com)* runs a free hour-long class on weekday mornings at 8 a.m. (except Tuesdays) at **Sculpture Court** near the Hong Kong Museum of Art in Tsim Sha Tsui, as well as a popular class on Saturdays at 8 a.m. at **Harcourt Garden,** Harcourt Road, Central. Run by the revered tai chi master William Ng, class sizes are limited to 40 students. You'll need your passport and, due to the popularity, advance registration is advised.

Street Markets

Of all of Hong Kong's street markets, the bazaar set up on Temple Street at night is one of the city's favorites and most colorful. Locals and tourists flock here for shopping bargains and food, to have their fortunes told, and to listen to amateur performers of Chinese opera. The market officially opens late in the afternoon, but is liveliest between 8 and 10 p.m.

Seeking out bargains amid Temple Street's nightly bazaar

Temple Street Night Market
🄰 Map p. 121

During the day, Temple Street is no different from other streets in the area, lined with restaurants and cheap clothing stores. Late in the afternoon, however, it's closed to traffic, and hundreds of vendors move in, erecting makeshift canvas stands and piling them with an incredible array of goods.

The market stretches south from Man Ming Lane, through the grounds of the Tin Hau temple across Kansu Street to Ning Po Street. For sheer variety, it's hard to beat anywhere in Asia. Stands are full of fake designer clothing and watches, cheap jeans and tops, cigarette lighters fashioned into anything from hand grenades to small statues of naked women, silk ties patterned with cartoon characters, swimsuits, sunglasses, shoes, pirated CDs, audiotapes, alarm clocks that ring constantly, toys, Chinese bric-a-brac, silks, magazines, and untold knickknacks.

Escape the bustle at one of the *dai pai dongs* (sidewalk restaurants) set up at intersections along the street, such as Nanking Street. You can dine on seafood, drink beer, and watch the crowds surge past.

At the Tin Hau temple, people stand around watching groups of men playing chess, while along Pak Hoi Street fortune-tellers read palms and faces.

The market is also a theater for shrill-voiced Cantonese opera singers and small orchestras of men playing percussion instruments, banjos (yue chin), xylophones, and dragon-headed fiddles.

Mong Kok Markets

Mong Kok presents a coarser side to Hong Kong. The area is an impossibly crowded mix of tenements, people, noise, and traffic-clogged streets. Though it's off the regular tourist route, it's worth heading there for its number of interesting markets.

The most popular of these markets is the **Bird Garden** (Yuen Po St.), with its pretty courtyards and moon gates. Birds—especially melodious ones—are favored pets among Chinese. The Bird Garden's stands have hundreds of birds including finches, mynahs, sparrows, parrots, and cockatoos. Cages with ornate carvings and delicate porcelain water bowls are for sale, along with special seeds and other bird food.

Next to the Bird Garden, one block back from Prince Edward Road West, off Sai Yee Street, is the **Flower Market,** worth a look for its color, scents, and array of flowers imported from all over the world.

Back on Prince Edward Road West, head west toward Nathan Road and turn left onto Tung Choi Street. The first section of the street is taken up by dozens of shops and a market selling goldfish and aquariums; the area is known as the **Goldfish Market.** The Chinese believe that aquariums filled with goldfish bring good luck and provide calm and beauty.

Farther south along Tung Choi Street, around Nelson and Argyle Streets, the **Ladies Market,** which, despite the name, sells clothes for both sexes as well as an excellent selection of Chinese curios and souvenirs. The market kicks off in the late afternoon. Just off from the Ladies Market on Nelson Street is the **Mong Kok Computer Centre,** an indoor clutter of shops and stalls selling the latest in computer technology at extremely low prices. ∎

Mong Kok Markets

Map p. 121

Get Caught in a Crush, Hong Kong Style

Hong Kong is famed for its crowds, and at their frenzied height the city's streets feel far busier than Manhattan or Picadilly. Perhaps the most renowned location for crowds is the working-class neighborhood of Mong Kok, one of the most densely populated residential areas in the world. Come after work hours, at 8 p.m. or later, when workers pile onto the pedestrian streets to eat and shop. Elsewhere, the prime shopping district of Causeway Bay offers the perfect Hong Kong photo-op. At the crossing of Yee Wo Street, in front of the Sogo department store, watch waves of shoppers surge across the road as the lights turn green. Again, after work is the best time to see the crowds.

New Kowloon

Until the British leased the New Territories from the Chinese for 99 years in 1898, the Hong Kong border was at Boundary Street, running east-west along the peninsula and demarcated by a bamboo fence. Land north of here is, strictly speaking, the New Territories, but the area's crowded neighborhoods have more in common with Kowloon.

Hong Kong Island forms a spectacular backdrop to a New Kowloon container terminal. The area is a mixture of industry and urban living.

The highly urbanized, somewhat dour districts of New Kowloon have a number of appealing attractions that will appeal to you, and, like most areas in Hong Kong, they are easy to reach by public transportation.

In the middle of high-rise housing complexes, the riotously ornate and active Wong Tai Sin Temple draws people from all over Hong Kong. Visitors come to pray for good fortune and have their futures predicted. Kneeling in a plaza in front of the temple, these worshippers ask specific gods questions while shaking a container filled with *chim* (numbered bamboo sticks). The number of the bamboo stick that falls out is then matched with a message obtained from a fortune-teller in a nearby arcade.

The amazing Chi Lin Nunnery, built in strict adherence to Tang dynasty architecture and form and following the principles of *feng shui,* also has

INSIDER TIP:

The shopping is various and good in Mong Kok, from the Jade Market to the Bird Market.

—TIFFANY TRENT
National Geographic contributor

its share of religious followers. Most visitors, however, come simply to wander through the nunnery's beautiful gardens and to admire the magnificently crafted timber buildings. Go early to experience the serenity of the place—and beat the busloads of tourists, who start arriving midmorning.

The streets of Kowloon City—with their abundance of inexpensive restaurants (featuring cuisines from all over Asia, including Cantonese, Korean, Malaysian, Thai, and Vietnamese), cheap clothing outlets, and down-to-earth atmosphere—make an interesting diversion after taking in the gardens of

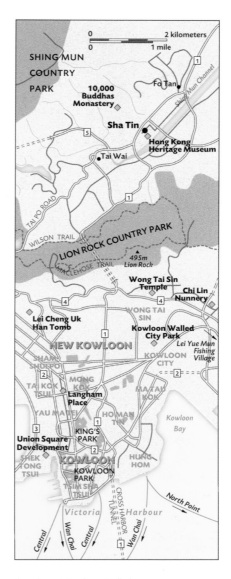

the adjacent Kowloon Walled City Park, one of Hong Kong's most traditional Chinese-style parks. The park sits on the site of what was once Hong Kong's most infamous area—an impossibly overcrowded, dangerous, and crumbling slum known as Kowloon Walled City.

Lost in Translation

Most of the signs in Hong Kong are bilingual, but even if the English is fluid and correct, they still might need cultural translation. In city parks, you will see many signs stating "do not release fish and terrapin into the pond." Obviously, introducing foreign species into an ecosystem falls somewhere between harmful and disastrous, but it seems odd that it is prevalent enough to warrant a sign. It is common practice, as Buddhists believe that releasing a store bought animal into the wild will save its life. Spitting indoors is tolerated in rural China, so the propensity of "no spitting" signs is necessary. Also, dishes in smaller restaurants aren't easily translated, so you shouldn't avoid a meal just because it is named "shaking beef" or "tofu made by a pockmarked woman."

Wong Tai Sin Temple

 Map p. 143

✉ 2 Chuk Yuen Village, Wong Tai Sin

☎ 2327-8141

$ $ (donation)

🚇 MTR: Wong Tai Sin, exit B2

www.siksikyuen .org.hk

Wong Tai Sin Temple

Wong Tai Sin Temple is one of Hong Kong's most popular places of worship, because of its resident deity's ability to grant the wishes of its devotees— wishes almost exclusively centered around money. People flock here to earn enough merit for a big win at the horse

INSIDER TIP:

The Wong Tai Sin Temple fortune-telling is especially active during the Lunar New Year.

—TIFFANY TRENT
National Geographic contributor

races, the Mark Six lottery, or any other windfall the powerful Wong, god of good fortune and healing, may bestow.

The image of Wong, which is housed in the ornate **main temple,** was brought to Hong Kong from Guangdong in 1915 and originally kept in a temple in Wan Chai until it was moved here in 1921. The main temple sits

under a roof of bright yellow tiles and pinewood ceilings, supported by bold red pillars. Elaborate painted designs, gilded dragons carved in relief, timber features under the eaves, and altar carvings that depict the life and times of Wong complete the building's impressive features. Buildings in the temple grounds were rebuilt in 1973.

The plaza in front of the main entrance to the temple (you cannot enter the temple, only view the Wong Tai Sin image through the doors) is crowded with devotees offering fruit, burning incense, and shaking out bamboo fortune sticks. The sound of these rattling *chim* is unceasing. You can get them from a small kiosk at the side of the plaza. Cast them on the ground in front of the temple, write the numbers down on the paper supplied, and take it to the adjacent **oblation and fortune-telling arcade** for a reading. The arcade is lined with dozens of fortune-tellers' booths where you can have your chim, face, or palms read. Some of the fortune-tellers speak English.

Late afternoon on Friday is

a good time to visit the temple for the extraordinary sight of hundreds of suited businessmen and well-dressed businesswomen praying, casting chim, and making offerings in the plaza.

To the right of the main hall is the smaller **Three Saints Hall,** dedicated to Taoist deities, where devotees crowd at an altar in front. Walk past the hall and the large Memorial Hall to the octagonal **Confucian Hall,** with its sweeping eaves and tiled roof features of

bubbling stream, a carp-filled pool, rock gardens, and bridges. A rock archway leads to a bamboo grove and a copy of the Nine Dragon Wall from the Imperial Palace in Beijing set in front of a small pond. The garden also features a 60-foot (18 m) artificial waterfall.

Kowloon Walled City Park & Kowloon Walled City

This traditional Chinese-style park sits on the old site of the notorious Kowloon Walled

Kowloon Walled City Park

Map p. 143

Tung Tsing Rd., Kowloon City

2716-9962

Bus: 1 from Star Ferry

Devotees looking for good fortune pray at the richly ornate Wong Tai Sin Temple.

lions, fish, birds, and mythical creatures. Between the Memorial Hall and the Confucian Hall is the entrance to the elaborately landscaped and peaceful **Good Wish Garden** (closed Mon.), full of colorful pagodas topped with ornate eaves, curved pathways, a

City, once an enclave of tightly packed, crumbling apartment buildings connected by passage-ways and dark alleys, and home to a variety of sweatshops and illegal factories. Adjacent to the Walled City Park, the streets of Kowloon City are an inexpensive way to indulge in two of Hong Kong's most popular pastimes—shopping and eating.

The Walled City was originally a garrison town built by the Qing government in 1847. When the British took possession of the New Territories (including New Kowloon) in 1898, the sovereignty of the Walled City remained in the hands of the Chinese, even after the British forced Qing officials out in 1899. The occupying Japanese pulled down the wall surrounding the city to extend nearby Kai Tak Airport. After World War II, thousands of refugees fleeing communist China moved in, and it became a haven for triads, drug users, prostitutes, assorted criminals, and, curiously, hundreds of illegal dentists (Chinese qualifications were not recognized in Hong Kong). After lengthy government compensation negotiations with residents, and the agreement of China, the city was finally abandoned and bulldozed in the mid-1980s. In its place the Kowloon Walled City Park was built.

You enter the park's South Gate on Carpenter Road to a plaza shaded with banyan trees and the **Yamen Building,** a three-hall structure originally used as the administrative office of the assistant magistrate of Kowloon. It now has photographs and a model of the Walled City.

Archaeological digs during demolition revealed two stone plaques bearing the inscriptions "South Gate" and "Kowloon Walled City." These now sit to the east of the entrance to the

Lung Nam Pavilion in Kowloon Walled City Park. The park, which replaced the notorious Walled City slum, was inspired by the Jiangnan garden style of the early Qing dynasty.

original South Gate, at one time the main entry to the city. Other relics unearthed, including some of the wall's foundation stones, a cannon, a flagstone path, and drainage ditch, are now features in the park.

The western section features small bridges straddling a carp-filled brook and stream, bordered by a winding covered walkway. Just

Chi Lin Nunnery is a monastic complex of lotus ponds, gardens, and magnificently crafted timber structures.

to the south, a bridge crosses an artificial lake full of turtles to one of eight elegant pavilions spread throughout the park—**Lung Nam Pavilion,** with its sweeping tiled eaves, timber lattice, moon gate entrances, red windows, and patterned walls. Between the water features and the Yamen Building, the enclosed **Garden of Four Seasons** is worth a look for its numerous species of bonsai trees.

The winding paths in the park's eastern section lead to a couple of hillock pavilions—the elaborately designed **Mountain View Pavilion** and **Hill Top Pavilion.** Sadly, views to the imposing **Lion Rock** to the north are now obstructed by a high-rise.

Follow the covered walkway from Mountain View Pavilion to the Ming-style **Twin Pavilion** and **Chess Garden,** with four giant

stone Chinese chessboards built into the ground. On weekends public tours of the park begin at 9 a.m., 11 a.m., 3 p.m., and 4 p.m., although these are offered in Cantonese only.

Kowloon City

The row of parallel streets bounded by Prince Edward Road West, Junction Road, and Carpenter Road is the best place to explore. Start in front of the Regal Kai Tak Hotel on Sa Po Road and zigzag west toward Junction Road. The streets are crowded with people and more than a hundred restaurants. You can dine on excellent Chinese, Taiwanese, Korean, Vietnamese, Thai, and Malaysian food. The area is especially renowned for the quality and number of its Thai restaurants.

A number of cheap clothing stores here sell slightly damaged clothing or overruns. With a bit of rummaging, you may come up with designer clothing for a fraction of the price you would pay in a department store or boutique in the more upscale shopping precincts. Most of these stores don't having fitting rooms or offer refunds.

Chi Lin Nunnery

Chi Lin Nunnery is a monastic complex of lotus ponds, gardens, and magnificently crafted timber structures, modeled after the architectural style of the Tang dynasty (618–907), a period of great cultural achievement in China. A total of 95,000 pieces of timber were

Chi Lin Nunnery
- Map p. 143
- 5 Chi Lin Dr., Diamond Hill
- 2354-1882
- MTR: Diamond Hill

Nan Lian Garden

- Map p. 143
- 60 Fung Tak Rd., Diamond Hill
- 2329-8811
- MTR: Diamond Hill, exit C2

www.nanliangarden .org

used in the construction of this splendid and serene place.

The design follows the ancient rules of Chinese architecture and *feng shui* (see p. 113). The main halls, built on a north-south axis, have ancillary halls to the east and west. The main buildings face the

INSIDER TIP:

Enjoy a range of fantastic oolongs and Pu-ehr teas at Nan Lian Garden's teahouse while gazing out over a pool of 400 colorful carp.

—IAN BAKER
National Geographic field researcher

sea and back onto a mountain, and are in a style known as "one court, three yards, and three doors." The gilded, flamboyant images of Buddha in the nunnery's halls are typical of the Tang period.

Enter the nunnery complex at the Shanmen ("first door" or "mountain gate") to the first yard, a tranquil place with four large lotus ponds and numerous bonsai plants. Long, colonnaded corridors with mullion windows flank the yard. Beyond the "second door" steps lead to the **Hall of Celestial Kings**—the "second entrance"— which guards the nunnery and serves as a reception hall. Inside the main door is the Maitreya Buddha, a heavenly being who will descend to Earth to save humanity. The Maitreya is surrounded on its altar by images of the Celestial Kings

holding spears, swords, and staffs. From the veranda there's a lovely elevated view of the plaza, lotus ponds, and timber structures.

Passageways on either side of this hall take you to the "second yard" and the magnificent Main Hall at its northern end. Just beyond the left passageway is the small **Jai Lan Hall** or Drum Tower. The Bodhisattva Jai Lan (the "courageous, vigilant, and diligent guardian" of Buddha's teachings) sits in a grotto on the ground floor.

Opposite the Drum Tower on the right passageway lies the **Ksitigarbha Hall** or Bell Tower, where Bodhisattva Ksitigarbha is housed. The bell on the upper floor has a chime so clear as to "awaken people's minds and soothe suffering spirits." Two

Kwun Yam

Kwun Yam, the Goddess of Mercy, is the Chinese incarnation of the Buddhist Bodhisattva Avalokitesvara. Legend holds that he was Prince Bu Xun, who lived on the southern coast of India. He renounced the material world and became the disciple of Buddha, vowing to deliver people from all suffering. Bodhisattvas are traditionally asexual, but during the Yuan dynasty, images of Kwun Yam as a female were erected in temples as it was believed many of the bodhisattva's tasks, such as bestowing and delivering children, were more appropriate for a female deity.

The magnificent Chi Lin Nunnery copies the graceful Tang dynasty style of architecture.

halls flank the yard. On the right is the **Hall of the Bhaisajyaguru** (medicine master), whose gilded image, holding a medicine bowl in its hands and honored by followers seeking longevity and good health, is attended by the Suryaprabha (sunlight) and Candraprabha (moonlight) bodhisattvas. To the left is the **Hall of Avalokitesvara** (also known as Kwun Yam, Goddess of Mercy; see sidebar opposite). Here devotees pray for worldly needs such as health, wisdom, peace, and wealth. The bodhisattva sits on a lotus upon a rock, in the middle of the ocean, pondering the reflection of the moon in the water, a symbol of the impermanent and illusory nature of life.

Chi Lin's grandest structure is the **Main Hall,** an architectural wonder. Twenty-eight columns of thick yellow cedar support a roof made from 28,000 tiles weighing 160 tons (145 mt). Instead of nails, a highly elaborate bracketing system, typical of ancient Chinese architecture, was employed, allowing the load of the heavy roof to transfer gradually to the columns. Traditional craftsmen from Anhui Province in China carried out the work.

Inside the Main Hall is a striking image of Buddha Sakyamuni, sitting on an altar flanked by two standing disciples, Mahaka-gapa and Anada, and two sitting bodhisattvas, Marjusri and Samantabhadra.

The north door of the

Main Hall leads to the "third yard"—unfortunately off-limits to visitors—which holds the Patriarch, Ancestral, Prayer, and Dharma Halls. In the nunnery's northeastern corner, the **Ten Thousand Buddha Pagoda** houses more than 10,000 Buddha images.

Next door to the nunnery is the new, meticulously landscaped **Nan Lian Garden,** whose rock pools, waterfalls, brooks and bridges, as well as period pavilions and a wooden mill, are based on Tang dynasty style. It can get busy on weekends, when you may be ushered along by "garden ambassadors"; a weekday visit is recommended. ■

Chi Lin Nunnery

Shanmen

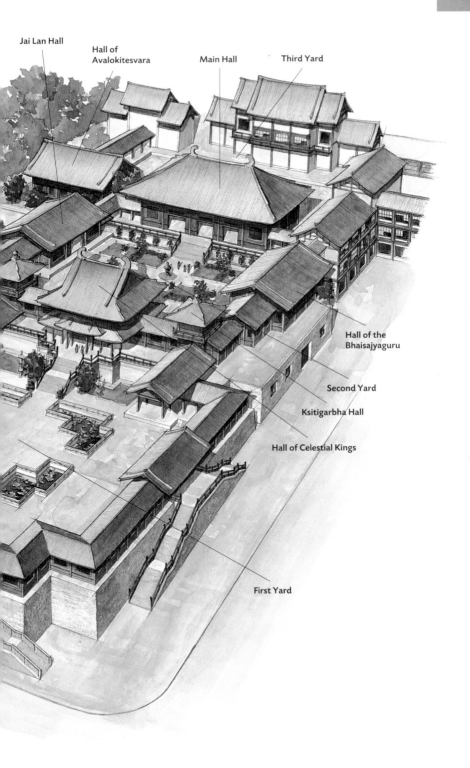

Jai Lan Hall

Hall of
Avalokitesvara

Main Hall

Third Yard

Hall of the
Bhaisajyaguru

Second Yard

Ksitigarbha Hall

Hall of Celestial Kings

First Yard

More Places to Visit in Kowloon

Lei Cheng Uk Han Tomb

The tomb, a branch of the Hong Kong Museum of History (see pp. 134–136), dates back to the Han dynasty (206 B.C.– A.D. 220). It was discovered in 1955 when workers were leveling the area to make way for a housing project, and consists of four barrel-shaped brick chambers in the form of a cross, centered by another domed chamber. The tomb, about 1,600 years old, lies protected inside a temperature-controlled vault. Funerary pottery and bronze objects unearthed at the site are displayed in an adjacent exhibition gallery. The tomb's inhabitants remain a mystery, but it is thought it was built for a high-ranking Chinese official.

🅰 Map p. 143 ✉ 41 Tonkin St., Sham Shui Po ☎ 2386-2863 🕒 Closed Thurs. & Sun. 🚇 MTR: Cheung Sha Wan, exit A3

Lei Yue Mun Fishing Village

The colorful and lively fishing village of Lei Yue Mun, lying at the eastern end of Victoria Harbour, has evolved into one of Hong Kong's premier seafood venues. Although the place has lost some of its character and been dolled up to resemble an ancient Chinese fishing village, it still maintains enough atmosphere to make for a good dining excursion. Buy live seafood from one of the many market stalls—ask the price before buying—and take it to a restaurant to have it prepared.

🅰 Map p. 143 (arrowed from map) ✉ Lei Yue Mun 🚇 MTR: Kwun Tong, exit A1, then bus 14C

Rosary Church

The small, whitewashed Rosary Church is one of Hong Kong's oldest Catholic churches, built in the late 1880s. Its well-proportioned Gothic revival style features pointed arches, tracery windows, buttresses,

a bell tower, and two stair towers.

🅰 Map p. 127 ✉ 125 Chatham Rd. ☎ 2368-0980 🚌 Bus: 5, 8, from Star Ferry; MTR: Jordan, exit D

Sham Shui Po

This impossibly crowded neighborhood on the border of Mong Kok along Boundary Street has an enormous street market along Apliu Street. The stands concentrate mainly on computer and electronic goods, including MP3 players, CDs, CD players, and televisions (both new and second-hand). You will also find cheap clothing, toys, novelties, and more. The market is open from noon to midnight.

Some very good clothing bargains can be found at the **Cheung Sha Wan Road Fashion Center,** between Yen Chow and Wong Chuk Streets, although some stores only sell to retailers—look for the signs on the door. Most Hong Kongers come to the area for the massive **Golden Computer Arcade and Computer Centre** (*Fuk Wa Street*), a maze of computer hardware and software stalls, some selling cheap game systems and games.

🅰 Map p. 121 (arrowed from map) 🚇 MTR: Sham Shui Po

Union Square

Kowloon's rise to rival Hong Kong Island is evident at the ambitious and impressive Union Square development in West Kowloon. Aside from the upscale residential and office buildings, Union Square is already home to the sleek **Elements** shopping mall (*www.elementshk.com*). It will also host Hong Kong's tallest building, the International Commerce Centre, which, on completion in 2010, will stand 118 stories high and feature an observation deck on the 100th floor. The Ritz-Carlton Hotel will occupy the top 15 floors.

🅰 Map p. 143 ✉ Union Square 🚌 Bus: 8 from Star Ferry

New towns, mountain trails, long beaches, ancient buidings, and pockets of rural life in the "Land in Between"

New Territories

Walled village decoration in Kam Tin

New Territories

The New Territories takes in a 307-square-mile (796 sq km) swath of land between Boundary Street in Kowloon and the border with the People's Republic of China—an area twice the size of Kowloon, Hong Kong Island, and the outlying islands combined. This is where many Hong Kongers come to breathe fresh air and escape the clamor of the city.

GUANGDONG

Sham Chun River
Man Kam T
Lo Wu
Ponds
Lok Ma
Chau
Lung Yeuk Ta
Heritage Tra
Liu Man
Shek Tong
Sheung
Shui
Ancestral Hall
Fanlin
San Tin
Wai
HONG KONG
GOLF COURSE
Fanling
Deep Bay
(Hau Hoi Wan)
MAI PO
NATURE
RESERVE
Tai Fu Tai
Mansion
Ponds
Hong Kong
Wetland Park
Fairview
Park
Kai Keung Leng
572m
Lam Tsuen
Spirit Trees
Ponds
Ponds
LAM TSUEN
Shui Tau
Tsuen
Kam Tin
COUNTRY PARK
Tai To Yan
565m
Lam
Tsue
Ping Shan
Kat Hing Wai
Yuen Long
Kadoorie Farm
& Botanic Garden
Miu Fat
Monastery
Shek Kong
TAI MO SHAN
COUNTRY PAR
Tai Mo Shan
957m
Ching Chung Koon
Monastery
Ho Pui
Reservoir
SHING MUN
COUNTRY
Black Point
(Lan Kok Tsui)
Castle Peak
Monastery
Tuen Mun
TAI LAM COUNTRY PARK
PARK
Yuen Yuen
Institute
Shing Mu
Redou
583m
Castle Peak
MACLEHOSE TRAIL
Shek Lung Kung
474m
Sam Tung
Uk Village
Museum
Tap Shek Kok
Castle
Peak
Bay
Tai Lam Chung
Reservoir
Chuk Lam
Sim Yuen
Tsuen
Wan
Tak
Wah
Park
Kwai
Chung
Pearl
Island
Sham
Tseng
A.C.P.E.
Center
TING
KAU
BRIDGE
KAM SHA
COUNTR
PAR
OUTLYING ISLANDS
p. 201
Ma Wan
TSING MA
BRIDGE
Tsing
Yi
Stonecutters Island
(Ngong Shuen Chau)

Settlers from mainland China began arriving in what is now the New Territories between the 10th and 15th centuries. They built villages surrounded by sturdy walls for protection, and farmed the fertile soil.

The arrival of the British had little effect on their way of life, even after the New Territories were leased from the Chinese in 1898. The completion of the Kowloon–Canton Railway in 1910, and a network of roads built by the 1920s, had only marginal impact. Rural village life continued unhindered until the start of World War II.

By the 1960s, the population of the New Territories was around 400,000, but Kowloon and Hong Kong Island to the south were bursting at the seams. To ease this, the government began massive infrastructure programs that saw the creation of large-scale housing developments with clusters of residential towers, some as high as 40 floors, rising above what were once paddy fields. These "new towns," including Tsuen Wan, Tuen Mun, Fanling, Sheung Shui, Tai Po, Sha Tin, and Ma On Shan, now house most of the nearly four million people living in the New Territories.

NOT TO BE MISSED:

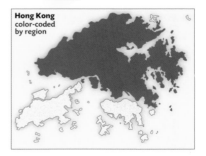

Hong Kong
color-coded
by region

Although much of the area's tradition, architecture, and environment has been lost, a surprising amount still remains. There are gloriously ornate Buddhist and Taoist temples, remnants of 500-year-old walled villages inhabited by descendants of the pioneering clans, imposing clan and ancestral halls, and isolated villages in lush valleys. Large tracts of beautiful countryside, interlaced with walking trails, are set aside as country parks. At Mai Po, on the western edges of the New Territories, the protected marshlands and tidal bay form one of the world's most important wetland areas, where migratory birds stop on their way from north Asia to Australia.

The development that has changed the face of New Territories has made it easier to get around. A string of expressways links new towns, and a cheap and efficient public transportation system of trains, a light railway, buses, and minibuses crisscrosses the area. ■

Tsuen Wan & Sam Tung Uk Village Museum

At the last stop on the MTR line, just north of the enormous Kwai Chung container terminal, lies this bustling new town of factories and towering residential blocks. Tsuen Wan, the gateway to the western New Territories, lies close to several interesting monasteries, country park walking trails, and a vestige of New Territories' history, the Sam Tung Uk Village Museum.

Peaceful gardens and ponds enhance the temple architecture of the Yuen Yuen Institute.

Yuen Yuen Institute

- 🏔 Map p. 154
- ✉ Wai Rd., Lo Wai, Tsuen Wan
- 🚇 MTR: Tsuen Wan, then Minibus 81 from Shiu Wo St.

On Tsuen Wan Market Road, a five-minute walk from the MTR station, is **Tak Wah Park** *(take exit B and follow footbridge over Sai Lau Kok and Castle Peak Rds.).* This relaxing area has ponds filled with carp and catfish, Chinese pavilions, grottoes, and an old run-down clan hall.

One of the main attractions in Tsuen Wan is the **Yuen Yuen Institute,** one of a number of monasteries tucked into the hills just north of the town and a ten-minute taxi ride from Tsuen Wan MTR station. The institute is a religious, one-stop shop, catering to worshippers of Buddhism, Confucianism, and Taoism; its impressive main building is a copy of Beijing's famed Temple of Heaven. You can walk around the pavilions and ponds in the peaceful grounds and enjoy a vegetarian lunch at the canteen.

The monastery of **Chuk Lam Sim Yuen,** or Bamboo Forest Monastery *(Minibus 85 from Shiu Wo St., just south of Tsuen Wan MTR station, exit B),* was originally built from bamboo matsheds (woven slats of bamboo used as walls for dwellings) in 1927. The monastery is home to three of the largest Buddha statues to be found in Hong Kong.

Shing Mun Country Park, in the hills northeast of Tsuen Wan, has a number of hiking trails. Follow the western bank of the Shing Mun Reservoir through dense forests into Shing Min Valley, on to Lead Mine Pass, and haul yourself up the 2,122-foot (647 m) Grassy Hill to superb views. Alternatively, take an easy amble around the 1.2-mile (2 km) **Pineapple Dam Nature Trail.** The park's visitor center *(closed Tues.)* has displays of the area's primeval vegetation and the building of the reservoir, along with a history of local agriculture and mining.

Adjacent to Shing Mun Country Park is **Kam Shan Country Park,** famed for its bands of macaque monkeys that hang around the road leading into the park. The monkeys have become used to being fed by humans, a practice officials are anxious to discourage. They may casually wander up to you and snatch anything you are carrying.

Winding over the hills between the two country parks is the **Smugglers' Ridge Trail** and **Shing Mun Redoubt,** a network of bullet-scarred, crumbling, overgrown pillboxes, bunkers, and trenches, part of a string of defensive positions built across the New Territories in the 1930s and known as the Gin Drinker's Line. The redoubt was overrun within hours of the Japanese launching their attack on Hong Kong on December 8, 1941.

Sam Tung Uk Village Museum

Part of New Territories' history is preserved at this restored walled village. A five-minute

Sam Tung Uk Village Museum

- Map p. 154
- 2 Kwu Uk Ln., Tsuen Wan
- 2411-2001
- Closed Tues.
- MTR: Tsuen Wan, exit B3

www.heritage museum.gov.hk

EXPERIENCE:
Learn to Play Mah-jongg

The constant click of mah-jongg tiles often provides the soundtrack to Hong Kong—the game is both a pastime and passion for many in the city. Officially, private gambling on mah-jongg is illegal in Hong Kong, except at licensed mah-jongg "schools." Many of the games which take place in bars, restaurants, and businesses, however, see money changing hands. The game requires four players and is based on assembling the best hand of tiles. If you want to try and learn the game, the YWCA (3/F, 1 MacDonnell Rd., tel 3476-1340, www .esmdywca.org.hk) regularly runs month-long courses, which are open to members of the public of both genders. More experienced players can try their luck in one of the many "schools" in Yau Ma Tei.

---

walk from the Tsuen Wan MTR station *(take exit B3 and walk east along Sai Lau Kok Rd.),* you'll see the distinctive whitewashed walls and tiled roof of the Sam Tung Uk Village Museum to the left. The museum provides an interesting, if somewhat sanitized, examination of early life in the New Territories.

Sam Tung Uk was a Hakka village, built in 1786 by the Chan clan. (The Hakka were settlers from the Chinese mainland who arrived in Hong Kong in the late 1600s.) The Chans moved from

INSIDER TIP:

For an exceptional breakfast experience and view toward some of the outlying islands and the South China Sea, eat at Victoria Peak's Peak Café.

—IAN BAKER
National Geographic field researcher

Guangdong Province in the 1750s and settled in Tsuen Wan. Clan leader Chan Yam-shing built three rows of village houses at Sam Tung Uk, and his descendants added annexes. The family's ancestral altar was placed in a hall at the back of the compound and the Chinese characters for "Chan's Family Ancestral Hall" were engraved on the granite lintel above the door frame.

The name Sam Tung (literally "three-beam dwelling") comes from the design of the village that incorporates three roofed halls, each with a *tung,* or main supporting beam, along its central axis.

After entering the main doorway, you come to an **Orientation Hall,** which highlights the history of the village and the Chan clan and charts the work carried out to restore the village. It's interesting to see how plain the village was in the 1970s before restoration began (it was fully restored and opened as a museum in 1987).

On the way from the Orientation Room to the village's Front Lane is one of the structures used as living quarters. It has areas for cooking, sleeping, and eating, as well as a cockloft for storage. The building, one of the four individual houses built beside the main halls, is full of artifacts and reproductions of furniture and cooking utensils collected from Hakka villages in Guangdong. The tiny side houses along the village walls also have small exhibits of artifacts such as traditional paper figurines and Chinese New Year prints. You can wander the narrow lanes past these structures.

The **Assembly Hall,** one of the village's three interconnecting main buildings that line up along a central axis behind the entrance to the museum, is hung with brightly decorated lanterns. The other two buildings are the **Entrance Hall,** and the **Ancestral Hall,** at the rear of the village, behind the Assembly Hall. The altar in the Ancestral Hall, where tablets inscribed with the names of ancestors were kept, still stands, but the tablets have been moved. They are in the new Sam Tung Uk village, which was built by the government to house residents of the village before it became a museum.

Behind the museum, a small park with a pond provides a pleasant place to rest under the trees. ∎

EXPERIENCE: Brew Up at a Traditional Tea Ceremony

Despite tea's popularity in the city, Hong Kong's renewed interest in the traditional Chinese tea ceremony is a little over ten years old. Today the ceremony is very much in vogue with Hong Kongers both young and old. This has seen a rise in the number of teahouses offering the ceremony, ranging from old-fashioned wooden tea shops to smart boutiques.

Jabbok Tea Shop *(120 Argyle St., Mong Kok, tel 2761-9133).* Jabbok Tea Shop is one of Hong Kong's oldest teahouses, and the owner is considered an expert on the tipple. In addition to excellent tastings, they offer lectures and literature, and even have an exclusive members-only teahouse and garden in the New Territories.

Lock Cha Tea Shop *(Upper Ground Floor, 290A Queen's Rd. Central, Sheung Wan—entrance on Ladder St.—tel 2805-1360, www.lockcha. com).* Set halfway up the steps of Ladder Street, Lock Cha's dark, wooden interior is piled high with sacks of tea and popular with locals. Although the staff rarely speak English, they are happy to take you through an old-fashioned tasting. Lock Cha also runs a more tourist oriented teahouse in the Museum of Tea Ware, where Lock Cha's owner runs regular tea appreciation classes, in partnership with the Hong Kong Tourism Board *(tel 2508-1234, www.discover hongkong.com).*

Luk Yu Tea House *(Luk Tea Building, 24 Stanley St., Central, tel 2523-1970).* There

A woman carefully pours tea during a tea ceremony. The custom is reestablishing itself in tea houses.

are no modern reproductions here: The early 20th-century art deco, stained glass, wood paneling, and ceiling fans are genuine at this tea house that opened in 1933. You get a real feeling for old Hong Kong with the individual wooden booths and the marble tabletops. The ambience is busy and loud, but customers seeking some privacy can reserve one of the partitioned booths. Here is one of the best places to sample bo lai, a fermented black tea among the most common in the city, lung ching green tea, jasmine tea and sui sin, which is derived from narcissus or daffodils. You can eat here also. The

Cantonese cuisine includes shark's fin and bird's nest soups, and prawns stir-fried with Chinese mushrooms and bamboo shoots. Dim sum is also served. Wine is very limited; most customers drink beer or tea.

Ming Cha *(7 Star Star St., Wan Chai, tel 2520-2116, www.mingcha.com.hk).* This teahouse's modern, minimalist interior is a haven from the pulsating streets outside and a refreshing break from the standard Hong Kong tea house. Ming Cha has an outstanding selection of teas and the expertly trained staff can take you through the tea ceremony blow-by-blow on the spot.

Airport Core Program Exhibition Center

Despite its less-than-enticing name, the Airport Core Program Exhibition Center (ACPEC) is an interesting place. It traces the building of the massive infrastructure projects that went into creating and supporting Hong Kong International Airport on Lantau Island, and has unsurpassed views to the mightily impressive Tsing Ma and Ting Kau Bridges.

The ACPEC provides stunning views of the 1.4-mile (2.6 km) Tsing Ma Bridge, the world's longest road and rail suspension bridge.

Airport Core Program Exhibition Center

- 🅐 Map p. 154
- ✉ 401 Castle Peak Rd., Tsuen Wan
- ☎ 2491-9202
- 🕐 Closed Mon.
- 🚇 MTR: Tsuen Wan, exit B, then Minibus 96M

When Britain announced in 1989 its plan to build an enormous airport at Chek Lap Kok, it neglected to tell China. Officials on the mainland were outraged, both by the oversight and because they saw the project as too ambitious and expensive, an unnecessary strain on Hong Kong's coffers, which they would soon inherit. At 16 billion dollars, the airport was the most expensive infrastructure program in the world. Originally due to be completed in 1997, symbolically before Britain handed Hong Kong back to China, it did not open until May 1998.

ACPEC has models, diagrams, and photographs charting the progress of many projects, including land reclamation in Central, construction of the Western Harbor tunnel, the Airport Express train line, and bridges, as well as the airport. A 10-minute video in English and Cantonese describes the construction every 30 minutes.

A **viewing terrace** at the back of the center gives spectacular 180-degree views to the Tsing Ma Bridge, at 1.4 miles (2.2 km) the world's longest road and rail suspension bridge, and the smaller Ting Kau Bridge. Beneath and beyond the bridges barges, tankers, tugboats, and numerous other vessels cut white wakes through the busy harbor's deep green waters. ∎

Tuen Mun Monasteries

Away from the endless rows of high-rise apartment buildings that characterize Tuen Mun are a number of Buddhist and Taoist monasteries worth exploring. They vary from the sedate and rustic to the expansive and busy. Most feature excellent vegetarian lunches, while all can be reached by the New Territories' Light Transit Rail (LTR) system.

Tsing Shan Monastery

Ting Shan Monastery, also known as Castle Peak Monastery, nestles in the foothills of Tsing Shan (Green Mountain) overlooking Tuen Mun. Its elaborate but faded shrines and worn appearance add character to the place. The present monastery was built in 1918, but, according to legend, it was founded in the fifth century by the famous and somewhat scurrilous monk Pei Tu, who is said to have stolen a golden Buddhist statue from a house where he was a guest. He was chased to the banks of a stream, where he magically turned his rice bowl into a boat to cross, hence his name, which translates to "cup ferry." Take the path behind the temple leading to a shrine and statue of a four-faced Buddha under an overhanging rock, and a view over sprawling Tuen Mun. From Tsing Shan Tsuen LTR station, save yourself the climb up the steep hill and take a taxi.

Ching Chung Koon Monastery

The atmosphere at this large complex, one of Hong Kong's most important Taoist shrines, is often hectic; its expansive grounds fill up on weekends and during festivals with worshipers and sightseers. The bold **main** temple building sports a heavily ornate orange roof supported by red pillars, with a riot of swirling colors under its eaves. Carved timber fixtures, frescoes,

Ching Chung Koon Monastery is one of Hong Kong's most famous Taoist shrines.

Castle Peak Monastery

- Map p. 154
- Off Yeung Tsing Rd., Tsing Shan Tsuen, Tuen Mun
- LTR: Tsing Shan Tsuen

Ching Chung Koon Monastery

- Map p. 154
- Tsing Chung Koon, Tuen Mun
- LTR: Ching Chung Station

Miu Fat Monastery

- Map p. 154
- Castle Peak Rd., Lam Tei, Tuen Mun
- LTR: Lam Tei Station

and antique artifacts complete the picture. The temple's major image is one of Taoism's legendary Eight Immortals, Liu Tung Bun. Liu is flanked by the sect's founder, Wong Chung Yeung, and Liu's student, Qiu Chang Chun. On the main altar are the magic sword used by Liu to slay demons, a fly switch to whisk away bad luck, and a gourd of herbs to heal the sick.

At the front of the altar stand two exquisite 300-year-old stone statues of goddesses, and a glass case with a thousand-year-old jade

Dragons

From Beowulf and St. George to J.R.R. Tolkien's *The Hobbit,* **the dragon in western tradition symbolizes war, destruction, and burning villages. This is all a misunderstanding, as the Chinese dragon symbolizes growth and power. Traditionally, dragons represented the concept of the yang (in short, all things masculine). They are associated with the five elements, wind, water, earth, fire, and the celestial bodies. They provide mankind with water, food, and even knowledge. Although benevolent, the dragon can be tumultuous, causing destructive storms and famines. Some skeptics don't believe that dragons are still alive today, but go to the Drunken Dragon Festival in Macau, have some rice wine, and decide for yourself.**

seal. Past the main temple are **two ancestral halls** packed with thousands of wooden ancestral tablets where paper offerings are burnt during commemorative services. Behind these lie a Chinese garden with a bridge winding over a pond to a small pavilion.

The temple is famous for its bonsai trees, and a bonsai festival is held each spring. At the building to the left of the main temple, you can buy tickets for the monastery's renowned vegetarian lunches.

Miu Fat Monastery

Gilded dragons set with mosaics and tiny mirrors wrap around the pillars at the entrance, statues of lions and elephants carved from stone guard the door, and porcelain figurines of mythical beasts line up along the ridges of the sweeping roof and eaves of this elaborate Buddhist temple.

Continue up the stairs to the vegetarian restaurant and on to the **main shrine** on the third floor. Here, thousands of gilded Buddha plaques are embedded in the walls, and murals painted on the ceiling depict scenes from Buddhist mythology. The main shrine holds the statues of the **Three Precious Buddhas.** Walk behind it to view the hundreds of ancestral tablets inscribed in gold and the huge statue of Avalokitesvara (see pp. 148–149), whose thousand hands stretch out to help the suffering.

The monastery is now adding a huge complex, a departure from the traditional temple next door. It will host a shrine and administrative offices and stand 42 feet (13 m) tall, with the glass top designed to look like a lotus flower. ■

Kadoorie Farm & Botanic Garden

Set in a steep, deeply wooded valley on the northwestern edge of Tai Mo Shan Country Park you will find a surprising amount of biodiversity on display. Two brothers, Lawrence and Horace Kadoorie, from one of Hong Kong's most influential families, started this unique place in the 1950s to help immigrants flooding across the border from China learn farming techniques.

The Kadoorie Farm & Botanic Garden has grown into a place of conservation and education, a sanctuary for the territories' rich variety of plants and animals, and an intriguing place to visit.

A zigzag of roads and paths takes you up the valley's steep slopes to the summit of **Kwun Yam Shan** at 1,974 feet (602 m). You can either walk or take the free shuttle bus. On the lower slopes a road winds past organic vegetable fields to greenhouses and nurseries full of subtropical flowers, enclosures for waterfowl and deer, an aviary, a lotus pond full of carp, and insect and amphibian houses.

Injured birds of prey are nursed back to health in the **raptor roost** at the top of the lower slopes. Here the road narrows to a path and views open onto terraced orchards. A shady path leads to a cascade called the Great Falls. Nearby, colorful butterflies flutter among flowers chosen for their specific nectars at the **Butterfly Garden.**

Farther up the slope, a stream runs alongside an enchanting fern walk to gardens growing tea and medicinal herbs. From here you can climb to the **Kadoorie Brothers Memorial Pavilion** for marvelous views back down the valley. Cross near to the top of Kwun Yam Shan with its ancient

An injured black kite receives attention at Kadoorie Farm's raptor sanctuary.

stone altars, believed to have been built about 500 years ago to call upon the blessing of the Goddess of Mercy, Kwun Yam, and a much more recent statue of the goddess. Nearby in the **Post Office Pillars** viewing area, the huge stone pillars that once held up Hong Kong's General Post Office now frame views of the Lam Tsuen Valley. ■

Kadoorie Farm & Botanic Garden

⬛ Map p. 154

✉ Lam Kam Rd., Tai Po, New Territories

☎ 2483-7200; call ahead for tours

 MTR East: Tai Po Market station, then bus 64K

www.kfbg.org

New Territories Drive

The drive begins in Tsuen Wan and follows Castle Peak Road in an arc close to the mainland Chinese border, before heading south through the verdant hills on Route Twisk and back into Tsuen Wan. Along the way you'll take in ocean views and some exceptional natural scenery.

Mangroves give way to mudflats at the protected Mai Po Nature Reserve.

About 1 mile (1.6 km) after picking up the start of Castle Peak Road in Tsuen Wan, you will skirt a scenic coastline on the way to the Ting Kau Bridge, linking Tsing Yi Island. A half mile (800 m) after passing under the bridge is the **Airport Core Program Exhibition Center ❶** (see p. 160). Head out to the terrace at the back for views of the spectacular Tsing Ma Bridge.

Continue on past the bridge to **Sham Tseng ❷,** famous for its restaurants serving roast goose. A mile (1.6 km) beyond, views take in the high peaks rising from the eastern end of Lantau Island. The road then dips under the Tuen Mun Highway to the **Gold Coast ❸,** a modern resort fronted by **Golden Beach ❹,** one of the area's better stretches of sand. From the Gold Coast, you will pass more beaches as the towering residential complexes of Tuen Mun come into view. At the T-junction, turn right on Castle Peak Road

NOT TO BE MISSED:

Mai Po marshes • Tai Fu Tai Mansion • Lok Ma Chau • Route Twisk

as it starts to head inland and skirts the eastern fringes of Tuen Mun.

After 7 miles (11 km), exit Castle Peak Road to Hung Tin Road on the right and loop onto Yuen Long Highway, bypassing busy Yuen Long town center. Follow the highway for 3 miles (5 km) to Pok Oi Interchange, and take the Pat Heung exit to rejoin Castle Peak Road.

At the next traffic circle, take the Mai Po turnoff. Two miles (3.2 km) farther down Castle Peak Road is the sign for the **Mai Po Marshes ❺** (see pp. 166–169); take a left turn on Tam Kon Chau Road and continue to the entrance. You can only enter the reserve if you have reserved a visit, but the countryside is striking, with patchworks of ponds and marshlands set against a hilly backdrop.

Return to Castle Peak Road and head north for 1 mile (1.6 km) to a narrow road on the left signposted to Fan Tin Tsuen. The village is home to several old clan halls and the **Tai Fu Tai Mansion 6** (see p. 200).

Back on Castle Peak Road, follow the signs for **Lok Ma Chau 7**, 1.5 miles (2.2 km) farther north, and enjoy uninterrupted views across the border to Shenzhen. Rejoin Castle Peak Road, this time skirting the Fanling Highway as it heads east for 3.3 miles (5.3 km). It ends at a T-junction. Turn left and follow the Fan Kam

Road, through the Hong Kong Golf Course, for 8 miles (13 km) until it joins Kam Tin Road. Turn left here and after another 1.3 miles (2 km) you join the scenic **Route Twisk 8**, which winds past Shek Kong, once a British Army base but now occupied by the People's Liberation Army. The route continues through the mist-shrouded hills of Tai Mo Shan and Tai Lam Country Parks for 5.5 miles (8.5 km) before arriving back at the eastern edge of Tsuen Wan.

See area map p. 154
Castle Peak Rd., Tsuen Wan
40 miles (65 km)
6.5 hours
Route Twisk, Tsuen Wan

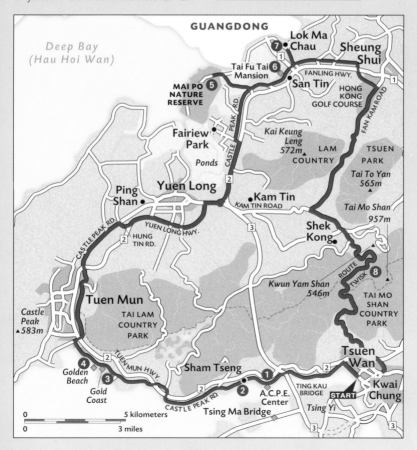

Mai Po Marshes

In the unlikeliest of spots in the northwestern New Territories, the Mai Po Marshes lie sandwiched between the high-rises of Yuen Long to the south and those of the Shenzhen Special Economic Region across the border to the north. The marshes and the mudflats of adjacent Inner Deep Bay make up one of the world's most important wetlands. The area's significance is underscored by Hong Kong Wetland Park, a nature reserve that lets visitors explore its biodiversity.

Countless thousands of migratory and resident birds seek haven in Mai Po's wetlands each year.

The area provides a unique habitat for huge numbers of resident species and a crucial stopping-off point for vast flocks of migrating birds. About 60,000 birds gather in the ponds, marshes, mangroves, and mudflats during the winter. More than 340 different species have been recorded here, many of them endangered, including a quarter of the world's remaining 600 black-faced spoonbills.

What brings them to the 3,700 acres (1,500 ha) of Mai Po and Inner Deep Bay is the opportunity to rest and refuel on their long migratory journeys between north Asia and Australia.

One of Mai Po's biggest attractions for the birds is the man-made, **earth-walled ponds** known as *gei wai*. The ponds attract fish, crabs, and oysters, which flourish in the environment.

Mai Po Nature Reserve

The Mai Po Nature Reserve, which is managed by the World Wide Fund for Nature Hong Kong, is active in promoting the site's importance. The **Education Center** has displays highlighting the area's geology, ecology, and settlement, and the exhibition gallery's interactive exhibits feature the art of gei wai–building, farming techniques, wetland ecology,

. . . .

Mai Po's network of paths, bridges, and boardwalks brings you within feet of thousands of birds.

. . . .

the area's abundant land-based wildlife species, and, of course, birdlife and migration.

Mai Po's network of paths, bridges, and boardwalks, with access for the disabled as well as ten **observation hides,** brings you within feet of thousands of birds. A **floating boardwalk** runs out into the mangroves of Deep Bay. Request a boardwalk permit when you reserve a visit.

Although it's unlikely you will see any on your visit, Mai

Bird Flu

Hong Kong put avian flu on the map, so it's a good idea to have at least a working knowledge while visiting, and what better place to start than a bird sanctuary? Avian flu is, simply put, a strand of influenza caused by viruses adapted to birds. Entire populations of domesticated birds, such as chickens and turkeys, have been slaughtered to stop the spread, which can rapidly infect other populations. In 1997, the virus first jumped the species barrier, killing six people in Hong Kong. Mai Po is closed by the government about once a year (most recently in February 2008) when birds are found to have contracted avian flu.

Po also attracts a wide variety of mammals, including mongooses, pangolins, and leopard cats. Despite the determined efforts at conservation and protection, the reserve remains under threat from development in the surrounding areas. Pollution in Deep Bay, flowing down from the manufacturing centers in southern China, and agricultural waste from Hong Kong, have had an impact, as has air pollution.

Access to the reserve is limited, and you need a permit, so make a reservation well in advance. You can rent binoculars at the site. Children under five years of age are not admitted.

Mai Po Nature Reserve
- Map p. 154
- Mai Po Wildlife Education Center, Tam Kon Chau, Yuen Long
- 2526-4473
- $$ (guide fee)
- MTR to Sheng Shui Station, then bus 76K

www.wwf.org.hk

Hong Kong Wetland Park
- Map p. 154
- Wetland Park Road, Tin Shui Wai
- 2708-8885
- $
- Closed Tues.
- MTR: Tin Shui Wai Station, then LTR to Wetland Park Station ; Bus: 967 from Admiralty

www.wetlandpark.com

Hong Kong Wetland Park

Set up to replace a section of the evershrinking wetlands, and as a center for education and tourism, these man-made wetlands attached to the Mai Po marshes are slightly less wild, but just as rewarding.

The 151-acre (61 ha) park attracts much of the wildlife that also calls the marshes home, and is designed to provide a more interactive learning experience than the Mai Po Nature Reserve. It has a huge **visitor center,** with a number of exhibitions on biodiversity around the world, including frozen tundras and a tropical swamp, and interactive displays on how humans interact with and affect wetlands.

However, it is outside, in the actual wetlands, that the park really impresses. Themed walks allow visitors to see the local wildlife in their natural habitat, with fixed binoculars, telescopes, and even closed-circuit television set up along the paths. The park can get very busy, particularly on weekends. Bringing your own pair of binoculars is advisable.

The park's star is Pui Pui the crocodile, who was moved to an enclosure here after being found in the Yuen Long area. ∎

Mangrove

Pied kingfisher

Black-capped kingfisher

Japanese yellow bunting

Leopard cat

Black-faced spoonbill

Dalmatian pelicans

Pangolin

Spotted greenshank

Spoon-billed sandpiper

Asian dowitcher

Shrenk's bittern

Mudskippers

Gray-headed lapwing

Black-faced
spoonbills

Oriental stork

Designated a Wetland of International
Importance in 1995, the Mai Po marshes
are some of the most important wetlands
in the world. They make a major stop-off
and feeding area for birds migrating
between Asia and Australia.

Imperial eagle

Chinese egrets

Otter

Mandarin ducks

Silky
starling

Black-headed
ibis

Bandicoot rat

Baikal teal

Dragonfly

Far Eastern curlew

Reed

Ping Shan Heritage Trail Walk

The short Ping Shan Heritage Trail offers the chance to see a collection of centuries-old and other related structures without too much effort. The buildings are part of the mini-empire of the Tang clan, the largest of Hong Kong's "Five Great Clans" who settled in the New Territories in the 11th century.

Tang clan boys received schooling at the meticulously restored Kun Ting Study Hall.

Hop off the LTR (Light Transit Railway) at Ping Shan and cross over the tracks. Head left along the sidewalk to Ping Ha Road, turn right, and follow it for about a half mile (0.8 km) to a small park on your right. The trail starts behind the park in the recently converted Ping Shan police station, a whitewashed, two-story building with wide verandas and now home to the **Ping Shan Tang Clan Gallery and Visitors Centre** (tel 2617-1959, closed Mon.). Built in 1899, the building houses relics and exhibitions related to the Tang clan, plus trail information. The trail's first stop is the 1767 **Hung Shing Temple ❶**, whose three carved timber altars are a riot of red and gold embroidery.

Continue along Ping Ha Road for a short distance to the lane on your right. The building on the corner, embellished with a brightly decorated lintel and superbly decorated inside, once served

NOT TO BE MISSED:

Kun Ting Study Hall • Tang Ancestral Hall

as the **Ching Shu Hin Guest House ❷** for important visitors. The gloriously ornate **Kun Ting Study Hall ❸** lies next door. Here boys of the Tang clan were educated. The hall was built in 1870 and has recently been fully restored to show off its carved granite columns, wall and eave plaster moldings, and wildly colorful murals.

Follow the lane a little farther until a square opens to your right and two large ancestral halls come into view. The one on the left is the **Tang Ancestral Hall ❹**, its sheer size proclaiming the power and wealth the family wielded in the area.

Built about 700 years ago and now splendidly restored, its three large halls and two courtyards feature stone pillars rising to support the finely carved painted roof beams 25 feet (8 m) above, while pottery dragon-fish top its sweeping eaves. In the first courtyard you will see a red stone wall leading to the gate, built to keep evil spirits out. Beyond this spirit wall is another courtyard and the main hall where ancestral tablets recording the names of this line of the Tang clan stand on a red altar. The hall also features a history of the clan hall and is popular with the many Tang descendants now living in Europe, the United States, Canada, and Australia.

Next door is the smaller 16th-century **Yu Kiu Ancestral Hall ❺**. This hall contains the ancestral tablets of a different branch of the Tang clan, and is designed in similar style to the main hall, although on a less grand scale.

From the square the trail continues for a short distance to the simple **Yeung Hau**

Temple ❻. Over a low wall, you can see its three chambers and red altars with an imposing statue of Yeung Hau, flanked by the earth god, and the goddess of expectant mothers, suitably adorned with pottery children in her lap.

Retrace your steps to a turn on the right and follow the trail to the small walled village of **Sheung Cheung Wai ❼** to explore its few narrow lanes. Just beyond the village is a well-tended and richly ornamented brick shrine to the earth god. The trail now snakes to the three-story **Tsui Shing Lau Pagoda ❽**, the only ancient pagoda remaining in Hong Kong.

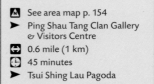

⚐ See area map p. 154
► Ping Shau Tang Clan Gallery & Visitors Centre
↔ 0.6 mile (1 km)
🕐 45 minutes
► Tsui Shing Lau Pagoda

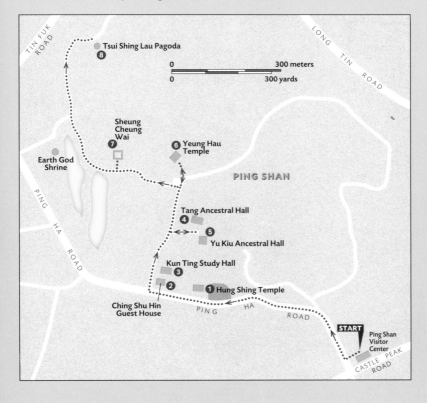

Kam Tin

In 1069, the Canton (Guangzhou) government administrator Tan Fu-hip visited Kam Tin and was so enamored with the beauty of the place that he later returned with his family and ancestral graves and settled here. This was the beginning of the Tang clan in Hong Kong, which went on to become the biggest of Hong Kong's "Five Great Clans."

Kam Tin
⬛ Map p. 154

Subsequent generations of the Tangs built walled villages around Kam Tin and in other parts of Hong Kong as protection against pirates, bandits, and neighbors. Remnants of these villages, and

A corner tower at Kat Hing Wai walled village

those of other clans, can be found in some parts of the New Territories, but **Kat Hing Wai** *(Bus 51 from Tsuen Wan Station, or 64K from Tai Po Market KCR)* is the most popular among visitors. The village is south of Kam Tin Road. Don't expect a quaint village set among cultivated fields, or a sparkling museum piece. Four hundred members of

INSIDER TIP:

If you ascend Kwun Yam Shan (Goddess of Mercy Mountain), you'll be able to see ancient terraces from old tea plantations near Tai Mo Shan, the highest peak in the New Territories.

—TIFFANY TRENT
National Geographic contributor

the Tang clan live here, mostly in homes that have long since replaced the original buildings, and the village and its surroundings have not escaped the gritty urbanization found in many of the villages and towns of the New Territories.

The fine, high stone walls of

the village, with imposing gray-brick corner watchtowers and a chain-iron gate guarding its only entrance, lend the 500-year-old village an impressive air, although the modern pink and purple houses jutting above the wall inside the village compound can take the edge off the experience.

Shui Tau Tsuen

From Kat Hing Wai, head west for about 200 yards (180 m) along Kam Tin Road to Mung Yeung Public School and take the lane on the right for a half mile (0.8 km) to the village of Shui Tau Tsuen, set amid fields dotted with water buffalo. The

Hong Kong's Great Clans

The so-called "Five Great Clans" began arriving in Hong Kong from China in the 11th century, settling in the fertile regions of the New Territories, where they built fortified walled villages and farmed the surrounding countryside. The Tang clan was the first to arrive, taking up residence in the Kam Tin area, before spreading throughout Hong Kong. They were followed by the Hau, who made their home near the present-day new town of Sheung Shui. Next came the Pangs, who carved out their territory near Fanling. The Liu arrived in the 15th century, followed by the Man a century later. The clans eventually became landlords of the New Territories, Kowloon, and Hong Kong, but the Tangs remained the most powerful. Many ancestors of the Five Great Clans still live in the New Territories.

At the gate, you'll be asked by one of the wizened old ladies guarding the entrance to slip a HK$1 coin into a hole in the wall.

Inside, the narrow lanes still follow the original geometrical pattern. The main lane, lined with souvenir stands, runs through the center of the village and ends at a small, rather nondescript temple and ancestral hall. Here, and in other places around the temple, more weather-beaten ladies will approach you, happy to don their distinctive wide-brimmed bamboo hats and have their photographs taken for HK$10. After the temple, spend some time wandering through the village lanes, past the open doors of dimly lit homes with flickering televisions. The village is quite small, so it won't take long.

village still retains a splendid row of ornate 17th-century houses, notable for the sweeping, carved timber, boat-prow features along the ridges of their roofs, decorated with sculptured fish and dragons.

Beyond the two restored study halls near the entrance to the village, take the lane that separates them for a few hundred yards to the village's imposing ancestral halls. The largest is the **Tang Ching Lok Ancestral Hall** (closed Mon.–Fri.), dating back to the late 1700s. Above the entrance to the hall are brightly colored murals of mountains, river scenes, and people, while inside the names of prominent ancestors are listed on the altar. ■

Fanling & Sheung Shui

These two towns are the MTR's last stops before reaching Lo Wu and the border with mainland China in the northern New Territories. (Lo Wu is closed to visitors unless traveling through to China.) Once traditional rural centers, they have grown into bustling new towns, but still hold a number of attractions reminiscent of the more traditional ways of the New Territories.

Fredrik Jacobson of Sweden tees off on the 18th hole during the final round of the 2002 Omega Hong Kong Open at the world-renowned Hong Kong Golf Club in Fanling.

Fanling

Map p. 154

Both Fanling and Sheung Shui have a series of walled villages and ancestral halls. These were built over the centuries by members of the "Five Great Clans" of Hong Kong (see p. 173), who made their way across from mainland China to settle and farm in the New Territories from about the 11th century onward.

Fanling

The walled village of **Fanling Wai** was built by the Pangs, one of the Five Great Clans, during the Ming dynasty. It's a ten-minute walk from the Fanling MTR station. From the station's eastern side, follow the sidewalk north to a traffic circle, then continue north along San Wan Road to the Pang's ancestral hall. A lane beside it leads to the village; follow it past a luxuriant banyan tree, then bear left for a short distance to a murky fishpond, built to provide good *feng shui* to the walled settlement behind.

Three-story modern houses extend behind the walls, replacing the more humble dwellings of old, but the sturdy corner watchtowers hint at how difficult capturing the village would have been for bandits or rival clans. Fanling still maintains the typical grid system of walled villages, with tightly packed houses separated by narrow lanes.

From near Fanling MTR station, Sha Tau Kok Road runs to Lung Yeuk Tau, just outside the town. The **Lung Yeuk Tau Heritage Trail** incorporates five walled villages and six unwalled ones known as *tsuens*, a village network set up by the Tangs. Several structures have been declared monuments and are protected, including the **Tang Chung Ling Ancestral Hall** *(closed Tues.)*, dating from 1525. The central chamber of the rear hall, adorned with elaborate dragon's head carvings, holds the ancestral tablets of the clan's most important members. The hall is decorated with fine woodcarvings, moldings, and murals.

Most of the original wall and layout of the village still exists at **Lo Wai,** whose wall and entrance gate have been restored. Lo Wai was the first settlement built in the area.

Ma Mat Wai entrance tower is worth a look for its chain-ringed gates and red stone lintel, but most of the wall has been demolished.

More impressive are the fully restored enclosing walls and corner watchtowers at **Kun Lung Wai** (also known as San Wai). Built in 1744, this village is the most authentic remaining in the area, although most of the original buildings within the walls have been knocked down and replaced.

Though you can get to some of the villages by Minibus 54K from Fanling MTR station, the entire trail can be difficult to follow. If you want to try, contact the Antiquities and Monuments Office *(136 Nathan Rd., Tsim Sha Tsui, tel 2208-4400, www.amo.gov.hk)*.

Across the pedestrian bridge over Fanling Highway from the MTR station is **Fung Ying Seen Koon,** a Taoist temple amid lush landscaping, with paths, waterfalls, and benches for meditating.

Sheung Shui

One of Hong Kong's finest ancestral halls is **Liu Man Shek Tong Ancestral Hall** *(closed Mon., Tues., & Fri.)* in the walled village of Sheung Shui Wai, about 15 minutes from the MTR station Sheung Shui. Take exit B1 to San Wan Road and walk north following the train line to San Po Street. Turn right here and cross Po Wan Road into Sheung Shui Tung Hing Road. The first lane

---

Tones

As if it wasn't already difficult to understand, Cantonese is a tonal language. Words and concepts are not only designated by the symbols, but also the tone in which they are pronounced. The language has nine tones, so the same syllable could mean nine different things. A deft mastery of the tones is as imperative as learning the words themselves.

---

on the left enters the village.

Built by the Liu clan in 1751, the village hall's exterior is enlivened with carved timber decorations, traditional Chinese murals, and pottery figurines on the roof's ridge. Inside the hall, an intricately carved altar holds tablets with the names of the founding ancestors and others who have played important roles in the clan's history. ∎

Sheung Shui
Map p. 154

Sha Tin

The sandy fields from which Sha Tin gets its name are nowhere to be seen today. All the sand has gone into making the concrete to build the huge residential towers that dominate this new town, which now houses more than half a million people. For visitors, the town's main attractions are the magnificent Ten Thousand Buddhas Monastery and the excellent Hong Kong Heritage Museum.

Sha Tin
 Map p. 155

Sha Tin is probably the most attractive of the rather drab and often intimidating new towns constructed in the New Territories. Edging the Shing Mun River Channel that cuts through the center of town is a green and shady ribbon of parkland.

An elaborate reconstruction of a Chinese opera shed at the Hong Kong Heritage Museum in Sha Tin

This is one of the few new towns visited by people from other parts of Hong Kong. Most come here to indulge in their favorite pastimes: shopping at the vast **New Town Plaza** (directly connected to the Sha Tin KCR station), one of the largest and busiest retail centers in Hong Kong, and gambling on the horses at the huge **Sha Tin Racecourse.** If you are in Hong Kong during the racing season, from mid-September to June, join 70,000 other bettors on a Saturday (sometimes Sunday) for a memorable and pulsating day at the races (see pp. 92–93). The hillside **Ten Thousand Buddhas Monastery** (see pp. 178–179) also attracts the throngs on weekends.

A few attractions are worth visiting before you reach Sha Tin Central. Get off the train at Tai Wai MTR station, and change to the Ma On Shan line, which has a dedicated Che Kung Temple Station. You'll find **Che Kung Temple** on the opposite side of the road. Much less elaborate and ornate than other Taoist temples in Hong Kong, it honors Che Kung, a Song dynasty general.

Inside the temple hall is a 36-foot (11 m) bronze statue of the general, standing with a distinct military air amid plumes of smoke from burning incense. Typical of Taoist temples, legions

Porcelain

When something as ubiquitous as ceramics gains the nickname "China," you know that it is important in this part of the world. Ceramics have existed in China for 11,000 years, and they have shifted from their utilitarian beginnings to the ornate designs characteristic of the Qing dynasty.

Although it is impossible to present an overarching aesthetic for Chinese ceramics, most think of the subtle blue on white glaze, often depicting birds and trees, which gained popularity during the Ming dynasty (1368–1644). Be wary of any items purported to be antique that you come across in a store or market, though, as China is also well known for its counterfeits.

of fortune-tellers inhabit the grounds. Small paper windmills placed around the temple are said to bring good luck when the wind sets them twirling.

As you continue north on Che Kung Miu Road to the intersection of Lion Rock Tunnel Road, follow the path to the right through a small village and underpass to the old walled village of **Tsang Tai Uk** ("Tsang's big house"), a Tang-clan strong-

INSIDER TIP:

As antidote to the bustle of Hong Kong and Kowloon, venture out to the New Territories, where the pace is slower and life more traditional.

—MARK GRAHAM
National Geographic Traveler magazine writer

hold built in the mid-19th century. A few clan members still live there. The ancestral hall, with its red timber altar embellished with gilded carvings, lies at the back

of a large, rectangular courtyard. The tops of the corner towers in the surrounding wall are shaped like the handles of a wok. Although somewhat faded, it's still possible to get a feeling of how this once thriving village looked in its heyday.

The **Hong Kong Heritage Museum,** a ten-minute walk along Lion Rock Tunnel Road, over Che Kung Miu Road and the Shing Mun River Channel, sits on the waterfront. It has an in-depth, interactive exploration of the region's history. The **New Territories Heritage Hall** on the first floor leads you through a series of incisive exhibits highlighting the area's natural environment, prehistory, trade and coastal defense, the life of fishermen and villagers, the advent of British colonization, and the huge new town developments that began in the early 1970s. Next door, the **Cantonese Opera Heritage Hall** reconstructs a shed opera theater with opera models in dazzling costumes. The **T. T. Tsui Gallery of Chinese Art** on the second floor has an extensive and varied range of Chinese artifacts including Tang dynasty terra-cotta figures and porcelain. ■

Sha Tin Racecourse
- Penfold Park, Sha Tin
- 2695-6223
- MTR East: Racecourse Station

Hong Kong Heritage Museum
- 1 Man Lam Rd., Sha Tin
- 2180-8188
- Closed Tues.
- $
- MTR: Che Kung Temple

www.heritage museum.gov.hk

Ten Thousand Buddhas Monastery

High in the hills just to the northwest of Sha Tin, which guarantee excellent *feng shui,* sits the Ten Thousand Buddhas Monastery, which was founded in the 1950s. It's the area's biggest attraction after the horse races. Be prepared for a steep climb to the main temple.

Nearly 13,000 gilded ceramic Buddhas, made by Shanghai craftsmen, were donated by worshippers.

Ten Thousand Buddhas Monastery
- 🅰 Map p. 155
- ☎ 2691-1067
- 💲 Donation
- 🚇 MTR: Sha Tin Station, exit B

The climb starts just beyond the ramshackle village of Pai Tau. You will have to clamber up more than 400 steps to reach the main hall. In some places, the path is wider and the concrete is newer, the result of repairs to the monastery after a mudslide in 1997. The temple was closed for two and a half years while the repairs, funded by donations from devotees, were carried out.

Shelves lining the walls of the **main temple** are stacked with almost 13,000 small Buddha statues, each one bearing a slightly different pose and expression and inscribed with the name of the person who donated it to the temple. Three larger gilded Buddha statues encased in glass stand in the temple's center.

The **terrace** in front of the temple is lined with fierce-looking, multicolored statues representing Buddha's 18 disciples, or lohans. Beyond these are two fantastical bodhisattva images, those midway between enlightenment and the material world; one rides an elephant, while the other rides a wild-looking lion. In the middle of all this is a statue of another bodhisattva, Wei To, who is the protector of monasteries, while a statue of Kwun Yam, the Goddess of Mercy, stands at his back.

The goddess faces a **red pagoda** which has nine levels, as this is an auspicious number in Buddhism, although it is actually only four stories high. Climb the levels for great views over the expanse of Sha Tin.

From here another 69 steps lead to the top level of the temple, where the mummified remains of the monastery's founding abbot, Yuet Kai, are sitting upright in a glass case in front of a giant gilded Buddha image.

The abbot, who was a philosophy professor from Kunming in southern China, spent his life devoted to the study of Buddhism. He arrived in Hong Kong after World War II and began building the temple.

When Yuet Kai died in 1965 at the age of 87, he was buried in a coffin on the hill. Eight months later, the body was exhumed for reburial and, according to devotees, the abbot not only showed no signs of decomposition, but also emitted a fluorescent glow. He was embalmed, layered in gold leaf, draped in robes, placed in a lotus position, and put on display in his present position as an example of piety.

Buddha's Five Remembrances

Central to the Buddhist tradition is the Upajjhat-thana Sutta, or "Subjects for Contemplation." These texts offer reflections to help navigate the inescapable turbulence of life. Most famous are the five remembrances listed below. It is thought that his reflection upon the third remembrance led Sid-dhartha (who became the Buddha) to abandon his royalty for a spiritual life.

- I am of the nature to grow old. There is no way to escape growing old.
- I am of the nature to have ill health. There is no way to escape ill health.
- I am of the nature to die. There is no way to escape death.
- All that is dear to me and everyone I love are of the nature to change. There is no way to escape being separated from them.
- My actions are my only true belongings. I cannot escape the consequences of my actions. My actions are the ground upon which I stand.

If you visit on a Sunday or a public holiday, you may find fortune-tellers in the temple hall, but be sure to ask how much it costs before letting them look into your future. ∎

Chinese Astrology

Behind the image of Hong Kong as a 21st-century city, with its gleaming skyscrapers and booming economy, a more ancient force can sometimes be seen at work. The moon, with its phases and movements, continues to hold sway over the lives of many people in the territory.

A *tanka* depicts all 12 animals in Chinese astrology. In modern Hong Kong, auspicious dates are still determined using the Chinese zodiac.

Visit Hong Kong during the Lunar New Year, usually in January or February, and you will find that it's the only time of year when the stores are closed. Most open again when the official holiday ends, usually after three days, but some may continue to keep their doors locked. They are waiting for an auspicious day to reopen; a day divined by *feng shui* experts or fortune-tellers according to the lunar calendar. To open earlier could mean poor business for the next 12 months.

Fortune-tellers pore over charts of the movements of the moon to calculate whether days will be good, bad, or average for major events in a person's life. The right day could mean the difference between a good or bad marriage. Young couples will consult the experts for auspicious days on which to tie the knot. To ensure they are among the lucky ones to get married on such a day, they will probably have to get in line for hours outside a marriage registry office three months in advance to reserve their date with destiny.

The moon has been used to divine such important occasions, along with harvests and festivals, for thousands of years in China. Since the lunar month differs in length from those used in the Gregorian calendar, the date for the start of the Lunar New Year changes every year, at least according to calendars in the West.

Each lunar year is governed by one of a dozen animals—rat, ox, tiger, rabbit, dragon (the only mythical beast in the list), snake, horse, goat, monkey, rooster, dog, and pig—creating a 12-year cycle. People are said to take on the characteristics of the animal in whose year they are born.

Both smart and charming, **rats** like to get their own way. They also love a challenge.

The dependable **ox** is able to achieve great things by adopting a careful, methodical approach. Not surprisingly, people born in this animal's year can be stubborn.

A **tiger** is sensitive and likes to be in control, but can also have a bad temper.

Rabbits can be a bit of a pushover with those willing to take advantage, and will handle problems at their own, slow pace.

Clever and powerful **dragons** are said to be lucky in love but lacking in compassion.

Snakes have the ability to charm, are hardworking, and also lucky with money.

Horses are natural-born wanderers and love to travel, but have an impatient streak.

Creative and artistic, **goats** need lots of support and understanding from those around them.

Monkeys love fun and are full of energy. Their devil-may-care attitude, however, can cause them problems.

The truth is all-important to the **rooster,** who likes to be in charge. Strutting is important, with appearance a priority.

The faithful **dog** can make a loyal friend, but can also be stubborn.

And **pigs**? Those born in the last year in the cycle are considered to be polite perfectionists, always willing to see the best in people.

Chinese Birth Signs

RAT: 1900, 1912, 1924, 1936, 1948, 1960, 1972, 1984, 1996, 2008

OX: 1901, 1913, 1925, 1937, 1949, 1961, 1973, 1985, 1997, 2009

TIGER: 1902, 1914, 1926, 1938, 1950, 1962, 1974, 1986, 1998, 2010

RABBIT: 1903, 1915, 1927, 1939, 1951, 1963, 1975, 1987, 1999

DRAGON: 1904, 1916, 1928, 1940, 1952, 1964, 1976, 1988, 2000

SNAKE: 1905, 1917, 1929, 1941, 1953, 1965, 1977, 1989, 2001

HORSE: 1906, 1918, 1930, 1942, 1954, 1966, 1978, 1990, 2002

GOAT: 1907, 1919, 1931, 1943, 1955, 1967, 1979, 1991, 2003

MONKEY: 1908, 1920, 1932, 1944, 1956, 1968, 1980, 1992, 2004

ROOSTER: 1909, 1921, 1933, 1945, 1957, 1969, 1981, 1993, 2005

DOG: 1910, 1922, 1934, 1946, 1958, 1970, 1982, 1994, 2006

PIG: 1911, 1923, 1935, 1947, 1959, 1971, 1983, 1995, 2007

Tai Po

Tai Po sits on the Lam Tsuen River where it flows into Tolo Harbor. Records dating back to the tenth century indicate it was an important market town and a center for pearl diving. The completion of the KCR (Kowloon–Canton Railway) in 1910 opened up the area, but it wasn't until the 1970s that Tai Po began its transformation from a sleepy village into a bustling new town.

Chinese bulbuls, Japanese white-eyes, and cuckoos are among the many birds you may see flitting about Tai Po Kau's subtropical foliage.

Tai Po
🄰 Map p. 155

The original Tai Po Market railway station, built in Chinese style with a pitched-tiled roof and swirling decorations, was completed in 1913 and now houses the small but fascinating **Hong Kong Railway Museum.** It has a selection of antique steam locomotives and carriages, and lots of wonderful memorabilia including old tickets, posters, and photographs. Information on its Tiffin Train Service, offered before World War II and popular with golfers on their way to the course at Fanling and or on their way to shooting parties in search of wild boar and barking deer, is a real delight.

Opposite the museum lies the entrance to the atmospheric **Tai Po New Market.** The wide pedestrian-only Fu Shing Street is packed with shops selling everything from shoes, bean curd, and bamboo Hakka hats to so-called thousand-year-old eggs. This is a great place to catch the hustle and bustle of New Territories' market life.

In the middle of all the commotion, about halfway along Fu Shing Street on the left, is an oasis of calm: the **Man Mo Temple.** Built in the late 19th century, it honors Man, the god of civil servants and literature, and fierce, red-faced Mo, the god of war and martial arts.

This small temple has a finely carved eaves-board under the roof ledge of its polished granite entranceway. Eight compartments surround a central courtyard, where senior citizens, shaded beneath palm trees, occupy themselves in quiet conversation and tranquil games of mah-jongg and cards.

Tai Po Kau Nature Reserve

Situated midway between Tai Po and Sha Tin, this 1,138-acre (460 ha) reserve is the oldest of the expansive nature reserves in Hong Kong. It was established in the 1920s to aid the reforestation of the New Territories, much of which had been stripped bare by a combination of village farming, building, and firewood collection. *(Take MTR East to Tai Po Market Station, then a taxi.)*

Five graded, color-coded trails cut through the reserve's dense and diverse woodlands; a map board at the entrance indicates their routes. The trails, ranging from a half mile (0.8 km) to 6 miles (10 km) in length, pass under canopied trees, along peaceful, gurgling streams, and over lichen-covered boulders on hillsides thick with ferns. This is a good way to see some of Hong Kong's best subtropical forests without having to clamber up the steep ridges and ravines

INSIDER TIP:

Walk through the Tai Po Kau Nature Reserve; it's world-renowned as an important bird area.

—DR. JODI ROWLEY
National Geographic field researcher

that are sometimes found along trails in the territories' country parks. The half-mile (0.8 km) nature trail is the easiest of the trails, but none of them are strenuous.

The reserve is rich in birdlife, with more than a dozen species recorded. It is also a favorite spot for photographing and watching the numerous butterflies that inhabit the park.

Mammals, including the armadillo-like pangolins, civet cats, and wild boars, live in the dense forests. You will rarely see them along the trails, but you can sometimes hear the odd "barking" call of the barking deer. ■

Hong Kong Railway Museum

✉ 13 Shung Tak St., Tai Po Market, Tai Po

☎ 2653-3455

🕐 Closed Tues.

🚇 MTR East: Tai Po Market Station, then minibus 25K

Plover Cove

This area of the northeastern New Territories, just below the border with mainland China, is one of the most sparsely inhabited and isolated areas in Hong Kong. Hakka immigrants from China originally settled here about 300 years ago, but the rugged terrain proved difficult to farm and the few hamlets built here remain isolated and all but deserted.

A number of villages around Plover Cove date back hundreds of years.

Plover Cove

🅰 Map p. 155

✉ Plover Cove Country Park Visitor Center, Bride's Pool Rd.

🕒 Open weekends and public holidays

🚌 Bus: 75K from Tai Po

The area is now home to two country parks, whose sometimes difficult trails reward hikers with stunning panoramas over steep mountain ranges and rolling hills to the waters of Tolo Harbor and Starling Inlet. **Plover Cove Country Park** to the east and **Pat Sin Leng Country Park** (both *www.afcd/gov.hk*) to the west are bounded by Plover Cove Reservoir and Starling Inlet, a tidal bay that stretches toward mainland China, and divided by a lush valley.

The gateway to the area is the village of **Tai Mei Tuk** *(Bus 75K*

from Tai Po Market KCR station), which sits close to the Plover Cove Reservoir dam wall and is popular with picnickers and day-trippers. The dam was built in the 1960s when drought and a growing population caused water shortages. Beyond the village, Bride's Pool Road climbs for about 400 yards (360 m) to the **visitor center,** which houses a small exhibition of the area's flora and fauna.

From the visitor center, you can follow the path onto Bride's Pool Road past barbecue sites, often crowded on weekends, but a better option is to head up the hill to the left onto the **Pat Sin Leng Nature Trail.** Along this 2.5-mile (4 km) hike you will have views over Plover Cove Reservoir toward Ma On Shan's high-rises on the edge of Tolo Harbor, and then across to the peaks of Plover Cove Country Park as you climb to about 1,300 feet

INSIDER TIP:

You don't have to go far from the concrete jungle to real jungle. Hong Kong has some fantastic trails through natural landscapes.

—DR. JODI ROWLEY
National Geographic field researcher

(400 m). Farther on, across deep green rolling hills and past Starling Inlet, the towers of Shau Tau Kok, which edges the border with mainland China, reveal themselves in the distance. The trail then plunges down to Bride's Pool Road, ending opposite the half-mile-long (0.8 km) **Bride's Pool Nature Trail,** which meanders through a small part of the heavily forested valley floor. The pool is a major water catchments, feeding the huge reservoir to its south. Pat Sin Leng Nature Trail starts at the country park's map board by a small green pavilion and winds along a ridge before dropping down to Plover Cove Reservoir.

Another option is to head along Bride's Pool Road north for another 3 miles (5 km) to the hamlet of **Luk Keng,** on the shores of Starling Inlet. The village is a crowded, haphazard mixture of old and new houses, and small temples. Minibuses run from Luk Keng to Tai Mei Tuk, and on to Fanling.

Between late March and August, the village, its ponds, and the remnants of old rice terraces become the biggest breeding area for egrets in Hong Kong. Huge flocks descend and congregate on the small island of **A Chau** to the left of the village.

You can rent bicycles in Tai Mei Tuk and cycle along Bride's Pool Road to Luk Keng. This 6-mile (10 km) ride traverses the valley that splits the two country parks. ∎

Cycling

Cycling in Kowloon or on Hong Kong Island is not only inadvisable, it's positively dangerous. However, parts of the New Territories are more cycle-friendly, with several of the new towns providing cycleways. The path between Tai Wai, just south of Sha Tin, and Tai Po follows the edges of Shin Min River Channel and Tolo Harbor. Bicycles can be rented from the numerous shops in Tai Wai and Tung Cheung Street in Tai Po.

A more pleasant ride is along Bride's Pool Road between the villages of Tai Mei Tuk and Luk Keng in the northeast New Territories. You can rent bicycles at shops in Tai Mei Tuk. Avoid weekends, as the paths get clogged with riders.

There are ten designated areas in Hong Kong's country parks where cycling is allowed, but you need a permit from the Country and Marine Parks Authority (*tel 1823*).

Sai Kung & Clear Water Bay

The eastern section of the New Territories is Hong Kong's playground. This is a strikingly scenic area of hiking trails cutting along verdant hillsides that plunge down to isolated beaches, coves, bays, dozens of deserted islands, and tiny villages nestled in steep valleys. In some of these surprisingly pristine and beautiful places, it's hard to believe you are only 40 minutes away from the crowds, noise, and high-rises of Kowloon.

White-sand beaches filigree Clear Water Bay's hilly coastline.

Much of this area is under the ordinance of Hong Kong's Country Parks, and there are numerous opportunities for recreation. You can hike, camp, and swim; rent sailboards and canoes; and charter boats—from small *kaidos* (motorized boats) to luxury launches—to reach isolated beaches and islands. Come during the week to best enjoy the splendors of the countryside. On weekends, especially Sundays, the beaches and hiking trails fill with people.

The pleasant fishing town of Sai Kung is the launchpad for visits to the country parks, and an ideal place to relax after a long hike or a day on the beach. At windswept Clear Water Bay peninsula, on the southeastern tip of the New Territories, the spectacular golf course at the posh Clear Water Bay Country Club edges the South China Sea.

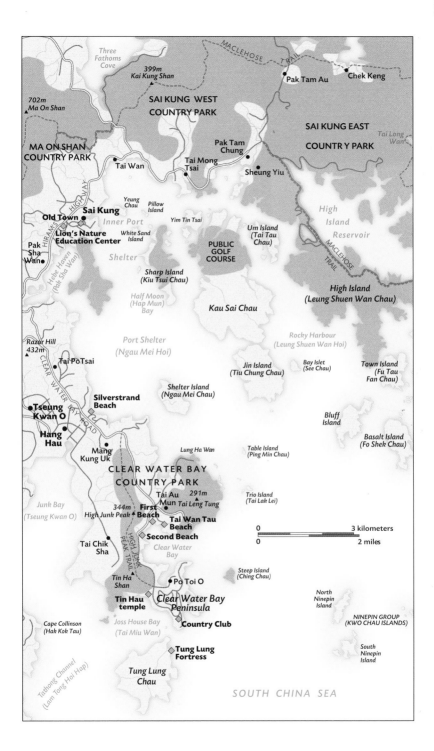

Three Fathoms Cove

MACLEHOSE TRAIL

399m Kai Kung Shan

Pak Tam Au   Chek Keng

702m Ma On Shan

SAI KUNG WEST COUNTRY PARK

SAI KUNG EAST COUNTRY PARK

Tai Long Wan

MA ON SHAN COUNTRY PARK

Pak Tam Chung

Tai Wan   Tai Mong Tsai

Sheung Yiu

High Island Reservoir

Yeung Chau   Pillow Island

Sai Kung
Old Town
Inner Port

Yim Tin Tsai

Lion's Nature Education Center

White Sand Island

Um Island (Tai Tau Chau)

Pak Sha Wan

Shelter

PUBLIC GOLF COURSE

High Island (Leung Shuen Wan Chau)

MACLEHOSE TRAIL

Sharp Island (Kiu Tsui Chau)

Half Moon (Hap Mun) Bay

Kau Sai Chau

Razor Hill 432m

Port Shelter (Ngau Mei Hoi)

Rocky Harbour (Leung Shuen Wan Hoi)

Tai Po Tsai

Jin Island (Tiu Chung Chau)

Bay Islet (See Chau)

Town Island (Fu Tau Fan Chau)

Shelter Island (Ngau Mei Chau)

Silverstrand Beach

Bluff Island

Basalt Island (Fo Shek Chau)

Tseung Kwan O

Hang Hau

Mang Kung Uk

Lung Ha Wan

Table Island (Ping Min Chau)

CLEAR WATER BAY COUNTRY PARK

Tai Au Mun   291m Tai Leng Tung

Trio Island (Tai Lak Lei)

Junk Bay (Tseung Kwan O)

344m High Junk Peak   First Beach

Tai Wan Tau Beach

0   3 kilometers
0   2 miles

Tai Chik Sha

Second Beach

Clear Water Bay

Steep Island (Ching Chau)

Tin Ha Shan   Po Toi O

North Ninepin Island

Tin Hau temple   Clear Water Bay Peninsula

Cape Collinson (Hak Kok Tau)

Joss House Bay (Tai Miu Wan)

Country Club

NINEPIN GROUP (KWO CHAU ISLANDS)

South Ninepin Island

Tung Lung Fortress

Tathong Channel (Lam Tong Hoi Hap)

Tung Lung Chau

SOUTH CHINA SEA

Clear Water Bay

 Map p. 187

Clear Water Bay Country Park Visitor Center

☎ 2719-0032

🕐 Closed Tues.

🚌 Bus: 91 from Choi Hung MTR

Here you will also find numerous hiking trails that are less demanding than the often rigorous treks farther north. Beaches nearby are easily accessible.

Clear Water Bay

At the southeastern corner of the New Territories is Clear

ged cliff face and can be reached by steps. Another, smaller beach, **Tai Wan Tau,** lies in the northern corner of the bay.

There are other beaches off Clear Water Bay Road before you reach these popular stretches of sand; the pretty **Silverstrand Beach,** backed by cliffside

Fish farms at Po Toi O. The hamlet still maintains its traditional fishing village character.

Water Bay, an almost untamed section of the area with a rugged coastline, bare hills, whitewashed villas, and exceptional panoramas of the South China Sea. The beaches and country park here also are popular on weekends, so it's best to visit during the week.

Most people come to the area for its two main beaches—**Clear Water Bay First Beach** and **Clear Water Bay Second Beach**—curving around deeply indented Clear Water Bay. These clean, white-sand, easily accessible beaches sit at the bottom of a jag-

mansions and apartments, is the most accessible. You will have to descend some steep steps to get there from the parking lot. The beach gained notoriety in the early 1990s after a number of fatal shark attacks, but shark nets have since been installed.

The headland from the northern border of Clear Water Bay forms the eastern section of **Clear Water Bay Country Park.** At the park's entrance is a visitor center, barbecue area, and the start of the circular **Tree Walk** track, a pleasant, short amble that

INSIDER TIP:

One of Hong Kong's most beautiful areas, Tai Long Wan ("Big Wave Bay") on the east coast of the Sai Kung peninsula, can be reached via an easy hiking trail that passes through small hamlets and rugged headlands.

—IAN BAKER
National Geographic field researcher

takes you through a cool, heavily forested section of the park. Near the start of the walk, a lookout offers splendid views of the Ninepins Islands group (Kwo Chau), Tung Lung Chau (see p. 214), other offshore islands, and to the fairways of the golf course of the exclusive Clear Water Bay Country Club across the bay.

From the parking lot at the entrance to the country park, you can take a well-marked track to the top of 955-foot (290 m) **Tai Leng Tung** for exceptional panoramas of islands and sea, then continue to Lung Ha Wan on the northern side of the headland.

A scenic coastal road with very little traffic, ideal for walking, winds south from the Clear Water Bay beaches for about 2.5 miles (4 km) to the entrance of the Clear Water Bay Country Club. About a half mile (0.8 km) before the entrance, a road drops down to **Po Toi O**, a fishing village scenically located on the edge of an inlet and a favorite spot for weekend junk cruises

(see p. 131). At the entrance to the country club, a sign indicates the start of the **High Junk Peak Country Trail.**

Tin Hau Temple: East of the sign and to the right of the entrance to Clear Water Bay Country Club, a series of steps takes you down to the Tin Hau temple which looks over Joss House Bay. The temple site dates back to 1266, making it one of the oldest in Hong Kong. Rock carvings there indicate the visit of a Song dynasty official in 1274. The present temple, built in 1878, was seriously damaged by Typhoon Wanda in 1962, but has since been renovated.

The main altar has three images of Tin Hau, the Queen of Heaven and protector of fisherfolk. In the intriguing goddess "bedroom" is a bed for each image, along with a washstand,basin, and mirror. The main hall features an 18th-century model junk, crewed with a deck full of carved sailors. A large plaza and pier have been built in front of the temple for the crowds arriving by ferry during the annual Tin Hau festival in April (see p. 50). At most other times, the temple is deserted. The large offshore

Sai Kung

This bustling fishing town is the starting point for hiking and beach trips to the surrounding countryside (see pp. 186–190). Many people also visit from Hong Kong's crowded districts to soak up the atmosphere of this agreeable town, breathe some fresh air, and dine at the

Live seafood is selected from quayside fish tanks before being carted off to nearby restaurants.

island of Tung Lung Chau, with its old Chinese fortress, sits at the entrance to rocky Joss House Bay.

If you are feeling energetic, you can return to the Clear Water Bay beaches via the 2.5-mile (4 km) **High Junk Peak Country Trail** which takes you up the barren hills of Tin Ha Shan for excellent views across the bay. A well-marked side trail takes you back down to the beaches just before the steep ascent to **High Junk Peak** (Tu Tue Yung).

renowned seafood restaurants lining the quayside. The town of Sai Kung makes for a pleasant day's outing, but avoid Sundays when crowds and traffic clog the place.

Start with a stroll along the **quay** at the end of Fuk Man Road, for a dose of fishing village atmosphere. The **harbor** buzzes with activity. A few fishing boats tie up alongside the wharf delivering their catch to the seafood restaurants, and junks take on

Golfing

If you are a golf fan, leave Sai Kung for Kau Sai Chau Island and Hong Kong's only public golf facility. Ferries leave from a private pier every 20 minutes. The Kau Sai Chau Public Golf Course *(tel 2791-380)* comprises two 18-hole courses (the North Course and the South Course) and was a gift from the benevolent Hong Kong Jockey Club. It is one of the most scenic in Asia, with spectacular views of the South China Sea, nearby islands, and the jagged hills of Sai Kung Country Park.

The facility also offers a large driving range and indoor and outdoor practice pitching and putting facilities.

You can rent clubs and shoes at the clubhouse. Reservations are essential and you will need a handicap certificate. The course is not particularly cheap by U.S. standards; a round of 18 holes will cost between HK$680 and $770 depending on the day (weekends are more expensive) and the course. Visitors pay up to twice as much as Hong Kong residents.

passengers for pleasure cruises to the splendid nearby islands, beaches, and pristine scenery around Shelter and Rocky harbors. Smaller boats *(kaidos)* ferry people to the scattering of islands and island beaches in the inner harbor, or take them for tours around the harbor. Peer into the huge fish tanks outside the restaurants for a staggering variety of sea life. Choose your fish—ask the price first—then take it to a quayside restaurant to be cooked for you.

During your amble along the quay, you are likely to be offered a pleasure trip on a kaido. Charter one for an hour's jaunt around the inner harbor or take the regular services to the white sandy beach at **Half Moon (Hap Mun) Bay** on Sharp Island (Kiu Tsui Chau). Less frequent services also run to beaches on Pak Sha Chau (White Sand Island) and Cham Tau Chau (Pillow Island).

Farther west along the quay, behind a small Tin Hau temple off Yi Chun Street, is Sai Kung's **old town,** a maze of alleyways brimming with activity and Chinese herbalist stores, noodle shops, convenience stores selling Chinese goods, and small family homes. This is an excellent area to get a look at a traditional village way of life.

North of Town: Back on the waterfront, backtrack past Fuk Man Road along the waterfront promenade that runs north for about a half mile (0.8 km). The beach here is not a particularly good one for swimming (although this does not deter the crowds of people who flock in on Sundays), but you can rent sailboards or relax at one of the restaurants or bars that look out over the beach. Just to the west of the beach, at the waterside village of **Tai Wan,** it's possible to canoe around Inner Shelter Harbor.

Unfortunately, the fringes of Sai Kung Town are undergoing extensive development, which is likely to destroy much of what is left of the town's character and village atmosphere. High-rise residential towers are planned for the area north of town, while Hiram's Highway, the road that runs down from Clear Water Bay

Sai Kung Country Parks

🅰 Map p. 187

✉ Sai Kung Country Park Visitor Center, Pak Tam Chung

☎ 2792-7365

🕐 Closed Tues.

🚌 Bus: 94 from Sai Kung Town

Road into Sai Kung, has been widened and rerouted to accommodate the growth of the area.

Sai Kung Country Parks

Sai Kung peninsula has some of Hong Kong's finest and wildest countryside, and four parks. The area has long been an isolated part of Hong Kong, characterized by tall peaks, an exposed, convoluted coastline, and small remote Hakka villages—features that now draw many hikers to the area. It's a splendid place for walking, with well-marked and well-maintained trails. You will also find Hong Kong's best beaches here.

Pak Tam Chung is as far as you can go into the parks by private car, although public buses travel to Wong Shek Pier and, on weekends and public holidays, Hoi Ha. Taxis are also allowed to enter the park. Pak Tam Chung is the place most people begin their hikes, and it also marks the start of the 63-mile (100 km) **MacLehose Trail** (see p. 198). The village has a visitor center where you can pick up information on hiking routes.

The four parks comprise 25,950 acres (10,500 ha) of the peninsula; they are Sai Kung East, Sai Kung West, Hoi Ha Wan Marine Park, and Wan Tsai. The largest and most popular is **Sai Kung East,** which contains High Island Reservoir—one of Hong Kong's main water sources—and trails leading to outstanding viewpoints and glorious beaches.

From Pak Tam Chung, head east along the road into the park to where the road forks at the top and the reservoir begins. To reach the spot where the dam meets the South China Sea in awesome fashion, it's about a 5-mile (8 km) walk—but not a particularly strenuous one.

The road begins by winding up hills, with the expansive High Island Reservoir spread out below. Farther into the walk, at the first dam wall, there are views of sheer headlands plunging into the jagged shoreline and whaleback islands scattered out to sea. At the end of the walk, you pass over

EXPERIENCE: Hunting for Squid

The blue waters around the Sai Kung Peninsula fill with boats of all kinds on sunny days. Yachts filled with elite partiers cut huge wakes that splash over the sides of smaller sampans. You can hire boats for just about anything, but one of the most unique trips is to go hunting for squid and cuttlefish—the harbor's other resident cephalopod. Many private fishermen offer tours, but you can also opt for the tours provided by many of the restaurants. The tours happen day and night, last three hours, and cost around HK$500 per person. As the boats usually wait to fill up with passengers before they leave, it's best to come with a group of friends, and some food and drinks. The actual fishing involves a hook, a line, and a lot of patience. You dangle the baited line into the water, wait, then try to avoid any spraying ink. Afterward, many tour operators will cook the fresh catch for you right on the boat.

Tai Long Wan—Big Wave Bay—ranks as Hong Kong's best beach.

the second dam wall and down to its base at the reservoir's eastern end. Here, the dam's main wall towers behind you spectacularly as you look out to sea. From the eastern end of the dam wall, a track runs down over a hilly pass to **Long Ke Wan,** a horseshoe-shape bay with a wide, white, sandy beach.

Hong Kong's best beach, **Tai Long Wan,** is about a 40-minute walk from Pak Tam Au, farther into the country park on the road to Wong Shek Pier. The track, just off the main road, winds down through the cool, heavily forested Ngau Wu Tun hill past stunning panoramas of Long Harbor to the tiny deserted village of **Chek Keng,** one of a number in the area left abandoned. After Chek Keng, you climb along a concrete path up the Tai Mun Shan over-pass to Tai Long Au and views to the white sand and rumbling surf of Tai Long Wan (Big Wave Bay), before descending down to the beach. A small village just before the beach sells noodles, water,

and soft drinks. The return walk is about 6 miles (10 km).

A shorter 3-mile (5 km) hike through **Hoi Ha Wan Marine Park,** one of the few remaining areas in Hong Kong where coral can be found, takes you past small ravines and old rice paddy terraces, looking out across the Hoi Ha Bay.

From Hoi Ha village, head east along the beach to a coastal path that skirts Ho Ha Bay. The track leads across a neck of land to Wan Tsai and heads north past stands of paperback, acacia, and casuarina trees. At the bluff on the tip of the promontory, you see out to Mirs Bay and a couple of small islands marking the marine park's boundary. To the southeast, across the deeply indented Long Bay, the peninsula's highest point, Sharp Peak (1,535 feet/468 m), rears dramatically. Return to Hoi Ha along the track running down the promontory's eastern side.

A warning: Dogs, both stray and domestic, are sometimes found along country park trails.

A Drive Along the Sai Kung Peninsula

The drive starts from where Clear Water Bay Road, running northeast from Kowloon, meets Hiram's Highway and dips down into the town of Sai Kung. This winding, scenic route follows the coast and into Sai Kung Country Park. You can return to Kowloon via the hilly Sai Sha Road that cuts through countryside, villages, and the massive Ma On Shan New Town to Sha Tin.

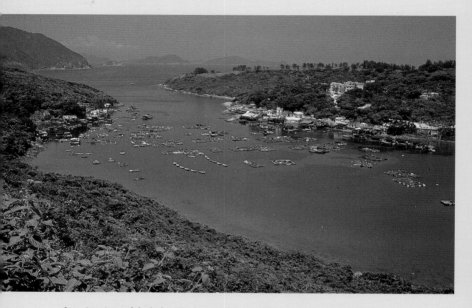

Stunning views of the lush, jagged coast of the Sai Kung Peninsula open up, with villages dotting the shoreline and islands scattering the channel beyond.

The green, looming 2,303-foot (702 m) peak of Ma On Shan, one of the highest in the New Territories, dominates the view as you turn left onto Hiram's Highway from Clear Water Bay Road. Notice the whitewashed villas and luxury developments built into the hills that edge the coast.

Hiram's Highway dips down to the coastal area of Sai Kung, and winds 1.2 miles (2 km) to the massive **Marina Cove ❶**, with its hundreds of villas wrapped around a boat marina. Continue on Hiram's Highway for another 1.2 miles (2 km) to the point where the road

NOT TO BE MISSED:

Sai Kung • Sai Kung Memorial • Wong Shek Pier

opens to views of the wide bay at **Pak Sha Wan ❷**, also called Hebe Haven. Dozens of bobbing pleasure craft shelter in the bay, which is almost totally enclosed by a narrow, curved peninsula. You can park here and sit on the deck of the Hebe Haven Yacht Club

(10½ Miles, Hiram's Hwy., tel 2719-8300) to enjoy a drink and bay views.

The highway winds its way past villages, wooded areas, and garden nurseries for another 1.8 miles (3 km) to the town of **Sai Kung ③** (see pp. 190–192), the main community in the area. Here, the road name changes to Po Tung Road for a short distance before becoming Tai Mong Tsai Road, and continues past the town about a half mile (0.8 km) to a small beach and seaside restaurants.

The road now hugs the contours of Inner Port Shelter, offering sea glimpses through the eucalyptus trees and grassy picnic areas that line the bay to the traffic circle at Shi Sha Road, which winds its way over the hills to the new

---

◭ See area map p. 155
▶ Hiram's Hwy. at Clear Water Bay Rd.
↔ 10.5 miles (17 km); 15.5 miles (25 km) including Wong Shek Pier
🕑 1.5 hours; 2 hours including Wong Shek Pier
▶ Wong Shek Pier

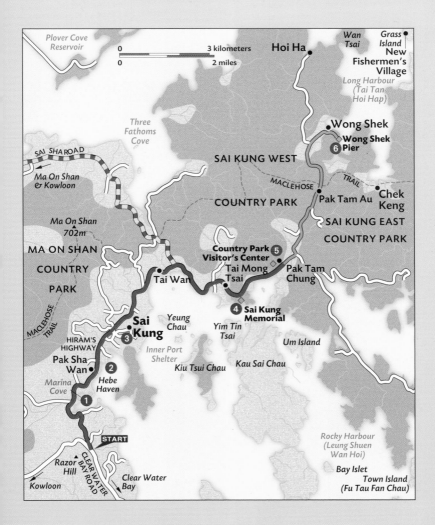

When It's Wet

Hong Kong's weather is fierce, unforgiving, and anything but subtle. During typhoon season, which is roughly May through November, the best driving advice for times when a storm is bearing down is to stay off the roads, or have someone else do the driving. If you must take the wheel, however, there are several precautions to heed.

Even in good weather, Hong Kong is notorious for its snarly traffic—traffic composed of notoriously bad drivers. Some seem to be manic; many appear to ignore other traffic all together. A major storm discourages most drivers

from taking to the roadways, but for the cars that brave the gusts and rain, keep a more than adequate distance. Don't count on observing turn signals; they are practically unheard of even in good weather. Slow down and keep out a sharp eye for flying debris, which ranges from leaves and branches to rooftops. Beware that the waves of intense rain that course across Hong Kong can reduce your visibility drastically. And avoid low-lying areas because flood waters rise quickly.

If a storm worsens, be prepared to seek shelter. If you need emergency help, dial 999.

town of Ma On Shan, near Sha Tin (see p. 176).

Past the traffic circle, views to the bay open up to the numerous islets of Inner Port Shelter and the larger islands of Sharp Island and Kau Sai Chau as the road dips, rises, and runs along the coast at the most scenic section along the route.

On one rise, about 3.5 miles (6 km) from Sai Kung, an obelisk overlooking the water at the **Sai Kung Memorial** ❹ pays tribute to the guerrillas and Sai Kung villagers who died during the Japanese occupation between 1941 and 1945.

A further 1.2 miles (2 km) brings you to the guarded entrance of Sai Kung Country Park at Pak Tam Chung (see p. 192). Park and head to the **Country Park Visitor Center** ❺ (Pak Tam Chung, Sai Kung, tel 2792-7365, closed Tues.), which houses a small but entertaining museum containing displays of coral found off the coast at Hoi Ha Wa Marine Park (see p. 193), geographic and topographic features of the park, typical park flora and fauna, and traditional village, fishing, and rural life in the area.

The only private cars allowed into the park are those that belong to the people who live there or their guests. But you can take a taxi, or, better still, catch the half-hourly No. 94 double-decker bus that slowly grinds its way

up the steep hills to the village of Pak Tam Au, before swooping down through forests and small villages to **Wong Shek Pier** ❻, at the southern end of Long Harbor. If you can, take the front seat on the top deck for the best views of the sheer peaks that dominate the park. The 5-mile (8 km) ride takes about 10 to 15 minutes.

You can rent sailboards and dinghies at the **Wong Shek Water Sports Center** (tel 2328-2311), take a walk along the waterfront, or relax at the picnic area on the water's edge.

If you want to return to Kowloon, you could take the alternate route along Sai Sha Road, which passes more villages and gives occasional sweeping panoramas of Three Fathoms Cove and Tolo Harbor, before coming to Ma On Shan. For those without their own transportation, the double-decker 96R runs along the whole route; the service runs Sundays at 15-minute intervals from Diamond Hill MTR. During weekdays, the 92 bus runs from Diamond Hill MTR as far as Sai Kung, where you can connect with the 94 bus, which serves Wong Shek Pier. Ferries also depart from Ma Liu Shui at the Chinese University of Hong Kong. From here, follow the expressway signs back to Kowloon.

Some can be a bit vicious but can be deterred with the threatening wave of a sizable stick, a useful aid when hiking.

Tap Mun Chau

Tap Mun Chau (Grass Island) guards the entrance to Long Harbor at the northeastern extremity of the Sai Kung Peninsula, where the narrow Tolo Channel runs into Mirs Bay and the nearby mainland China border. In the 1980s and early 1990s, it was a favorite dropping-off point for illegal immigrants arriving from the mainland, until Hong Kong's marine police got wise.

The island, with its busy fishing village, offers the agreeable combination of isolation and easy access. It is well worth visiting if you have the time. The best way to reach the island is via Wong Shek Pier, where the Tsui Wah Ferry Service (*www. traway.com.hk*) runs scheduled *kaidos,* with around six sailings during the week and double that number on weekends.

Private sampans at the pier, although they aren't cheap at around US$10 one-way, will make the 20-minute journey through the sheltered waters of Long Harbor to the island's pier, tiny village, and **Tin Hau temple.** The temple is notable for its well-crafted porcelain roof figurines and location. It's the last Tin Hau temple in Hong Kong before the open sea; fishermen traditionally visit these temples before sailing, to pray for a safe voyage (see Tin Hau, p. 94).

Tap Mun is named after the grassy and windswept hills that roll over the island. Plenty of trails crisscross these hills, making for pleasant walking. The northern half of the island is uninhabited and intensely quiet. Climb the track behind the village—there is a map board near the pier showing walking trails—to view the pounding surf on the island's east coast. The track then runs down to Tap Mun's only **beach** at Chung Wai, before

INSIDER TIP:

For great seafood, check out Tung Kee Seafood Restaurant in Sai Kung.

—IAN BAKER
National Geographic field researcher

climbing up and heading south to the **Balanced Rock,** a weird rock formation just off the island near its southeastern tip. It then continues around the southern tip of the island, past the newer houses of **New Fishermen's Village** and a Christian chapel, to the pier and main settlement.

There are a couple of restaurants in the village, and at press time, a small hostel was due to open its doors soon. Again, avoid visiting the island on Sundays, when crowds of people converge on it. The last ferry from the island leaves at 6 p.m. on weekends, but be sure to check the current schedule to confirm the correct times before you embark on your trip. ■

More Places to Visit in the New Territories

Chinese University of Hong Kong

The university's art museum houses an excellent collection of paintings and calligraphy by Guangdong artists from the Ming period to modern times, and artists from other regions from the Yuan, Ming, and Qing dynasties. There are also bronze seals dating from pre-Qing to modern times, and period collections of jade flower carvings, as well as other designs and ceramics.

🅜 Map p. 155 ✉ Ma Liu Sui ☎ 2609-7416 🚇 MTR East to Chinese University Station, then shuttle bus

Lam Tsuen Spirit Trees (Wishing Trees)

For many years, people tied bundles of colorful paper and an orange to either end of a red cord and launched it into one of two trees here—a bauhinia and a banyan—while making a wish. If the bundle caught a tree branch, then the wish would be granted. Anyone who managed to do it on the first attempt was considered a very fortunate person. According to legend, a fisherman was miraculously cured of illness by an earth god when he prayed at the trees, and since then they have been considered lucky. Unfortunately, disaster struck in 2005, when over-wishing caused a large branch on the main banyan tree to snap. Wishes now have to be tied to nearby wooden racks. You can buy these offerings for about HK$20. The trees are situated outside **Lam Tsuen Tin Hau Temple,** which was built in 1768. Inside there's a shrine dedicated to those killed in an inter-village incident in the 19th century.

🅜 Map p. 154 ✉ Lam Kam Rd., Lam Tseun, Tai Po 🚇 MTR East to Tai Po Market, then bus 64K

Lions Nature Education Center

Nestled in a pretty valley a few miles from Sai Kung, the center is a less grand version of the Kadoorie Farm & Botanical Garden (see p. 163). It was originally a government farm, but later developed into a center for conservation and education. Scattered among its 40 acres (16 ha) are a specimen orchard with more than 30 different types of fruit trees, herbal gardens, vegetable fields, a bamboo grove, and a fernery, along with ponds full of aquatic plants, an arboretum, and a nature trail. A series of halls contains an insectarium, a huge display of seashells collected from Hong Kong's coastline, a fishery exhibition highlighting Hong Kong's dwindling marine resources, exhibits featuring the life, methods, and tools of Hong Kong's minute farming community, and an explanation of the territories' country parks.

🅜 Map p. 155 ✉ Hiram's Hwy., Sai Kung ☎ 2792-2234 🕐 Closed Tues. 🚇 Bus 92 from Diamond Hill MTR

MacLehose Trail

This 62-mile (100 km) trail meanders over rugged ridges and through remote villages, skirting sandy beaches as it traverses eight New Territory country parks from Sai Kung in the east to Tuen Mun in the west. It climbs near the peaks of two of Hong Kong's highest mountains, Tai Mo Shan and Ma On Shan, along the way. The trail has ten sections, each graded by its degree of difficulty, some for serious hikers only, others relatively easy. The views along the entire route are

EXPERIENCE: Fortune-telling in Hong Kong

In keeping with the city's superstitious streak, many Hong Kongers remain firm believers in fortune-telling and look on a visit to a fortune-teller as no different from a check-up at the dentist or doctor.

Popular modes of fortune-telling include palm and face reading, as well as the reading of *chim* sticks, also known as fortune sticks. Like their western counterparts, Chinese fortune-tellers can delve into your love life, explore your career opportunities, or determine how many children you will

INSIDER TIP:

Visit the Kowloon street markets in the evening to have your fortune told—by palm reading, chim sticks, face reading, or blocks of carved wood.

—DANIELLE RIVERA
Hong Kong Tourism Board

have. However, the reason that Hong Kongers visit them is usually associated with prosperity—whether to ask for auspicious dates on which to open a business or figure out which numbers they should pick for the lottery.

Wong Tai Sin Temple is famed for its fortune-tellers, especially those reading chim sticks, which you will hear reverberating around the complex. You can buy the sticks from a small kiosk at the side

of the plaza. Cast them on the ground in front of the temple, write the numbers down on the paper supplied, and take it to the adjacent oblation and fortune-telling arcade for a reading. The arcade is packed with fortune-tellers, many of whom speak English and some of whom even have air-conditioning.

One of the best locations

to have your palm or your head read is the **Temple Street Night Market.** Here you will find a host of roadside tents—many of them boasting about which celebrities they have put on the path to success— offering a selection of readings, some of them in English. The fortune-tellers are at the end of the market toward the Tin Hau temple.

Bamboo containers of *chim* (flattened numbered sticks) are used when seeking advice from fortune-tellers.

Hong Kong's longest hike, the 62-mile MacLehose Trail traverses the length of the New Territories.

outstanding. Every November, an arduous team race called the Trailwalker takes place. Thousands take part, with some superfit teams taking only 13 hours to complete the journey.
www.afcd.gov.hk ☎ 823

Sheung Yiu Village

The fortified village of Sheung Yiu was built about 150 years ago by a Hakka clan named Wong. Now it has been partly restored to serve as a museum, containing Hakka furniture and a collection of cooking and farming implements. The village lies a pleasant 20-minute walk along the Pak Tam Chung Nature Trail from the gates of Sai Kung East Country Park (see pp. 192–193). Follow the signs from the Country Park Visitor Center.
🅰 Map p. 155 ✉ Sheung Yiu Village, Pak Tam Chung Nature Trail ☎ 2792-6365 🕒 Closed Tues. 🚌 Bus 94 from Sai Kung

Tai Fu Tai Mansion

Tai Fu Tai Mansion is an excellent, fully restored example of a traditional Chinese dwelling of the scholar-gentry class, built by Man clan member Man Chung-luen around 1865. The elegant facade is built on a granite-block base with a green brick wall, and is richly embellished by ceramic figurines and moldings on the niches. Above the framed entrance is a red wood board inscribed with gilded Chinese characters heralding the name of the mansion. A boat-prow ridge on the roof of the entrance hall has more moldings and exquisite ceramic figurines.

Inside, two side chambers frame the central courtyard, with three bedrooms at the front of the dwelling. Various other rooms are set against the mansion's outside wall, with the main hall at the rear of the courtyard. The rooms are decorated with plaster moldings, woodcarvings, and motifs on the walls.

The main hall retains some of its original black wood furniture, and under its eaves are two "honorific" boards engraved with gilded Chinese and Manchu characters. Portraits of Man Chung-luen and other clan members can be found at the back of the hall.

Nearby, the **Man Fung Lung Ancestral Hall,** thought to have been built at the end of the 17th century, has also been restored. While not nearly as ornate as Tai Fu Tai Mansion, it's worth a look for its imposing stone columns and beautifully carved supporting brackets.
🅰 Map p. 154 ✉ Tung Chan Wai, San Tin 🕒 Closed Tues. 🚇 MTR East to Yuen Long, then bus 76K

Rural charm, bustling waterfronts, glorious seafood, deserted beaches, and, in many cases, splendid isolation

Outlying Islands

At Pak Tai Temple, Cheun Chau

Outlying Islands

Hong Kong's waters are littered with 234 islands—from tiny scraps of rock jutting out of the sea to substantial slices of land taking in mountain peaks, long, lonely beaches, and communities of fishermen and farmers. The islands maintain a more isolated and rural feel than the New Territories, and pockets of a traditional way of life can still be found. Spend at least a day on one of the outlying islands.

Cheung Chau's bustling harbor: The island relies on fishing for much of its income.

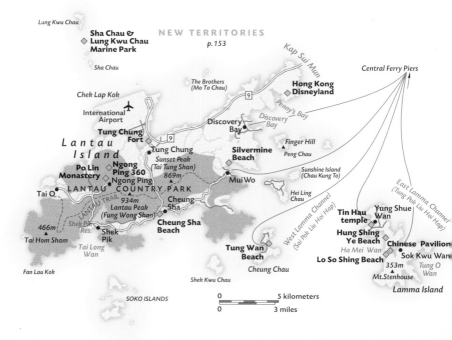

NOT TO BE MISSED:

About 100,000 people live in the outlying islands, less than 2 percent of the whole population of Hong Kong. During the past three decades, many people have abandoned their island homes and drifted across the water to the main urban areas of Hong Kong seeking their fortunes. Left behind are the older people, some of whom still cling to traditional ways. Ironically, a number of bedroom communities have sprung up on the bigger and more central islands for people seeking relief from Hong Kong's clamorous ways, including many Western expatriates.

Hong Kong's major islands are less than an hour away from Central District's Outlying Islands Ferry Terminal, an easy jaunt which is made more convenient by regular ferry services. On weekends and holidays, people pile onto these ferries and head for the beaches and seafood restaurants lining the quaysides of villages, or take to the innumerable hiking trails that ramble over hills and along sparkling coastlines.

One of the most popular outlying islands is Lantau with its precipitous peaks, peaceful hillside monasteries, fishing villages, and string of white-sand beaches. At Chek Lap Kok, on the north shore, stands Hong Kong's massive international airport and the latest of its new towns, Tung Chung. Surprisingly, these developments have had little effect on other areas of the island. Near the airport, at the northeastern tip, a huge Disneyland theme park opened in 2005.

People visit Cheung Chau for its crowded harbor, bustling waterfront, watersports, and easy hiking. Lamma, on which there are no cars, is favored for its seafood restaurants, splendid beaches, relaxed atmosphere, and great hiking.

Few people venture to the other outlying islands because of the time and effort involved to get there. If you can put up with a little legwork and irregular ferry schedules, however, they are worth the visit. A trip on the weekend to isolated Ping Chau in Mirs Bay in the northeastern New Territories carries with it a splendid ferry ride through the Tolo Channel, while windswept Tap Mun Chau (see p. 197) offers some wonderful solitude during the action-packed weekdays in Hong Kong. ∎

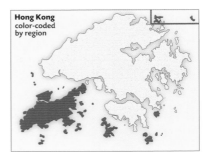

Lamma

Lamma is the closest of the big outlying islands to Hong Kong Island and the third biggest after Lantau and Hong Kong Island itself. This peaceful community of fishermen, farmers, and Western expatriates carries a distinct rural ambience. With villas and apartments clinging to green hills and overlooking the sea and waterfront restaurants, it almost conjures up a Mediterranean feel. There are frequent ferries to Lamma, a mere 30 minutes away.

Sok Kwu Wan is one of two villages on the delightfully rural and scenic Lamma.

Lamma

🗺 Map p. 202

☎ Hong Kong and Kowloon Ferry: 2815-6063

🚢 Ferry: Outlying Islands Ferry Pier 4, Central District, Hong Kong Island

www.hkff.com.hk

Yung Shue Wan, at the northern end of Lamma, is one of only two small villages on the island and the ferry gateway to the island. It's home to a large number of expatriates who prefer the rustic surroundings and cheaper rents to the noise, crowds, and expense of Hong Kong Island.

You can easily walk from Yung Shue Wan to the second village of **Sok Kwu Wan** along a well-marked concrete path. The 1.5-mile (2.4 km) trail, which opens up to fantastic views along some sections, can be walked in about 75 minutes. From Sok Kwu Wan, ferries run back to the Outlying Islands Ferry Pier in Central District

on Hong Kong Island.

Yung Shue Wan sits at the edge of a small bay, with houses spilling along its lowlands and up to the surrounding hills. The village's popularity with both expats and weekend tourists has led to an increasing number of bars and restaurants along the lone main street, ranging from snack bars to sophisticated cafés. Yet it has retained its charm and the squat buildings, lack of cars, and seaside location attract those who want to escape Hong Kong's urban chaos. It takes only a few minutes to walk through the village. A side path just past the main intersection takes you to a hundred-year-old **Tin Hau**

temple, dedicated to the Queen of Heaven and guardian of fishermen (see sidebar p. 94). Two stone lions guard the entrance, and inside are images of the veiled Tin Hau, complete with bridal headdress.

On the village's outskirts take the concrete path past fields of tall grass, banana groves, acacia trees, and brightly painted homes to **Hung Shing Ye Beach** (no shark nets). It's a pleasant stretch of sand, but you'll have to put up with the looming presence of the chimneys of Lamma's giant power plant.

At the beach, Lamma's highest peak, 1,076-foot (353 m) Mount Stenhouse, rears to the south. The path then leads north along bare hills to a tile-roofed **Chinese pavilion,** where you can pause to take in the fabulous views. On weekends and holidays, the coast is dotted with pleasure boats.

Down the road, Sok Kwu Wan comes into view over the hills. It sits on a fjordlike inlet clustered with fish farms. The scarred hills of an abandoned quarry across the bay

INSIDER TIP:

Lamma Island is free of cars. It offers great hiking and biking trails, plus renowned seafood restaurants and new age eateries.

—IAN BAKER
National Geographic field researcher

from the village dampen the view, but the vegetation is growing back. The trail then drops to delightful **Lo So Shing Beach**—nestled in a cove just before the village.

Sok Kwu Wan nuzzles the bay at the foot of a sheer hill. The colorful bay brims with pleasure craft and fishing boats dropping off their catch to fill the bubbling fish tanks outside the seafood restaurants lining the **quayside.** Take a seat along with the groups of gregarious diners for a seafood meal before hopping on a ferry back to Hong Kong Island. ∎

Typhoons

During the May to November typhoon season, Hong Kong is usually skirted by a couple of typhoons or tropical cyclones. Typhoons bring severe rainstorms and strong winds, which can affect business and public transportation. Although these storms' danger shouldn't be underestimated, Hong Kong is well prepared and quickly returns to normalcy.

A warning system alerts the public of impending typhoons. Warning Number 1 (the letter T) means a typhoon is within 500 miles (800 km) of Hong Kong. This is followed by Number 3 (an upside-down T), which means strong winds between

25 to 38 mph (41–62 kph) are blowing or expected. Next is Number 8 (a triangle), which means gale force winds between 39 to 73 mph (63–117 kph) are blowing or expected—businesses close and ferry service and public transportation are suspended. Number 9 (double triangles) means winds are increasing and a direct hit is imminent. Number 10 (a cross) is a direct hit, and winds are now above 73 mph (118 kph). All interior doors should be closed; you should shelter away from windows. Warnings are posted on Hong Kong radio and TV (in the right hand-corner) and in many buildings' lobbies.

Chinese White Dolphins

When construction work began in the waters off Chek Lap Kok to create the enormous new international airport in the early 1990s, Hong Kong rediscovered one of its lost natural treasures, the Chinese white dolphin, also known as the Indo-Pacific humpback dolphin or, more popularly, the pink dolphin.

Pollution and boat traffic threaten the estimated 200 Chinese white dolphins living at the mouth of the Pearl River Estuary near Lantau Island.

The creatures make their homes along coastlines, often at river mouths, or near mangrove forests. They are one of 80 cetacean species of dolphin that are found in small populations as far apart as Australia, South Africa, and along the Chinese coast up to the Yangtze River. Mention of them has been found in Chinese literature dating back to the Tang dynasty (618–907).

Chinese white dolphins (Sousa chinensis) are unique in color. Almost black at birth, maturing dolphins turn a light gray, then eventually change to their distinctive pale pink color.

They grow to about 10 feet (3 m) and can live for up to 40 years. Although young males tend to stray from their groups, scientists say the dolphins are territorial. Therefore, they are very unlikely to leave their habitat, which puts them at great risk of extinction.

Marine scientists in Hong Kong estimate the number of Chinese white dolphins living in the Pearl River Delta, whose brackish waters provide an ideal environment for them, at about 1,000, with between 100 and 200 living in Hong Kong waters, mainly in the waters north of Lantau Island.

The plight of these dolphins captured public attention during the construction of the airport, a project that involved flattening the island of Chek Lap Kok near Lantau and reclaiming a large amount of land around it. Land reclamation during this project destroyed much of the dolphins' inshore feeding areas, while boat traffic continues to cause underwater disturbance, injury, and death. Water pollution—mainly sewage from Hong Kong and chemicals from Pearl River tributaries—and overfishing have added to their troubles.

The storm of media attention sparked scientific studies examining the dolphins and their habitat and put pressure on authorities, which eventually led to serious attempts to preserve them and create safer habitats. The Hong Kong government created artificial reefs to attract fish to feed the dolphins, established a 4.5-square-mile (12 sq km) marine park, and put restrictions on land reclamation and other public works in areas where they are seen.

Dolphin-watching is becoming an increasingly popular pastime in Hong Kong, where they are often spotted in the waters near the airport. One company, **Hong Kong Dolphin-watch** (see p. 132), organizes regular dolphin-watching trips (the company will take you out again free of charge if none are seen). ■

EXPERIENCE: Helping Hong Kong's Wildlife

It comes as no surprise that the waters surrounding Hong Kong, a city with unparalleled urban growth, are filled with threatened species. Development is not the only villain, the local wildlife also suffer from polluted waters and overfishing. Due to these factors, the once numerous manta rays are now absent, reef sharks are on the verge of extinction, and good luck finding the green turtle, which hasn't been seen in over four years. Luckily, activists have teamed up with the local government to combat these problems, resulting in many great environmental groups that are always in search of a helping hand.

The **Ocean Park Conservation Foundation Hong Kong** (tel 2553-5840, www.opcf.org.hk/eng) was established in 2005 when the Ocean Park Conservation Foundation and the Hong Kong Society for Panda Conservation joined together. Based in Ocean Park, the foundation offers volunteer positions. The application form can be downloaded from their website.

Hong Kong Dolphin Conservation Society (www.hkdcs.org) was founded in 2003 to spread information and awareness about the dangers posed toward Hong Kong's dolphins, porpoises, and whales. You can become a member of the society by paying $100HK. This secures you a dolphin badge, a newsletter, discounts, and the ability to partake in HKDCS activities. Once a member, you can volunteer to help in the society's various undertakings.

Greenpeace China is based in Hong Kong. This group of activists is always in the news for their aggressive stance on environmental issues. They are always looking for volunteers. Catch up with them at: 8/F, Pacific Plaza, 410–418 Des Voeux Road West, Hong Kong, tel 2854- 8300, www.green peace.org/china/en.

Finally, one cannot overlook the **World Wildlife Fund Hong Kong.** Active all over the world, they have been in Hong Kong since 1981, with five offices— Wanchai, Tai Po, Central, Mai Po, and Hoi Ha Wan—and nine volunteer committees. Visit www.wwf.org/hk/eng to download a volunteer form, or call 2526-1011. If you prefer to help from your computer, go to www.panda.org to join the WWF Passport program, which specializes on online activism.

Lantau

Lantau, the largest of Hong Kong's islands, at twice the size of Hong Kong Island, was little touched by development until the completion of the international airport on its northeastern coast in 1998. Its size has allowed it to absorb this massive project and, on the whole, still preserve a peaceful, bucolic atmosphere.

The fishing village of Tai O, on Lantau's western tip, features houses built on stilts in the water.

Lantau
- Map p. 202
- Ferry: Outlying Islands Ferry Pier 6, Central District, Hong Kong Island

wwnwff.com.hk

Ngong Ping 360
- Map p. 202
- Tung Chung, Lantau
- $$
- MTR to Tung Chung

www.np360.com.hk

The island's main tourist draws are the massive outdoor Buddha statue at Po Lin Monastery, Hong Kong Disneyland, and the spectacular Ngong Ping Cable Car. A 50-minute boat ride from the Outlying Islands Ferry Pier in Central District on Hong Kong Island brings you to **Mui Wo** (also called Silvermine Bay for the silver mines that once skirted the settlement). It lies at the edge of a deep bay carved out of the southeast coast. The village's slightly unkempt appearance is improved by scenic views to the island's rugged interior and a well-tended, generous sweep of sand at **Silvermine Beach,** popular with day-trippers during the summer.

Mui Wo is the starting point for the 44-mile-long (70 km) **Lantau Trail,** which is divided into 12 sections of varying degrees of difficulty. Although some sections require a lot of steep climbing, views along the trail are endlessly spectacular, and camping is allowed.

From the ferry pier at Mui Wo, buses regularly head off beyond the bay along South Lantau Road and the southern coastline, passing the village houses, restaurants, and vacation apartments that line the eastern sections of the long, narrow stretch of sand at **Cheung Sha Beach.**

Midway, Tung Chung Road cuts north across the island toward Tung Chung, Hong Kong's latest new town, opposite the airport at Chek Lap Kok. The town's major attraction is the **Ngong Ping Cable Car,** which offers breathtaking vistas over the South China Sea and Lantau's rolling mountains. The ride takes visitors from Tung Chung town center up to **Ngong Ping Village** (see p. 211). The Po Lin Monastery (see p. 210) and seated Buddha are easily accessible from here.

About a mile (1.6 km) beyond Tung Chung is **Tung Chung Fort.** Built in 1832, it is enclosed by a granite block wall, its three arched entrances engraved with Chinese character inscriptions. The six muzzle-loading cannon on the fort's ramparts once pointed out over the sea, ready to fire at marauding pirates.

Continue along South Lantau Road as it cuts inland, skirting Shek Pik Reservoir, passing the road to Po Lin Monastery and its gigantic Tian Tan Buddha, before winding its way down to the stilt houses perched over a tidal creek at the fishing village of **Tai O.** The village, partly built on Lantau Island and connected to a tiny island by a 50-foot (15 m) bridge, was once Lantau's biggest; its Tanka boat people make a living from fishing and trading salt with China. On holidays and occasional weekends, you might see the rope-tow ferry, once the only way to cross the small canal.

Despite the construction of concrete homes, the village manages to retain some of its ramshackle charm, not to mention the powerful odors of its fish-processing industry. You can bargain for a short *kaido* (small motorboat) trip along the canal for a closer look at the rickety stilt houses, and on to the harbor, dotted with houseboats and junks.

In contrast, on the east coast of Lantau is **Discovery Bay,** commonly referred to as DB or

INSIDER TIP:

See the world's largest Buddha at Po Lin Monastery. Enjoy the wonderful vegetarian fare.

—TIFFANY TRENT
National Geographic contributor

Disco Bay, a modern, planned bedroom community that successfully manages to expunge any feeling of being in Asia. Complete with marina, golf course, restaurants, and beach (the sand had to be shipped in), it is more interesting for its concept than anything else. Residents riding around in whirring golf buggies give it a slightly surreal atmosphere. High-speed ferries next to the Star Ferry Pier in Central District whisk residents and visitors to Discovery Bay in about 20 minutes.

North of Discovery Bay is

Po Lin Monastery
- 🗺 Map p. 202
- ✉ Lantau Island
- 💲 $
- 🚢 Ferry to Mui Wo, Lantau, then bus 2 from Mui Wo or Ngong Ping Cable Car

Penny's Bay, the site of the huge Disneyland theme park that opened in 2005 (see below).

Po Lin Monastery

The giant bronze Buddha statue at Po Lin ("precious lotus") Monastery—the biggest seated, outdoor image of its kind in the world—is Lantau's No. 1 attraction. Despite the crowds that

INSIDER TIP:

My wife and I started smiling as soon as we got on the special Hong Kong Disneyland subway shuttle, with mouse-ear windows, and never stopped enjoying ourselves.

—JAY PASACHOFF
National Geographic field researcher

flock here and the often carnival atmosphere, it's difficult not to be impressed by the grandeur of the place.

Before the 85-foot (26 m) Tian Tan Buddha statue was built at the end of the 1980s, Po Lin Monastery was a peaceful and serene religious retreat sitting in splendid isolation high up on the Ngong Ping plateau in the shadow of the towering Lantau peak. When it was completed, the number of visitors were naturally restricted by the narrow roads up the mountain.

The Buddha image, cast in 202 pieces at a factory in Nanjing, cost more than HK$60 million and took three years to build. It sits

on a hill above the monastery, at the end of a steep stairway. On the large platform encircling the statue are six bronze bodhisattva statues, each of them offering gifts to the Buddha.

The monastery grounds are about 150 yards (140 m) away from the steps leading to the big Buddha. The main temple holds finely carved gilded images of the historical Buddha, Shakyamuni, flanked by the Healing Buddha on the right and Amitabha on the left. The building is riotously ornate, filled with carved timber features, swirling colorful frescoes running above the doorways and windows, and tiered bulb-shaped lanterns dangling from the high, beamed ceilings.

To the left of the main temple are large dining rooms where you can enjoy a vegetarian meal *(purchase meal tickets from a booth at foot of steps to the big Buddha)*. Avoid weekends, especially Sundays, when it's crowded.

Hong Kong Disneyland

Hong Kong Disneyland is an American theme park with Chinese characteristics. The compact park, which was built on reclaimed land near Hong Kong Airport and opened in September 2005, contains several iconic Disney attractions, but concessions have been made, especially regarding Chinese superstitions (e.g., no clocks on Main Street, U.S.A.) and food, which is distinctly Asian.

Those looking for the California Disneyland experience

or even the Paris version are likely to be disappointed, because the park falls in some respects short of its sister sites in rides and attractions. That said, the park offers much for younger children and is slowly adding more attractions.

Inside the main gate you'll come to **Main Street, U.S.A.,** with shops—their shelves clogged with fluffy toys and other souvenirs—as well as cafés, restaurants, and an information center at the City Hall on Town Square. At the center, you can make dining reservations, exchange currency, leave messages, and obtain park maps. A trip on the **Hong Kong Disneyland Railroad,** which circles the park from Main Street, is a good way to become familiar with the park's attractions and layout.

Watery rides in **Adventure-land** take you down Jungle Rivers and to Tarzan's Island and Treehouse by raft. **Fantasyland** is home to the iconic Sleeping Beauty's Castle, as well as Mickey's PhilharMagic movie theater, which features a huge 3-D screen showing scenes from classics such as the "Lion King" and "The Little Mermaid" with added special effects. Recently opened is the famed "It's a Small World" attraction, which takes guests on a boat ride through a world of dancing, singing dolls. Unlike the original, it also includes many Disney characters in its cast.

The park's best area may be **Tomorrowland,** featuring the only adrenaline rush ride—the indoor roller-coaster Space Mountain—and the interactive laser game Buzz Light Year Astro Blasters.

There are two hotels adjoining the park—Hong Kong Disneyland Hotel, with its over-the-top "Victorian elegance," and the glitzy, enormous Disney's Hollywood Hotel (see p. 256).

Ngong Ping

The Hong Kong Tourism Board's blockbuster attraction, Ngong Ping 360, opened in 2007. **Ngong Ping Cable Car** links Tung Chung town center and a specially constructed **Ngong Ping Village.** The attraction's main draw is the panoramic views of Lantau and the South China Sea from the 4-mile (6 km) car ride. Ngong Ping Village is a "specially themed cultural village" that basically translates as

a theme park interpretation of a Chinese village, with a teahouse, theater, and overpriced concessions. Though the attraction has been plagued by problems since launching, such as weather closures and technical faults, it seems to have established itself as a major attraction. ■

Hong Kong Disneyland

- Map p. 202
- Penny's Bay, Lantau Island
- 1-830-830
- $$$$$
- MTR: Disneyland Resort Station

Flamboyant buildings and the world's largest seated Buddha image await visitors to Po Lin.

Cheung Chau Walk

Lying 7.5 miles (12 km) southwest of Hong Kong Island, the fishing island of Cheung Chau measures just under a square mile (2.4 sq km). Because of its small size and relatively tame topography, most of Cheung Chau's attractions can be visited on foot in less than two hours. This walk takes you through the bustling heart of the island to tranquil temples and appealing countryside.

A maze of lanes wanders behind Cheung Chau's waterfront promenade.

NOT TO BE MISSED:

Praya Street • Pak Tai Temple • Tin Hau temple

Start on busy **Praya Street,** facing the harbor, and head north to the end of the wall of apartments, shops, and restaurants. To the right, beyond a playing field, is the flamboyantly decorated **Pak Tai Temple ❶**. It features vibrantly colored glazed dragons and other figurines crowning its roof, carved granite pillars, gilded-wood altar carvings, and wall murals. Cheung Chau's Bun Festival is celebrated here each May.

Follow Pak She Street to the right past a mishmash of houses and shops until it crosses Kwok Man Street and becomes **San Hing Street.** Vegetable stalls, herbal medicine and incense shops, and clothes and bag outlets spill onto the lane, while on the balconies above laundry airs in the breeze. Life here is lived at close quarters, but it is surprisingly peaceful.

The lane opens into a small square; turn left and take Tung Wan Road to **Tung Wan Beach ❷**, a generous sweep of sand with a verdant headland at its southeastern corner. Follow the Cheung Chau Beach Road left along the beachfront for a short distance to a small park where an abstract sculpture honors Cheung Chau's most famous daughter, Lee Lai-san, who won Hong Kong's first-ever gold medal, for mistral sailing, at the Atlanta Olympics in 1996.

Back at the square, walk south on Hing Lung Main Street, which abruptly changes into Tai San Street. It is sometimes so narrow that shop awnings on either side of the lane almost touch. A block before it ends, turn right and follow the first alley on the left to its end. Go up some steps and to the right and you will see the **Hung Shing Temple ❸**, built to honor a sea god, overlooking the harbor. Fairy lights flicker over the main altar's wood flower carvings.

Take Tai Hing Tai Road left and continue

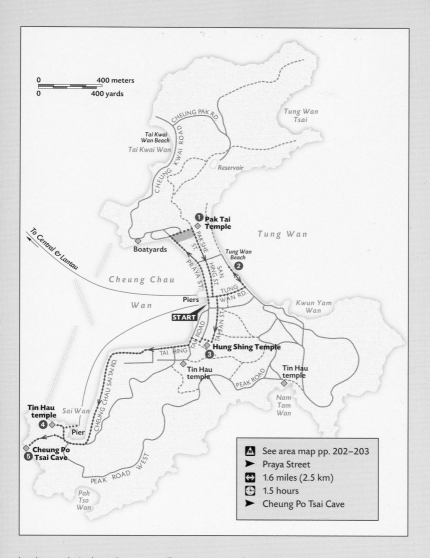

0 |———————| 400 meters
0 |———————| 400 yards

To Central & Lantau

CHEUNG PAK RD

Tai Kwai Wan Beach
Tai Kwai Wan

Tung Wan Tsai

CHEUNG KWAI ROAD

Reservoir

❶ **Pak Tai Temple**

PAK SHE ST

Boatyards

Tung Wan Beach
❷

SAN HING ST

Tung Wan

Cheung Chau
Wan

PRAYA ST

Piers

START

TUNG WAN RD

Kwun Yam Wan

TAI SAN ST

TAI ROAD

TAI HING

Hung Shing Temple
❸

Tin Hau temple

PEAK ROAD

Tin Hau temple

CHEUNG CHAU SAI TAI RD

Tin Hau temple
❹
Sai Wan
Pier

Nam Tam Wan

❺ **Cheung Po Tsai Cave**

PEAK ROAD WEST

Pak Tso Wan

See area map pp. 202–203
► Praya Street
↔ 1.6 miles (2.5 km)
🕐 1.5 hours
► Cheung Po Tsai Cave

---

heading south. As the path curves, you'll see magnificent views of the hundreds of junks in the harbor, backed by the green peaks of nearby Lantau Island. A little farther on the left, colorful figurines decorate the roof at a Tin Hau temple.

Tai San Street now hugs the coastline and becomes Cheung Chau Sai Tai Road. At its end, a wooded path to the right winds up a hill to another tranquil **Tin Hau temple ❹**.

Follow the path back to a short trail leading to the **Cheung Po Tsai Cave ❺**, where legend says the notorious pirate once stored his booty. Cheung Po Tsai is said to have commanded a fleet of more than 700 vessels in the early 1800s before being defeated by the combined navies of China, Britain, and Portugal. The Sao Feng character in the third installment of *Pirates of the Caribbean* is supposedly based on him. Return along the trail to Sai Wan Bay near the Tin Hau temple, where you can head back to Cheung Chau village by taking a *kaido* from its pier. The boat trip gives close-up views of the junks.

More Outlying Islands to Visit

Kat O Chau

This isolated, ungainly island spreads between Plover Cove and the Chinese border in the northeastern New Territories. Its small population spends its time catching, drying, and selling fish. Steep cliffs hold caves where pirates once hid their booty. The temples and shrines near where boats arrive at Kat O Wan ("crooked island") include a well-preserved **Tin Hau temple.** Ferries are extremely irregular. If you get stuck, negotiate a journey back to the mainland with a local *kaido* owner.

⚠ Map p. 203 🚆 MTR East: Sheung Shui, bus 78K to Shau Tau Kok Ferry Pier, then boat

Peng Chau

Horseshoe-shape Peng Chau lies just to the east of Lantau. Its 8,000 people are jammed into just over half a square mile (1.3 sq km) of land. Its narrow lanes packed with homes, shops, and restaurants, give it a lively Chinese character. Short walks include a climb to the island's highest point—**Finger Hill** at 311 feet (95m)—and some excellent views; check the pier's map board. An 18th-century **Tin Hau temple** stands on Wing On Street facing the ferry pier. Day-trippers head here on weekends to visit the seafood restaurants, but the beach at Tung Wan is not particularly inviting.

⚠ Map p. 202 ⛴ Ferry: Outlying Islands Ferry Pier, Central District, Hong Kong Island

Ping Chau

Set in Mirs Bay in the northeastern New Territories near the Chinese border, Ping Chau is part of Plover Cove Country Park (see pp. 184–185). Though most of its former residents are long gone, the island is popular for its pretty beaches and a loop trail that follows the coastline past strange rock formations and a couple of waterfalls. It's worth taking the trip to Ping Chau for the ferry ride, which passes through the wide, fjordlike Tolo Channel and on to Mirs Bay, stopping at isolated villages along the way. You can stay at the campground at **Kang Lau Shek** ("drum tower rock") on the island's southeastern tip or rent a room in Chau Tau, near the ferry pier.

⚠ Map p. 203 🚆 MTR East: University Station, then ferry from Mai Liu Shui Ferry Pier Sat., Sun., & public holidays

Po Toi

Po Toi is a group of islands lying on the southern fringes of Hong Kong, about 3 miles (5 km) southeast of Stanley on the south of Hong Kong Island. The rugged main island, Po Toi, is threaded with hiking trails leading to interesting landmarks and fantastic sea and island views from the top of the hills. Only a handful of people live there, running a few seafood restaurants overlooking Tai Wan Bay, near the island's only settlement.

At the ferry pier take the path south through **Wan Tsai,** past vegetable gardens and banana trees to some steps on the right. Head down these to a series of prehistoric rock carvings of stylized animals and fish and interlocking spirals. Continue along the path to the island's southern tip and the weird rock formations. The island is very popular with day-trippers on Sundays.

⚠ Map p. 203 🚤 *Kaidos* (small motorboats) from St. Stephen's Beach, Stanley, Sun., & public holidays. From Aberdeen on Tues., Thurs., Sat., Sun., & public holidays

Tung Lung Chau

This rocky island sits just off the Clear Water Bay Peninsula's (see pp. 186–190) southern tip, at the eastern entrance to Victoria Harbour. Follow the path from the small hamlet at the ferry pier to the well-preserved **Tung Lung Fort** on a headland in the island's northeast. The walk takes about an hour and offers spectacular coastal views. A path in the opposite direction takes you to a prehistoric rock carving believed to be the image of a dragon. ⚠ Map p. 203 🚆 MTR: Sai Wan Ho, then ferry from Sai Wan Ho Ferry Pier Sat., Sun., & public holidays

From the colonial charm of Macau to the frantic pace of modern China's Guangzhou and still within easy reach

Excursions

Ma Kok Mui Temple, Macau

Macau

Up until December 20, 1999, when the Portuguese handed it back to China, Macau was Asia's oldest European enclave. The city's recent gambling fever is evident in the huge casinos, but away from the gambling glitz, Macau has retained its Mediterranean charm. Lying just an hour away from Hong Kong, it makes an appealing day trip.

Sparkling new casinos and hotels are overtaking Macau.

Portugal was the first European nation to try its hand at trading with China. Persistence—and more than the odd threat—earned it a little piece of Chinese land on a tiny peninsula at the mouth of the Pearl River Delta in 1557. Over the centuries, Macau's influence waned as other European nations jostled for lucrative trade privileges. By the time Hong Kong was colonized in 1841, Macau was in terminal decline.

In 1966, China's Cultural Revolution was fomented in the enclave and rioting and killings ensued. Portugal threatened to abandon Macau because of the violence and, fearing a loss of trade, China backed down. Again in 1974, when Portugal began divesting itself of its colonies, it offered to hand Macau back to China, but this was rejected. It wasn't till after China reached a handover agreement with Britain in the 1984 Joint Declaration that a similar arrangement was made with Portugal. Under the 1987 Sino-Portuguese Pact, Macau, like Hong Kong, would enjoy a high degree of autonomy for 50 years beyond its handover.

NOT TO BE MISSED:

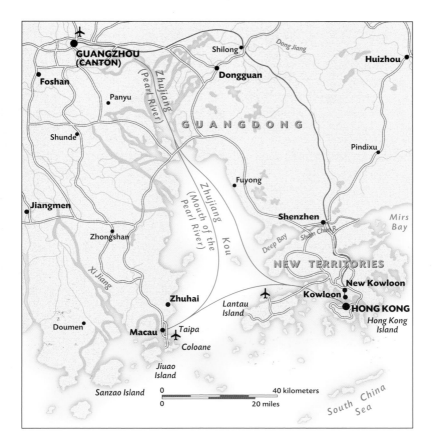

In 2001, Beijing ended billionaire Stanley Ho's monopoly on gambling in the city, before which, Macau's slightly forebidding casinos only attracted the dedicated gambler. Since then, a number of big-name casinos from Las Vegas have opened their doors and revolutionized both the industry and the island. These new mega-casinos, including the Sands Macao and the Venetian on the Cotai Strip, the world's biggest, have brought with them dining, shopping, and floor shows. In fact, Macau has now overtaken the Vegas strip in terms of annual gaming revenue.

The casinos have caused Macau's visitor numbers to skyrocket, with day-trippers from the mainland and Hong Kong helping the city record 27 million arrivals in 2007, just behind neighbor Hong Kong.

In an attempt to cash in on this boom, Macau built the massive Fisherman's Wharf shopping and entertainment complex in the outer harbor. Period themed European streets and larger constructions, such as an erupting volcano and a Roman amphitheater, are home to a mix of bars, restaurants, and shops.

However, aside from the rampant commercialism of the casinos, Macau has been left with a wealth of colonial heritage, making strolling a pleasure. In 2005, this compact part of the city was awarded a World Heritage site listing.

Getting to Macau is simple. Comfortable and fast Jetfoils leave the Macau Ferry Terminal in Hong Kong's Western District every 15 minutes. You will need to pass through immigration in both Hong Kong and Macau, though, so bring your passport. ■

Macau Peninsula

Macau has never experienced the spurts of unbridled growth characteristic of Hong Kong, a situation that is manifest in both its architecture and attitude. Its winding cobblestone streets, pastel-colored colonial buildings, restored early 20th-century mansions, baroque churches, fine parks, and slow pace effect a pleasant, leisurely atmosphere, evoking a Mediterranean air, a world away from the manic pace of Hong Kong.

The ramparts of Fortaleza do Monte overlook Macau.

Macau Grand Prix Museum & Macau Wine Museum

- **Map p. 224**
- Tourism Activities Center, 431 Rua Luis Gonzaga
- 8798-4108
- Closed Tues.
- $
- Bus: 1A, 3, 3A, 10A, 10B, 12, 17, 23, 28A, 28B, 28C, 32

Peninsula East: A ten-minute walk from the Macau Ferry Terminal is the Tourism Activities Center in Rua Luis Gonzaga Gomes, which houses two museums. The **Macau Grand Prix Museum** is a delight for car enthusiasts, displaying gleaming Formula 3 and other racing cars and motorbikes that have thundered around the streets of the city during the annual Macau Grand Prix (held in November) since 1954.

In the same building as the Grand Prix Museum is the **Macau Wine Museum,** which neatly presents varieties of wine from Portugal's different regions, along with a collection of winemaking tools and a mock-up of a cellar. The admission price includes a glass of wine.

Avenida de Amizade is the main thoroughfare running from the ferry terminal toward the center of the city. The avenue lined the waterfront before a huge slab of land was reclaimed. On the waterfront at the southeast corner of the reclaimed land is the Macau Cultural Center, which houses the **Macau Museum of Art.** Its five floors of permanent and temporary exhibits contain the city's most comprehensive collections of Chinese calligraphy and ceramics, plus paintings by Western artists.

Next door to the center is the **Handover Gifts Museum of Macau,** which houses a remarkable array of gifts presented to Macau by China's provinces when the city was handed back to the mainland in 1999.

To the east, **Fisherman's Wharf,** a huge dining and shopping complex cum theme park, juts out into the Outer Harbor. The park's faux houses are supposedly themed on various world cities, such as Amsterdam and Venice, although you'll be hard-pressed to spot the difference between the houses representing the various cities. Bizarrely, you'll find tourists taking pictures of fake European architecture, when the real thing lies just across the road. It also has a number of small children's rides.

Avenida de Amizade ends at the mustard-colored, barrel-shaped main tower of the **Lisboa hotel** (see p. 257). The area is dominated by the huge Grand Lisboa's lotus flower design. Nearby on the artificial Nan Van Lakes is the **Cybernetic Fountain.** It has 86 water spouts, the most energetic shooting plumes of water 250 feet (80 m) into the air. Every Saturday and Sunday night at 8:30 and again at 9:30, the fountain erupts into an entertaining sound and light show.

Peninsula South: On Rua

Central the cobblestone square of Largo de Santo Agostinho, opposite the Largo do Senado (Senate Square; see p. 222), has a number of old buildings. One of them, **São Agostinho** (St. Augustine's Church) was built by Augustinian friars in 1586, although the present

structure dates back to 1814.

This baroque-style church, built in cream-washed stone with white columns and motifs surrounding its windows, is notable for its spacious interior, and an altar dressed in marble, topped with a statue of Christ carrying the cross.

Opposite the church, beside the renovated **Dom Pedro V Theater,** which was the first European

theater in southern China and still hosts performances, is **São Jose** (Chapel of St. Joseph), part of a seminary set up in 1728 to train Chinese priests. The chapel was built 30 years later. It is laid out in a cruciform shape, with a three-tiered whitewashed facade topped

---

Macau Casino Rules

With the influx of American style casinos moving into town, rules at Macau's casinos are becoming increasingly relaxed. Nevertheless, there are a few ground rules to keep in mind. The legal gambling age is 18 for foreigners and 21 for Macau residents. The dress code is relaxed, although shorts, flip-flops, and sleeveless tops aren't allowed. Laptops, cameras, and backpacks all need to be checked (most casinos provide a free cloakroom service). Casinos use Hong Kong dollars and not the local Macau pataca, although ATM and currency exchange facilities are available.

Handover Gifts Museum of Macau

🅰 Map p. 225

✉ Avenue Xian Xing Hai, s/n, NAPE Macau

☎ 853/8504-180

Macau Museum of Art

🅰 Map p. 225

✉ Avenida Xian Xing Hai

☎ 8791-9814

🕐 Closed Mon.

💲 $

🚌 Bus: 1A, 23

Dom Pedro V Theater

🅰 Map p. 224

✉ Largo de Santo Agostinho

Travel to Macau

Hong Kong and Macau are well connected by a continuous stream of high-speed ferries; the journey takes 60 to 70 minutes.

From Hong Kong Island, ferries depart from the Shun Tak Centre with Turbojet (tel 2859-3333, www.turbojet.com.hk). Ferries run every 15 minutes between 7 a.m. and midnight, and less frequently overnight. Tickets cost HK$142 for economy class, oneway, more for weekend and night sailings. Similarly priced ferries also leave Tsim Sha Tsui's China Ferry Terminal with New World First Ferry (www.nwff.com.hk), every 30 minutes from 7 a.m. to 7 p.m., with a reduced service overnight. Both ferries dock at the Macau Ferry Terminal.

Tickets for both services can be bought at the ferry terminals with tickets almost always available for the next sailing, although booking ahead for weekends and night sailings is recommended.

Passengers arriving at Hong Kong International Airport can use Turbojet bonded ferries to take them directly to Macau, without having to pass through Hong Kong immigration and customs. Macau Express Link (tel 853-2886-1111) runs the same service between Macau Airport and Hong Kong.

Alternatively, HeliExpress (tel 2108-9898, www.heliexpress.com) helicopter service runs half-hourly trips to Macau from the Shun Tak Ferry Terminal to Macau Ferry Terminal. Tickets cost HK$2,200 oneway for the 16-minute trip, more on weekends and holidays.

with twin brick-roofed towers. A door next to the elaborate main altar leads to a beautiful cloistered garden and plant nursery.

Back on Rua Central, head south along Rua de São Lourenço to another of the city's impressive ecclesiastical sites. Dating back to the 1560s—its facade is a 19th-century addition—the imposing **São Lourenço** (St. Lawrence's Church) is fronted by a staircase and an ornamental gate.

The church's cream-and-white facade features square twin towers and a Chinese tile roof. Inside, gold and white beams along its high, timbered ceiling support chandeliers. A statue of St. Lawrence sits on the richly adorned main altar, dressed in multicolored vestments.

As you head south from St. Lawrence's Church, Rua Padre Antonio becomes Calcada da Barra when it reaches another square, Largo Lilau, and winds around to the **A-Ma Temple.** Dedicated to A-Ma, the Queen of Heaven (known as Tin Hau in Hong Kong), it is Macau's oldest temple, predating Portuguese settlement. The name "Macau" is derived from A-Ma Gau, the "bay of A-Ma."

The temple's prayer halls, pavilions, and courtyards wind by boulders, through moon gates, and past old ladies with begging bowls to the heavily wooded slopes of Penha Hill. The main shrine, to the right of the entrance, has statues of A-Ma and a model of a war junk complete with little cannon.

Opposite the temple, the **Macau Maritime Museum** juts from the entrance to the inner harbor with walls evoking sails and porthole windows. Among the dozens of superbly crafted scale replica boats is the impressive 1:40 scale model of the Portuguese naval training boat, the Sagres, under full sail.

From the museum, head east along Rua se São Tiago da Barra until it curves to become Avenida da Republica at the Macau Peninsula's southern tip and the start of Macau's second artificial lake, Sai Van. To the south, across the lake on the harborfront, you'll notice the huge, arched, black granite **Gate of Understanding,** built in 1993 to cement Macau's relationship with China. Farther east is the needle-shaped **Macau Tower,** soaring 1,110 feet (338 m), and by far Macau's tallest structure. The outdoor observation deck on the 61st floor allows stunning views of Macau, China, and, on clear days, Hong Kong, about 40 miles (65 km) away. Below the observation deck is a revolving restaurant.

The tower is part of the Macau Convention and Entertainment Center. At the center's entrance, next door to the Macau Tower, are several restaurants and cafés that open onto an expansive plaza with more cafés, a playground, fountains, and seating areas; a boardwalk runs along the waterfront.

If that isn't exciting enough, try the **Macau Tower Sky Jump:** You plummet from the top at 45 mph (75 kph) before being eased down to earth when the cable-car brakes click in just before ground level. **Skywalk X,** where you stroll along a tower ledge (attached to a harness) about 800 feet (230 m) up, provides another adrenaline rush.

Avenida da Republica winds around the northern shore of Sai Van Lake and makes for a pleasant amble, with shady trees, stone retaining walls, cobblestone footpaths, and small parks and benches giving a European feel.

The avenue ends near the **Residence of the Portuguese Consul,** built atop a small hill. Once the Bela Vista Hotel, one of Asia's most famous hotels, it is a castle-style colonial building constructed in the 19th century. Over the years, it has served as a boarding school, hostel for refugees, and hotel.

Peninsula North: The Goddess of Mercy, Kun Iam (known as Kwum Yam in Hong Kong), is honored at the elaborate Kun Iam Tong Temple on Avenida do Coronel Mesquita. The temple was established in the 13th cen-

Macau Maritime Museum

- 🅰 Map p. 224
- ✉ Largo do Pagode da Barra
- ☎ 2859-5481
- 🕐 Closed Tues.
- 💲 $
- 🚌 Bus: 1, 1A, 2, 5, 6, 7, 9, 10, 10A, 11, 18, 21, 21A, 34

INSIDER TIP:

Ferries from Macau to Hong Kong can fill up late on Friday and Saturday nights with Hong Kong gamblers heading home. You might want to book a return in advance.

—RORY BOLAND
National Geographic contributor

tury and its present structures date from 1627. A huge entrance gate featuring porcelain figures clustered along its roof ridges provides a suitably grand introduction to this lovely temple. In the main hall you'll find an image of Kun Iam attended by 18 arhats (Chinese sages) on either side; the image is lavishly clothed in embroidered silk. Behind the temple, terraced gardens feature fountains fashioned into Chinese landscapes.

Macau Walk

This walk begins in central Macau and wends its way north and then east past some of Macau's best-known attractions, ending with sweeping views of the city and harbor.

Colorful colonial buildings, including the Igreja de São Domingos, edge the Largo do Senado.

Start your walk at **Largo do Senado** (Senate Square), at the heart of old Macau. The square—with black-and-white mosaic stones laid in wave patterns and a lively fountain—is lined with a fine array of restored colonial buildings. The square also has the small, but useful, Macau tourism office. The **Leal Senado ❶** ("loyal Senate"), now the municipal council building, faces the square on the opposite side of Avenida Almeida Riberio. Originally completed in 1784, with its imposing facade of white plaster and green-shuttered windows added a century later, the building earned the name "loyal" because of Macau's resolute refusal to recognize Spain's occupation of Portugal in the 17th century. From its grand foyer, a stone staircase embellished with blue-and-white tiles leads to a delightful garden. Farther up the stairs are the wood-paneled senate chamber and library.

Standing out among the colonnaded and lively pastel-colored buildings around the square is the startling white facade of **Santa Casa da**

NOT TO BE MISSED:

Leal Senado • Igreja de São Domingos • Ruinas de São Paulo • Macau Museum • Camoes Grotto and Garden • Lou Lim Ioc Garden • Guia Fort

---

Misericordia ❷ ("holy house of mercy"), a mission set up in 1568 and one of the oldest in Asia.

At the square's northern end you'll see **Igreja de São Domingos ❸** (St. Dominic's Church), one of the city's best examples of Portuguese colonial baroque architecture, which infused local elements into 18th-century baroque style. It marries classical design with Chinese roof tiles, extensive use of timber, and large shuttered windows. Inside, the church is no less impressive, especially the cream-colored stone altar, decorated with white-stucco moldings and twisting columns, which climbs to the ceiling. The centerpiece of the altar is a 17th-century image of Our Lady of the Rosary, flanked by statues of St. Dominic and St. Catherine of Siena. The cross below Our Lady is that of the Dominican order.

Next to St. Dominic's is the **Museum of Sacred Art Treasures ④**. In addition to a room on its first floor devoted to the renovation of the church, the three-level museum carries about 300 works of sacred art, made unusual because many of the images and religious regalia were crafted in former Portuguese colonies in Africa, Malaya, India, and Macau using tropical woods and ivory, along with vestments made from Chinese silks.

Take a left turn at the museum along the narrow, cobblestone-paved Rua da Pahla, which soon becomes Rua São Paulo. It winds past small colonial buildings and balconied Chinese shop-houses to the grand stone stairway and imposing facade of the **Ruinas de São Paulo ⑤** (Ruins of St. Paul), one of the finest monuments to Christianity in all of Asia. São Paulo is by far the most impressive of Macau's many churches, even though only its remarkably well-restored tiered stone facade remains. Built in the early 17th century by members of the Jesuit order, it is a magnificent example of ecclesiastical architecture.

After the Jesuits were kicked out in 1762, the cathedral was converted into a barracks, which burned down in 1835. The facade is a masterpiece embellished with carvings and statues: A bronze dove symbolizing the holy spirit tops the facade, below which an infant Jesus is flanked by implements of crucifixion. On the third tier, the Virgin Mary guides Portuguese ships through the "Sea of Torments of Sin," including a seven-headed hydra with a Chinese inscription warning "The Holy Mother tramples the heads of dragons." Behind the facade is the crypt of the church's founder, Alessandro Valignano.

Just to the right of the church, at the top of the stairway, head right and take the escalators to the **Macau Museum ⑥** (tel 2835-9111, closed Mon., $). Built into the side of **Fortaleza do Monte ⑦** (Monte Fort), this excellent museum's three floors guide you through Macau's lively history and emphasizes the role played by both the Portuguese and Chinese in its development.

The museum's top floor leads out to the grounds—now pleasant gardens—of Monte Fort, where you can see sweeping views of Macau and check out the emplacements housing the original guardrooms and cannon. The fort was built by Jesuits between 1617 and 1626. The cannon were used only once, when the Dutch invaded in 1622. A cannonball fired by a priest hit one ship's powder keg, creating panic and allowing the Portuguese to drive back the invaders.

INSIDER TIP:

Visit Macau for the glitz but also for the timeworn temples and the traditional fishing villages.

—PAUL ROGERS
National Geographic Traveler magazine writer

Return through the museum to St. Paul, go down the stairs, and turn right to follow Rua de Santo Antonio to **Igreja de Santo Antonio ⑧** (St. Anthony's Church), on the site of Macau's first chapel, built in 1558. The church has burned down three times, the last time in 1930. The bulky, intimidating, gray facade was built in 1940.

Opposite St. Anthony's Church is the **Macau Protestant Chapel and Cemetery ⑨**. The tiny, whitewashed chapel fronts a small, well-tended cemetery with tombs and gravestones set amid green lawns and frangipani trees. Macau's mainly British and American citizens were laid to rest here in the 18th and 19th centuries. Gravestones tell tales of shipboard accidents, shipwrecks, fever, and disease. Among those buried in the cemetery are George Chinnery (1774–1852), known for his paintings of Macau, and Robert Morrison (1782–1834), a Protestant missionary to China, who translated much of the Bible into Chinese. If the door is locked, ring the bell.

Adjacent to the cemetery is the **Camoes Grotto and Garden ⑩** (Praca Luis de Camoes), a lush park of winding paths, boulders, shady

GUANGDONG

MACAU

IHLA VERDE

SUN YAT-SEN MEMORIAL PARK

Barrier Gate

ISTMO FERREIRA DO AMARAL

AVENIDA DO CONSELHEIRO HEIRO BORJA

Lin Fong Temple

AVENIDA DE VENCE

AVENIDA DO ALMIRANTE LACERDA

AV. DO CORONEL MESQUITA

Kun Iam Temple

Bacia Norte do Patane

0   400 meters
0   400 yards

RUA DA RIBEIRA DO PATANE

RUA VISCONDE PAÇO DE ARCOS

LUIS DE CAMÕES GROTTO & GARDEN **10**

Macau Protestant Chapel & Cemetery **9**

ESTRADA DO REPOUSO

LOU LIM IOC GARDEN **12**

AV. DO FERREIRA DE ALMEIDA

RUA DE SILVA MENDES

AV. SIDC

FLC GAR

Inner Harbor

RUA TOMAS VIEIRA

EST. A. LOUREIRO

St. Michael's Cemetery

109m Guia Hill

Igreja de S. Antonio **8**

Ponte 16

RUA DE S. ANTONIO

5

Ruinas de São Paulo

RUA SÃO PAULO

6 Macau Museum

EST. DO

CEMITERIO

11

Dr. Sun Yat-sen Memorial House

Chapel

13

14

Guia Fort & Lighthouse

3

Igreja de São Domingos

START

4 Sacred Art Museum

Fortaleza do Monte

7

RUA DO COMPO

Wine Museum & Grand Prix Museur (Tourism Activities Center

RUA DAS LORCHAS

Leal Senado **1**

São Agostinho

São Jose

LARGO DE S. AGOSTINHO

São Lourenço

RUA PADRE ANTONIO

2 Santa Casa da Misericordia

LARGO DO SENADO

RUA CENTRAL

Dom Pedro V Theater

AV. DA PRAIA GRANDE

AV. DE ALMEIDA RIBEIRO

ESTRADA DE SÃO FRANCISCO

RUA LUIS GONZAGA GO

RUA DO ALMIRANTE SERGIO

CALCADA DA BARRA

RUA DA PRAIA DOM PARTO

AV. DOUTOR MARIO SOARES

Hotel Lisboa

AVENIDA DE AMIZADE

LARGO LILAU

Penha Hill

Residence of the Portuguese Consul

Cybernetic Fountain

MACAU

AVENIDA DR. SUN YAT-SEN

A-Ma Temple

RUA DE SÃO TIAGO

Macau Maritime Museum

Barra Hill

Nam Van Lakes

TAIPA

AV. DOUTOR STANLEY HO

Sai Van Lake

AVENIDA DA REPÚBLICA

BRIDGE

Gate of Understanding

Macau Tower

Macau Convention and Entertainment Center

Taipa, Coloane

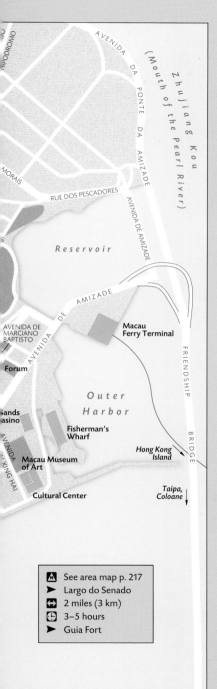

banyan trees, ferns, and bamboo groves climbing to a lookout with views to the Inner Harbor and mainland China.

From there, head to the rear of St. Anthony's Church, east along Rua Tomas Vieira, to a small traffic circle. On the circle's other side, take Estrada do Cemiterio and continue east to the hillside **St. Michael's Cemetery ⑪**. This Catholic cemetery is crowded with extravagant gravestones adorned with large statues of the Virgin Mary, harp-playing angels, and saints.

Continue east along Estrada do Cemiterio and turn left at Avenida do Conselheiro Ferreira de Almeida. Here you'll pass some lovely restored 1920s buildings, now housing government offices, before reaching the walled **Lou Lim Ioc Garden ⑫** at the junction of Estrada Adolfo Loureiro. Modeled on the famed gardens of Suzhou, the beautifully landscaped gardens are heavily wooded, with a large pond in front of a flamboyant colonial home (now an art gallery).

From here, continue along Estrada Adolfo Loureiro and cross Avenida do Conselheiro Ferreira de Almeida one block to Avenida Sidonio Pais. Turn right and walk a short distance to Rua de Silva Mendes and the **Dr. Sun Yat-sen Memorial House ⑬** *(Av. Sidonio Pais, tel 2857-4064, closed Tues.)*, the Moorish-style home built by Sun's family in the 1930s, replacing the original, more modest dwelling in which he lived during his visits to Macau. Inside you'll find memorabilia and photographs outlining Sun's four-decade struggle to overthrow the Qing dynasty and establish the Chinese Republic (see p. 34).

Keep heading north along Avenida Sidonio Pais to Flora Garden, where you can hop on a cable car *(closed 6 p.m., $)* for an 80-second ride to Guia Hill, at 360 feet (109 m), the highest point in Macau. Take the path to 17th-century **Guia Fort ⑭** to see the first lighthouse built (in 1865) on the China coast, the ruins of the fort, and the sweeping views of Macau from the cannon platform. Next to the still operating lighthouse is a simple chapel containing a fine image of the Virgin Mary holding the Baby Jesus.

A junk carved into a boulder at A-Ma Temple symbolizes the deity's relationship with the sea.

Walk north down Avenida do Coronel Mesquita and turn right on Avenida do Almirante Lacerda to **Lin Fong Miu** (Temple of the Lotus), with a bas-relief tableau of Chinese historical and mythological figures carved in the 19th century. The first hall through the entrance—guarded by stone lions—is dedicated to A-Ma. Beyond this, is a courtyard with a frieze of writhing dragons and a lotus pond.

Head north from here down Istmo Ferreira do Amaral to the 19th-century **Barrier Gate** (Portas do Cerco or "gate of siege"), constructed in grand style to mark the Macau–China border.

The Casinos: If you're visiting Macau to gamble, you'll have plenty of choices. Most of the main casinos are open 24 hours; it's best to avoid them on weekends and holidays because they're crammed. From the Macau Ferry terminal, several casinos run free shuttles.

The nearest casino to the ferry terminal is the **Sands Macao.** This bold Las Vegas import was the first to challenge the traditional Macau casinos, many of which were sleazy gambling dens. The huge main gambling hall with its slightly amateurish floor show is classic Vegas.

Farther along the waterfront on Avenida Dr. Sun Yat-sen is the gleaming wave structure of the **MGM Grand Macau**, one of the city's biggest casinos. Across the road the sleek curvature of the **Wynn Macau** runs along Rua Cidade de Sintra. More intimate than its bigger rivals, the Wynn attracts a well-heeled crowd.

Outside, across Avenida de Amizade, onto Avenida de Lisboa, are the Lisboa Hotel and its sister property the Grand Lisboa. The hotel was once the biggest game in town and is worth a trip inside to see how the city's casinos used to look. Now towering 40 stories overhead is the spectacular Grand Lisboa, which offers Las Vegas style with a Portuguese twist.

Further afield, and best reached using the free shuttle buses, is the **Cotai Strip,** reclaimed land connecting Coloane and Taipa island which is being developed to emulate the Las Vegas strip. Although it currently is a huge construction site, the strip will feature several big name resorts casinos and hotels. The flagship project, the huge **Venetian Macao,** has already opened its doors. The casino boasts canals, gondolas, and faux Venetian shops.

Macau's casino boom isn't without its critics, with prices rising in the city, profits going abroad, and many key workers being attracted by high paid casino jobs, locals are becoming increasingly vocal in their opposition to the city's gamble on casinos. ■

Macau's Islands

Despite the tag, Macau's two islands are no longer islands, thanks to the huge Cotai Strip, a land reclamation program that now connects the two islands. Taipa has an increasingly similar identity to one of Hong Kong's new towns thanks to rapid development, although it retains some of Macau's most authentic Portuguese sights, while nearby Coloane is sparsely populated and has, for now, suffered far less development.

Taipa

Charming **Taipa Village** is at the island's southern end. Here, narrow lanes are lined with quaint Chinese shop-houses, open-air restaurants, and pastel-colored colonial buildings. To the east of the village, **Our Lady of Carmel Church** stands in a cobblestone square atop a small hill. From here, take the garden path down to the small, banyan-shaded **Avenida da Praia,** with its restored mansions dating back to the 1920s, called the **Taipa Houses Museum** or Avenida da Praia Residences. The first of these is the **Macanese House,** a museum with louvered shutters and deep verandas, fashioned into a Macanese family home of the 1920s with period furniture. The other four residences, similar in design, house an exhibition gallery, displays on the regions of Portugal and the history of Taipa and Coloane, and a reception room and restaurant.

Coloane

A long causeway near Taipa Village links the two islands. Buses to the island stop at the small, pretty main square, **Largo Presidente A. R. Eanes,** at Coloane Village, but the rest of the village is mostly pretty shabby. Head left at the waterfront to the **Chapel** of St. Francis Xavier. The church, with its cream-and-white facade and blue timber doors, is a late addition to Macau's surfeit of churches, built in 1928.

Keep heading south along Avenida Cinco Outubro to **Tam Kong Temple,** dedicated to a Taoist god of seafarers. Porcelain figures decorate the temple's tiled roof. Inside, a 4-foot-long (1.2 m) carved whalebone dragon boat, filled with a crew of wooden men in red coats and yellow hats, adds interest.

....

Coloane village comprises buildings dating from the Qing dynasty, including a dressing hall.

....

From the village square you can hop on a bus for the short ride to **Ha Sa Beach.** The long curving beach gets its name from the color of its sand—Black Sand Beach.

The world's largest A-Ma statue crowns **Coloane Peak,** with the adjacent **A-Ma Cultural Village** *(closed Mon.)* adding more tributes to the Goddess of the Sea. The village comprises a number of buildings dating from the Qing dynasty, including an A-Ma "palace," a dressing hall, and a museum. ∎

Taipa
🅰 Map p. 225

Taipa Houses Museum
✉ Avenida da Praia, Taipa
☎ 2882-7103
🕐 Closed Mon.
🚍 Bus: 11, 28A

NOTE: **Getting there.** Buses run frequently from the Macau Peninsula to both Taipa and Coloane. From here, buses to Taipa village include Nos. 11, 22, 28A, and 33. Buses to Coloane Village include Nos. 21A, 25, 26A. These continue to Ha Sa Beach.

Guangzhou

This sprawling metropolis of ten million people is the engine that has driven China's emergence as an economic power. It has used its proximity and relationship with Hong Kong to power its way to prosperity. The city, once known as Canton to the western world, is the face of modern China, with gleaming high-rise towers, a relatively well-off population, and a vitality close to matching that of Hong Kong, just 75 miles (120 km) southeast.

Guangzhou's Ozhong Interchange at night exemplifies China's growing modernity.

This vitality is not surprising. Most Hong Kong people—the Cantonese—originally hail from Guangzhou and its province, Guangdong. Over the past two decades, they have transformed the city into the most modern and vibrant in China.

Guangzhou is easily accessible from Hong Kong, just a few hours by train or high-speed ferry. For those wanting a quick glimpse into the changing nature of modern China, it is an ideal excursion.

Guangzhou is not an attractive city, nor one that leans heavily on tourism. It exhibits all the characteristics of a modern Asian city hell-bent on growth. Its heavy traffic, sprawl, and constant din are intimidating, but a number of attractions—temples, parks, and museums—make it worth the visit, at least for a day or two. These attractions are relatively close together and not hard to find. Taxis are everywhere and their fares are cheap. A modern subway system, although limited, also runs between some of these sites.

Most visitors limit themselves to old Guangzhou, which spreads from the banks of the meandering Pearl River. Much of this area, with its riverfront promenades, colonnaded 1920s shop-houses, mazes of narrow, winding lanes, impromptu markets, and mercantile bustle, is amenable to walking.

Charming Shamian Island, once a British and French concession, retains nearly all of its colonial character. From there, amble east along the shaded riverfront promenade taking in the river traffic before heading north through the city's side streets to the imposing Gothic spires of the 19th-century Scared Heart of Jesus Cathedral. Farther north into the heart of the city are the ancient temple compounds of Guangxiao and Lui Rong, and to the west, the riotously ornate Chen Chan Temple.

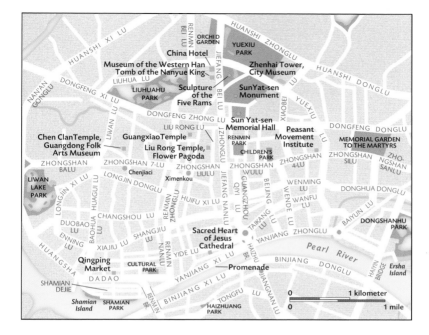

Near the landmark China Hotel is the impressive Museum of the Western Han Tomb of the Nanyue King, with its fascinating collection of relics buried with Wen Di (137–122 B.C.), the second emperor of the short-lived Nanyue dynasty. Opposite, the expansive Yuexi Park has a number of attractions worth visiting. Nearby, the Sun Yat-sen Memorial Hall honors the founder of modern China, while to the west, a peek into the life of China's other great leader, Mao Zedong, can be found at the quirky Peasant Movement Institute, housed inside a 14th-century Confucian temple.

Shamian Island & Around

The north bank of the Pearl River is among Guangzhou's oldest and most interesting areas, mixing hints of colonialism with vibrant street life. Beside the riverbank, parts of which are given

INSIDER TIP:

For an exotic experience, visit Guangzhou's Yumin seafood restaurant where crocodiles, later to end up on plates, roam the lobby with their jaws tied shut.

—KAREN E. LANGE
National Geographic writer

over to generous promenades, you can join the locals strolling and catching river breezes, then head into the city's winding laneways to catch the excitement of everyday street life.

A relic of Guangzhou's concessions to colonialism is found on **Shamian Island,** a small slice of land on the northern banks of

Get a Chinese Visa in Hong Kong

Many people who visit Hong Kong go on to mainland China; it is possible to get your Chinese visa while in the city. You can apply for a visa at the Chinese Ministry of Foreign Affairs Consulate Department (7/F, China Resources Bldg., 26 Harbour Rd., Wan Chai, tel 3413-2300, www.fmcoprc.gov.hk, Mon.–Fri. 9 a.m.–noon & 2 p.m.–5 p.m.). You'll need your passport and two color passport photos. Fees vary widely, based on the type of visa and speed of service. Though the standard charge for a single-issue visa is HK$150, citizens from several countries pay more. U.S. citizens pay a whopping HK$1,020. Visas are issued in four working days; two-day and three-day service are offered at a higher cost. Lines often stretch out the door, especially on Mondays or before public holidays; luggage and backpacks are not permitted inside.

Many people use China Travel Service (China Travel Bldg., 77 Queen's Rd., Central, tel 2315-7188), a quasi-government owned travel agency offering more efficient service at marginally higher prices. See www.ctshk.com for more offices in Hong Kong.

Certain nationalities can purchase a SEZ visa, valid only for the Shenzhen Special Economic Zone, on the Hong Kong/China border.

Shamian Island

Map p. 229
(SW corner)

the Pearl River and divided from the city by a narrow canal. This was once the British and French Concession granted by China in 1859, where Europeans built grand buildings, laid cobblestone streets, and planted rows of banyan trees and hedged gardens. Surprisingly, the place was left alone during Guangzhou's mad development scramble of the 1990s.

Over the last few years, the colonial buildings have been restored, and are now occupied by offices, restaurants, and boutiques. The main boulevard, **Shamian Dejie,** running through the center of the island east to west, has rows of neatly trimmed hedges, trees, and brick-paved plazas with seating areas. The island has very little traffic, making it a delightful place to stroll. Look for the statues representing the area's former colonial residents. Along its waterfront, outdoor restaurants sit in shaded **Shamian Park.** You can watch boats chug their way along the Pearl River while you sip a beer,

a pleasing experience. Shamian's quaintness and gentility sits in stark contrast to the manic pace of the rest of the city.

Across Shamian Island's canal is the colonnaded colonial facade of the city's most famous market, **Qingping.** One of the first markets of its kind in China, it was established soon after the introduction of free market economics in the late 1970s. Stores in the front arcades sell the usual collection of dried medicinal herbs including mushrooms, spices, sea horses, anise, bark, deer antlers, and so on. As you move farther into the market, stands along the warren of side streets offer the more mundane fish, fresh fruit and vegetables, flowers, potted plants, and goldfish. But as you go deeper, it gets a bit more bizarre. Although the authorities have cracked down on some of the market's wilder excesses, it is still an interesting exploration of Cantonese culinary habits: a takeaway menagerie of live civet cats, dogs, deer, monkeys, centipedes, cockroaches, scorpions, toads, frogs, and tortoises, all of them destined for the pot. Even more disturbing are the rare sights of tiger paws and rhino horns laid out on mats.

Back on peaceful Shamian Island, beyond Shamian Park, head east along the wide waterfront boulevard past people practicing tai chi, playing badminton, and chatting on park benches. You'll leave the island across a small bridge and onto Yangjian Xi Lu (Yangjian Road West). After several hundred yards, the street opens up to the waterfront and a gener-ous **promenade,** with banyan branches arching over the sidewalk, a favorite spot for strolling lovers in the evenings and tai chi practitio-ners in the early morning.

A few blocks from the water-front on Yide Lu (Yide Road) is China's oldest Catholic church, the imposing **Sacred Heart of Jesus Cathedral,** known as *shi shi jiaotang,* stone house in Chinese. This Gothic-inspired edifice, with its twin spires, heavy timber doors, flowered window lattices, and stained-glass features, is a surpris-ing find in an area of balconied shop-houses, rundown tenements, and bustling narrow laneways. Construction began in 1863, and it was consecrated in 1888. Note the carved Chinese-style lions jutting out from its walls.

Just northeast of Shamian Island on Huangsha Avenue, the **Cultural Park,** an odd, faded mix-ture of attractions, includes a roller-skating rink, an amusement park with wonderfully antiquated rides, a fishing exhibition with empty fish tanks, a sad-looking Dolphin

Performance Hall, and a mildly interesting Hang Dynasty Hall.

Old Guangzhou

Although Guangzhou is a huge, sprawling city, many of its main attractions are a relatively easy distance from one another and can be reached by short taxi rides. In between these sights, you'll see Chinese city life at its most vibrant; from wide avenues lined with shiny high-rise office towers and clogged with traffic to bustling side streets with colonnaded shop-houses and narrow lanes brimming with people and activity.

Picturesque Shamian Island has a more relaxed air than the rest of Guangzhou.

Start your tour at Zhongshan 7-Lu *(Zhongshan Rd., Section 7)* at the **Chen Clan Temple,** next to the Chenjiaci subway station. It is one of the most beautiful and ornate ancestral halls in China and one of the very few to survive the Cultural Revolution of the 1960s and 1970s.

Guangzhou
🅰 Map p. 229

Chen Clan Temple & Guangdong Folk Arts Museum
🅰 Map p. 229
✉ Zhongshan 7-Lu
☎ 8181-4559
💲 $
🚇 Subway: Chenjiaci

This expansive temple complex comprises 19 buildings dotted with garden courtyards and linked by a network of long verandas. The roof ridges and eaves of the halls are lined with thousands of brilliantly colorful, expressive porcelain figurines depicting a confusion of mythological scenes, while intricate stone bas-reliefs, featuring similar scenarios, are sculpted above the doorways. The sturdy main doors, decorated with paintings of Chinese guardians Qin Qiong and Wei Chigong, open to the vaulted ceiling supported by carved timber beams, while sublimely decorated lanterns hang from above. Panels crafted into beautiful patterns screen the entrance hall from the first courtyard. From there, verandas embellished with latticework and topped with more porcelain figurines lead to the complex's other halls, each featuring similar exquisite detailing.

A number of the halls host the **Guangdong Folk Arts Museum,** which displays arts and handicrafts from all over China, but especially from Guangdong Province. The collection, dating mainly from the Qing period up until recent times, includes some magnificent examples of embroidery, porcelain work, enamelware, ceramics, papercuts, stained-etched glass, shell patchwork, basketwork, and lacquerwork. Carvings have been fashioned from jade, stone, ivory, ox horn, shell, and wood.

Particularly impressive are the two gilded shrines—fashioned into sedan chairs—for holding ancestral tablets, flanking the altar in the main hall. These exquisite pieces feature Taoist religious tableaus (there is also one of dozens of clambering crabs!) carved in wood with extraordinary detail. Also worth a lot closer inspection are the miniature ivory carvings—less than half an inch (1 cm) in size. They are so small a magnifying glass has been set up to view them.

Hop back on the subway for one station (Xinemkou) to the **Guangxiao Temple** on Hongshu

Balconied shop-houses still line the streets in the city's older sections.

Lu (Hongshu Road). It is one of Guangzhou's oldest temples, dating back to the fourth century. Past the pot-bellied Laughing Buddha at the entrance, its neatly trimmed hedges and shady banyan trees make for pleasant strolling. The restored buildings feature an ingenious bracketed timber roof system, supporting broad and sweeping multi-eave roofs, with ridges lined with porcelain figurines. Inside the spacious main hall are three large gilded Buddha images side by side.

Nearby to the east, on Liu Rong Lu (Liu Rong Road), stands the 197-foot (60 m) **Flower Pagoda,** with nine external and 17 internal floors, the impressive centerpiece of **Liurong Temple** ("temple of the six banyan trees"), dating from around the sixth century. You can climb to the top of this octagonal structure for outstanding views of sprawling Guangzhou. Behind the pagoda, the main shrine, rebuilt in 1984, holds three large gilded Buddhas.

Just south of the temple on Gangta Lu is **Huaisheng Mosque.** Many Muslims claim a mosque was first constructed on the site in the seventh century, making it quite probably the first mosque in China. There are several decent halal snack shops nearby.

In 1983, bulldozers accidentally unearthed the tomb of Wen Di, the second emperor of Nanyue (137–122 B.C.), a localized dynasty of five kings, which lasted less than a century. The excavated tomb was turned into the **Museum of the Western Han Tomb of the Nanyue King,** just east of the China Hotel on Jiefang Bei Lu

(Jiefang Road North). It re-creates the tomb's setting; you descend stairs from a grassy knoll into the tomb chambers, where the king, along with an accompaniment of human sacrifices, including his concubines, cooks, guards, and musicians, were buried. The museum houses the remains of Wen and the others along with the

Shenzhen

On the China side of the Hong Kong/China border is the city of Shenzhen. Accessible by rail from Hong Kong, the city is popular for both bargain-hunting shoppers and tourists who want to say they were in China. Lo Wu is a beachside entertainment district popular with expats. Flights from Shenzhen's airport to internal China destinations are cheaper than from Hong Kong proper.

thousands of jade, gold, bronze, iron, crystal, and fabric funerary objects buried with them, including Wen's burial shroud, made from a thousand pieces of jade.

Across from the museum is the biggest of Guangzhou's parks, the 232-acre (93 ha), hilly and heavily wooded **Yuexiu Park.** On one of its hills, near the south gate, sits one of the city's main attractions: the **Sculpture of the Five Rams,** a rather unattractive concrete rendering of goats climbing a hill, although after viewing it, you are left to wonder why. Erected in 1959, it is the symbol of

Museum of the Western Han Tomb of the Nanyue King

▲ Map p. 229
✉ 867 Jiefang Bei Rd.
☎ 3618-2920
$ $

Sun Yat-sen Memorial Hall

- ▲ Map p. 229
- ✉ Donfeng Zhong Rd.
- ☎ 8355-2030
- 💲 $

Museum of the Peasant Movement Institute

- ▲ Map p. 229
- ✉ 42 Zhongshan 4-Rd.
- ☎ 8333-3936
- 🕐 Closed Mon.
- 💲 $

Guangzhou, whose name means "city of rams" (or Goat City). Myth holds that hundreds of years ago, five celestial beings riding five rams through the air arrived in the city, presenting rice stalks to the locals to indicate that the region would forever remain free from famine.

INSIDER TIP:

Chinese twenty-somethings with money congregate at the Baby-face Club on Guang-zhou's Pearl River. The Flaming Lamborghini is one of the club's popular drinks.

—LESLIE CHANG
National Geographic writer

Take the path to the sculpture's right down the hill to pretty Nanxui Lake, cross a bridge, and head right up the hill to **Zhenhai Tower.** The tower was first built in 1380 (today's version dates from 1928) and was used by the French and British troops during the Opium Wars (see pp. 31–33) because of its position overlooking the south of the city. It now houses the **Guangzhou City Museum,** with exhibits tracing the history of the city from neolithic times to the present.

To the right of the tower, on another hill, stands a marble and granite obelisk commemorating the revolutionary, Sun Yat-sen (see pp. 34–35), who mastered the overthrow of the Qing dynasty in 1912. The monument was built in 1929, four years after his death.

The obelisk overlooks the gigantic **Sun Yat-sen Memorial Hall,** set behind a broad expanse of manicured lawns and entered at Dongfeng Zhong Lu (Dongfeng Road Central). Built in 1931 on the site of the Qing governor's residence, the huge building, measuring 154 feet (47 m) high and 233 feet (71 m) long, is done in heavily ornate, traditional style, with sweeping roofs topped with blue tiles. Inside, a domed ceiling rises above a 3,200-seat theater.

Next to the memorial hall is a small exhibition hall with a collection of historical photographs; unfortunately for foreign visitors, captions are only in Chinese.

To the west of the memorial hall, on Renmin Bei Lu (Renmin Road North), is pretty **Liuhau Park.** Here, you can rent rowboats and paddle around the city's largest artificial lake.

Guangzhou has a number of revolutionary museums. Among the best is the **Museum of the Peasant Movement Institute,** housed inside a Confucian temple dating to 1370. Outstanding temple architecture consisting of garden courtyards and swooping tiled roofs mixes with more prosaic examples of peasant movement studies in its rooms.

Established in 1924, the institute is famed as the place Communist Party leaders Mao Zedong and Zhou Enlai lectured young party members. The temple's halls are a museum with much of the original furnishings in place, including classrooms, dormitories, library, and Mao's quarters. One small room dedicated to Mao has much Mao paraphernalia. ∎

Travelwise

Tram driver, Hong Kong Island

TRAVELWISE

PLANNING YOUR TRIP
When To Go
Climate

Hong Kong, which sits on the South China Sea, just south of the Tropic of Cancer, has a subtropical climate. Winter (Dec.–Feb.) can see temperature fluctuations between 50°F (10°C) and 76°F (25°C), as cool Arctic winds blow across the Asian continent. The temperature can drop to zero on some peaks in the New Territories, but rarely sinks below 45°F (7°C) in urban areas. There is little rain and humidity is relatively low. Spring is marked by a sharp increase in humidity. Summer (June–Aug.) is hot, with humidity reaching 90 percent and over, and is subject to bouts of heavy rain. Best times to visit are March to April and late September to November, when humidity drops and there's little or no rainfall.

Hong Kong lies in a typhoon region and may be buffeted by severe rainstorms and fierce winds, which can occasionally force the complete shutdown of businesses and public services for 24 hours or more. The typhoon season is May to November, but the most typhoon-prone month is August. The suspension of transportation and other services is governed by a series of numbered signals (1 for caution, 3 for worsening, 8 for take immediate shelter, etc.), which are posted widely and repeated on TV and radio. During a Number 8 signal, shops, offices, and most public transportation shut down.

The average temperatures for Hong Kong are:
Spring: March to May 72°F (22°C)
Summer: June to Aug. 85°F (30°C)
Fall: Sept. to Nov. 74°F (24°C)
Winter: Dec. to Feb. 63°F (17°C)

What to Take

Winter and spring can be cool, especially after sunset, so a sweater or jacket is advisable. In summer, air-conditioning in restaurants, bars, movie theaters, offices, and on public transportation can be cool enough to warrant a light jacket.

An umbrella is a must in summer. Also bring a light waterproof jacket. Some of the top restaurants expect men to wear a jacket, if not a tie, but most settle for neat, casual attire.

From mid-spring to late fall, lightweight, loose, cotton clothing is advisable. T-shirts and neat shorts are acceptable streetwear, especially during the oppressively hot and humid summer months. A lot of your time will be spent on foot, so bring comfortable walking shoes. Sandals—not flip-flops—are acceptable. If you plan on hiking in Hong Kong's country parks, bring a sturdy pair of hiking boots.

No matter what you wear, dress neatly, as people in Hong Kong often measure you by your appearance. Although it is a cosmopolitan city, women should refrain from wearing revealing clothing.

Insurance

Arrange adequate medical and travel insurance to cover worst-case possibilities before leaving your home country. Only third-party cover is provided in car rental agreements.

Theft or loss of property covered by personal insurance should be reported as soon as possible to the Hong Kong police. You will need to go in person to a police station where you will be given a stolen-property form to fill in. The process is efficient and police are dutifully polite to visitors.

Entry Formalities
Visas

Citizens from the United States, Canada, Australia, and the European Union can stay up to three months without a visa, provided they have a passport valid for at least three months beyond their departure date. British citizens can stay up to six months visa free. Visitors may need to prove to immigration officers on arrival that they have sufficient funds and an onward ticket before being allowed to enter, although this is a rare occurrence.

If you wish to stay longer than the visa-free period, you will need to apply for a visa at an SAR counter of a Republic of China embassy, consulate, or visa office before arrival.

Visitors are not allowed to enter employment (paid or unpaid) or establish or join any business.

The Hong Kong Immigration Department is at Immigration Tower, 7 Gloucester Rd., Wan Chai, tel 2824-6111, www.info.gov.hk/immd.

Hong Kong citizens are required by law to carry their identity cards at all times. Visitors must also carry some form of identity with a photograph. Police have the right to stop you and ask for ID, although this happens very rarely to foreigners. A driver's license with photograph is adequate.

Macau

Residents from the United States, Canada, Australia, and a number of other countries can stay in Macau for up to one month without a visa; citizens of the European Union get three months and British citizens get six months. Passports need to be valid three months beyond the length of visit.

Guangzhou

Hong Kong is the easiest place to obtain visas for China. All visitors to China need a visa. Single or multiple entry visas—each stay is for 30 days—can be obtained in Hong Kong from travel agents or from China Travel Services *(tel 2315-7188, www.ctshk.com).* Agents charge a commission on top of the normal visa costs, which range between HK$100–700 depending on the number of entries and how quickly you want the visa, but the service is well worth it. You will need two passport-size photographs. Obtaining a visa from the Visa Office of the Ministry of Foreign Affairs of the People's Republic of China *(7th Floor, Low Block, China Resources Bldg., 26 Harbor Rd., Wan Chai, tel 3413-2300)* is cheaper, but it is often crowded and can be frustratingly slow. Visas are usually issued within two to three days. You can get an express visa in 24 hours by paying extra. U.S. citizens pay more for their visas than other nationalities.

Customs

Though Hong Kong is a duty-free port, there are restrictions on the amount of alcohol, cigarettes, and perfumes you can bring into the country. Adults (18 and over) can import duty-free a maximum of 60 cigarettes or 15 cigars or 75 g of tobacco, plus a liter of spirits, 60 ml of perfume, and 250 ml of eau de toilette. Duty has been removed for wine brought in a passenger's own baggage.

The import of animals or animal parts is strictly controlled. Firearms, narcotics, copyright-infringed goods, and products deriving from endangered animals, such as ivory or tiger skins, are prohibited. Firearms must be declared and handed into custody until departure.

Cars can be brought in for personal use without payment of duty. There are no currency restrictions.

Drugs & Narcotics

Although penalties for importation of drugs are not as harsh as some countries in Asia, they are still severe. You should clearly label medicines for personal use and obtain a statement from your doctor if you are bringing in a large amount of pharmaceuticals. For smaller amounts, bring a doctor's prescription.

HOW TO GET TO HONG KONG
Airlines

Hong Kong is a key regional hub for east Asia and is connected to all parts of the world by numerous airlines. The territory's chief airline, Cathay Pacific, operates daily flights from Australia, Canada, Europe, London, and a few major U.S. cities—Los Angeles, New York, and San Francisco. Hong Kong's second airline, Dragonair, has budget flights to a number of Chinese and regional destinations. From the United States, Continental and United are among the airlines offering regular scheduled flights. Qantas flies daily between Australia and Hong Kong.

The flight time is 18 hours from New York, 15 hours from Los Angeles, 13 hours from London, and 8 hours from Sydney.

Useful Numbers in Hong Kong

British Airways, tel 2822-9000 or 800/AIRWAYS
Cathay Pacific, tel 2747-1234 or 800/233-2742
Continental, tel 3198-5777
Qantas, tel 2842-9000 or 800/227-4500
United, tel 2810-4888 or 800/864-8331

Airport

Hong Kong is served by Hong Kong International Airport at Chek Lap Kok, which opened on Lantau Island in 1998—28 miles (45 km) from Central District on Hong Kong Island. About three-quarters of the airport site was constructed on land reclaimed from the sea. The terminal building, designed by British architect Sir Norman Foster, is Hong Kong's single largest building. Its winglike roof and glass walls have been critically acclaimed as a landmark in modern architecture.

The fastest airport-to-city link is the Airport Express high-speed train, which runs at 15-minute intervals between 5:50 a.m. and 1:15 a.m. and takes under 25 minutes to the Central interchange on Hong Kong Island, where it connects directly with Hong Kong's subway system or Mass Transit Railway (MTR) at Hong Kong Station. Outside the station is a taxi stand. There is also a stop at Kowloon. You can check in your baggage at airline counters at Hong Kong station before boarding the train to the airport. One-way tickets cost HK$100 ($13) for adults and HK$50 ($6.40) for children. Return tickets, valid for a month, cost HK$180 ($23).

An airport bus operates every 15 minutes. It takes one hour to Central and costs HK$40 ($5).

Airport money exchange bureaus are open between 6 a.m. and 11 p.m. daily, but the exchange rates are on the low side. There are ATMs in the arrivals hall.

Departure tax, included in airline fares, is HK$120 ($15). Security tax and fuel surcharges are also usually included in the airfares.

Because of the distance from the airport to the city, taxis are expensive and take longer than the train. Expect to pay HK$350 ($45) to Central District and HK$280 ($36) to Tsim Sha Tsui.

HOW TO GET TO MACAU

The **TurboJet Company** runs fast ferries from the Macau Ferry

Terminal at the Shun Tak Center, 200 Connaught Road Central—above the Sheung Wan MTR station in Hong Kong's Western District. Ferries run every 15 minutes from 7 a.m. to 1:45 a.m. Between 2:30 a.m. and 6 a.m., departures vary from 45 to 90 minutes. The trip takes about one hour and immigration procedures are efficient and speedy. You can buy tickets at the terminal just before your trip, although it is advisable to book on weekends. For inquiries tel 2859-3333, for reservations tel 2921-6688.

HeliExpress (tel 2108-4838) runs a half-hourly helicopter service between Hong Kong and Macau from 9 a.m. to 11 p.m. daily, departing from its helipad at the Shun Tak Center. It costs HK$1,700 ($219), including tax and insurance surcharge, one way and takes about 16 minutes.

HOW TO GET TO GUANGZHOU

Guangzhou is easily reached from Hong Kong in less than two hours by through-trains departing from Hong Kong Mass Transit Railway (MTR) station in Hung Hom. There are 12 services a day and immigration procedures are efficient. Fares are HK$230 ($30) for premium class and HK$190 ($25) for first class. For reservations and inquiries tel 2947-7888. Tickets can also be purchased from China Travel Services (tel 2789-5401) and travel agents.

GETTING AROUND
Traveling in Hong Kong
By Car

Because of the limited opportunities for driving, car rental is not as common in Hong Kong as it is in other major tourist destinations. It is also expensive. Renting a car for the day could cost you well over $100.

Visitors with a driver's license from their own country are permitted to rent and drive cars. Driving is on the left. Three road toll tunnels connect Hong Kong Island to Kowloon. Street parking in busy areas such as Central, Causeway Bay, and Kowloon can be very difficult, if not impossible, and traffic police are very vigilant in enforcing restrictions, but you can usually find room in the city's underground and covered parking lots.

Cars are banned on Lamma, Cheung Chau, and most other outlying islands, and movement restrictions operate on Lantau Island, where a bridge connects only with the airport.

It's against the law to drive or travel in a car, front or back seat, without wearing a safety belt. Hong Kong has a large number of motorcycle traffic police who diligently stop cars with unbelted occupants.

The police frequently set up roadblocks to check for illegal immigrants; carry your driver's license and passport at all times.

Drink-driving laws are enforced. As a rule, don't drive if you have drunk more than one pint of normal strength (5 percent alcohol by volume) draft beer, or two 200 ml glasses of wine, or one single measure of spirits.

Road atlases are widely available in bookstores.

Renting a car

Should you choose to rent a car, Avis has a desk at Hong Kong International Airport, as well as a downtown partner office at G/F Parklane Hotel Car Park, 310 Gloucester Rd., Causeway Bay, tel 2882-2927, www.avis.com.hk.

By Public Transportation

Hong Kong has a highly efficient, inexpensive, and integrated public transportation system, combining government and private companies. Most times, you never have to wait more than a few minutes between rides.

Timetable Information

Bus, train, and subway (known as the MTR—Mass Transit Railway) maps and timetables are available at Hong Kong Tourism Board (HKTB) offices (see pp. 241–242).

Bus

Hong Kong has one of the world's largest fleets of double-decker buses in the world. On some roads in Central in the rush hours, traffic jams are caused solely by continuous walls of buses. Elsewhere they are often the quickest, cleanest, and most comfortable means of getting around.

All of the buses are air-conditioned—even in winter—so you should take a lightweight jacket for journeys of 20 minutes or more.

Double-decker services generally operate daily between 6 a.m. and midnight, in addition to a night bus service marked N. Fares are posted on the counter beside the driver. You put the exact fare into a box, also beside the driver (no change is given) or wave your Octopus card (see p. 239) over a small electronic device. Many drivers speak little English.

In addition, fleets of 16-seater minibuses (called maxicabs in some areas) ply the main routes. Red minibuses run prescribed routes on Hong Kong Island and Kowloon. Green minibuses take the roads in the New Territories. They do not run to any timetable and they pick up and drop off passengers along the route—you have to shout to the driver when you want to get off. Some services between Hong Kong Island and Kowloon run all night.

The payment system varies. Change is given on red minibuses—you pay when leaving—while you are required to put the exact fare into a box next to the driver when you board a green minibus.

Trams

Hong Kong is one of only two places in the world still operating double-decker trams (the other place is the British seaside town of Blackpool). A journey on a tram is something every visitor should experience. Try to get a seat upstairs at the front. Tracks run from Kennedy Town in Western District to Shau Kei Wan at the eastern end of Hong Kong Island. Trams also run every few minutes to the racetrack at Happy Valley. There is a flat fare of HK$2 for any distance. You enter at the rear of the tram and pay on leaving at the front by placing HK$2 in a box next to the driver or using an Octopus card. No change is given.

Peak Tram

A funicular tram, built in 1888, carries passengers up the steep mountainside to the top of Victoria Peak. The service, which operates daily from 7 a.m. to midnight at 15-minute intervals, takes 12 minutes. You can return to the city by bus 15 to the Star Ferry terminus.

Harbor ferries

Fleets of ferries crisscross Hong Kong's harbor, linking Hong Kong Island and Kowloon with the outlying islands and satellite towns along the New Territories' coast.

The most famous ferry is the Star Ferry, which operates between the Central District and Wan Chai on Hong Kong Island, and Tsim Sha Tsui and Hung Hom on Kowloon. The familiar olive-green-and-cream ferries, with burnished-wood interiors, run every five to ten minutes between 6:30 a.m. and 11:30 p.m. daily, and the trip takes eight minutes. A similar service runs between Tsim Sha Tsui and Wan Chai, and Central and Hung Hom at less regular intervals.

Ferries and hydrofoils operate regular services daily to the islands of Lamma, Lantau, Peng Chau, and Cheung Chau. Journeys take up to an hour. A regular fast hydrofoil takes 25 minutes between Hong Kong Island and Discovery Bay on Lantau Island. All these ferries run from the Outlying Islands Ferry piers in front of the ifc building. For timetable information details of daily harbor tours, tel 2508-1234.

Trains

Hong Kong's extensive, efficient train service is now universally known as the MTR (Mass Transit Railway), including what was formerly known as the KCR. The MTR runs the Hong Kong metro, as well as the interconnected suburban rail systems that service the New Territories, as far as the Chinese border at Lo Wu and Lok Ma Chau. Just about everywhere you want to go in Hong Kong is serviced by the MTR, aside from the south side of Hong Kong Island, where a line is planned. Currently there are nine lines, as well as the Airport Express and Light Rail.

For tourists, the primary metro line is the blue Island Line, which runs most of the length of north Hong Kong Island, from Sheung Wan in the west, through Central, Wan Chai, and Causeway Bay, to Chai Wan in the east. Jumping-off points for Kowloon are the Central and North Point stations. In Kowloon, the red Tsuen Wan Line runs from Central on Hong Kong Island, through Tsim Sha Tsui, Jordan, and Mong Kok, to Tsuen Wan in the northwest. For the New Territories, the East Rail Line runs from East Tsim Sha Tsui in Kowloon, through Sha Tin and Fanling, to Lo Wu and the border in the north. Both the Airport Express and dedicated Disneyland Line run from Hong Kong Station, through Kowloon Station.

The MTR system is fast, safe and spotlessly clean. Trains run between 6:00 a.m. and 1:00 a.m., depending on the line. Times and fares can be found at tel 2881-8888, www.mtr.com.hk.

The MTR also runs intercity routes to Zhaoqing, Beijing, Shanghai, and Guangzhou from Hung Hom station.

Ticket Information

Octopus cards are the easiest way to move around. Otherwise, all MTR stations have automated ticket machines as well as customer service desks. Feed tickets into the turnstile and then pick them back up, before feeding it back in at your destination, where it will be retained. Try to avoid travel during rush hours (8 a.m.–10 a.m. and 5 p.m.–7 p.m.) as it can get very crowded.

Taxis

Hong Kong boasts around 18,000 metered taxis. Fares are low compared with most Western cities.

Urban red taxis can operate throughout Hong Kong, aside from some areas on Lantau. (A limited number of blue taxis service Lantau.) Green New Territories taxis are confined to rural areas in the New Territories, and can't pick up fares in Kowloon or Hong Kong Island.

Flag fall is HK$16. There's a surcharge of HK$20 for crossing the harbor via one of the tunnels. Taxis are not permitted to pick up or drop passengers where there is a yellow line along the roadside, usually in congested locations.

Most drivers speak a little English and will know the location of the major hotels and tourist areas. Otherwise, bring your destination written in Chinese.

Taxi drivers are almost universally honest. However, if you need to make a complaint, taxi numbers are displayed on the dashboard. To lodge a complaint against a driver, tel 2889-9999.

To trace lost property, tel 1872-920.

PRACTICAL ADVICE
Communications
Post Offices
Though there are numerous post offices and sub-post offices, they are sometimes hard to find and crowded. The main offices are adjacent to the ifc building on Hong Kong Island and at 10 Middle Road in Kowloon. Both are open 8 a.m. to 6 p.m. Monday to Saturday and 8 a.m. to 2 p.m. on Sunday. Smaller offices close at 5 p.m. Monday to Friday and at 1 p.m. on Saturday, and are closed on Sunday and public holidays. For the locations of other offices, tel 2921-2222.

Telephones
The large variety of public phones cost HK$1 for a five-minute local call. Some are coin only or card only; others take both phone cards and credit cards. Stored-value phone cards for HK$50, HK$150, and HK$200 can be bought at convenience stores.

Local calls from private phones (not cellular) are free and Hong Kong people see it as their inalienable right to use phones in restaurants, bars, and stores free of charge for local use. Businesses will often put their phones in a convenient place for customers—and passersby—to use. Check with your supplier for cellphone compatibility. All Hong Kong phone numbers are eight digits and there are no area codes. To call Hong Kong from overseas, dial the international access code, then the country code 852 before the number. To call outside Hong Kong, dial 001 first.

To make collect calls, dial 10010. Directory inquiries, 1081.

Conversions
Although the British Imperial system still remains, Hong Kong uses the metric system for weights and measures. Speed and distances are in kilometers:
1 mile = 1.6 km

Weights are in kilograms and tonnes:
1 kg = 2.2 lbs
1 tonne = 0.98 ton

Volumes are in liters:
1 liter = 1.75 pints

Temperatures are in Celsius:
0°C = 32°F

Electricity
All appliances operate at 220 volts. The standard plug connection is the British-style square three-pin, now used by all major hotels. Older buildings still use a mix of round two- and three-pin plugs. Adaptor plugs are widely available in stores and electrical goods shops.

Holidays
Banks, post offices, government offices, and most commercial offices close on Sundays and public holidays. Most shops, restaurants, and bars remain open, except during a few days over Chinese New Year—Hong Kong's quietest time of the year when many locals travel abroad. Dates vary from year to year, but usually fall mid-January to mid-February. Several other annual Chinese holidays are linked to the lunar calendar. Many Chinese shops operate as normal on Christmas Day.

Established holidays include:
January 1
(New Year's Day)
January/February
(Chinese New Year)
Late March/Early April
(Good Friday, Easter Saturday, Easter Monday)
Early April
(Ching Ming)
April/May
(Buddha's Birthday)
May 1
(Labor Day)
July 1
(Hong Kong Establishment Day,

marking the end of British colonial rule)
August 17
(Sino-Japanese War Victory Day)
September
(Mid-Autumn Festival)
October 1
(China's National Day)
December 25
(Christmas Day)
December 26
(2nd Christmas Day)

Liquor Laws
Hong Kong has very liberal rules. Alcohol can be bought virtually anywhere, from street stands and convenience stores to harbor ferries. It's possible to get a drink around the clock seven days a week. Many bars open from late morning until 3 a.m. the next day, some for 24 hours. It's illegal to sell alcohol to anyone under 18.

Media
Newspapers
Hong Kong has a free and open media. There are two local English language daily newspapers, the *South China Morning Post* and *The Standard*. They carry local and international news and features, including sections devoted to English and European soccer and U.S. baseball, football, basketball, and hockey. The *Asian Wall Street Journal* is also published here. The *Post* gives special emphasis to events in mainland China. Several weekly free *What's On* guides are also widely distributed in bars and restaurants. There are numerous Chinese-language daily newspapers. Several regional weekly news magazines are based in Hong Kong, notably the *Far Eastern Economic Review, Time Asia,* and *Asiaweek*. International newspapers and magazines, including *USA Today* and the *International Herald Tribune,* can

be found in bookstores and newsstands. Newsstands at the Star Ferry concourse in Tsim Sha Tsui have a huge selection of British, U.S., Australian, Canadian, Asian, and European newspapers.

Radio
Thirteen stations offer music, news, and other entertainment on FM and AM bands. Most are Cantonese, but several have English services. The shortwave BBC World Service, with international news every hour on the hour, is retransmitted on a local medium wave frequency to provide excellent reception.

Television
There are two English-language free-access terrestrial television stations. Most hotels also provide numerous cable and satellite channels featuring CNN, CNBC, and BBC World, plus movie and sports channels.

Money Matters
The Hong Kong dollar is the unit of currency, pegged to the U.S. dollar (around HK$7.79 to US$1). The Hong Kong dollar is divided into 100 cents. Coins come in denominations of 10, 20, and 50 cents, and $1, $2, $5, and $10; notes are in $10, $20, $50, $100, $500, and $1,000.

The notes come in three different types for each denomination and bear the names of three different banks: the Standard Chartered Banking Corporation, the Bank of China and the biggest, the Hong Kong and Shanghai Banking Corporation (HSBC).

Large bank branches, especially in the Hong Kong Island central business district, offer exchange services for travelers' checks and cash. There are currency exchange bureaus at the airport and in the main shopping districts frequented by foreign visitors, and their exchange rates are usually lower than banks. Both banks and exchange bureaus charge a commission. Ask what it is before exchanging.

Hotels will also exchange cash and travelers' checks for guests, but at higher rates than banks or exchange bureaus.

Automatic teller machines (ATMs) attached to banks are widely available in Hong Kong; most MTR stations have at least one. HSBC "Electronic Money" machines provide 24-hour cash withdrawal in local currency for Visa and MasterCard holders. American Express cardholders have access to Jetco (network of Hong Kong banks) ATMs and can withdraw local currency and travelers' checks at the "Express Cash" ATMs. A growing number of ATMs now belong to the Maestro and Cirrus networks. Check with your home bank for charges.

Opening Times
In many respects, Hong Kong is a 24-hour city. Shops and department stores are open seven days. Most big stores will open about 10 a.m. and close at about 8 p.m. or 9 p.m. Smaller shops, especially in Kowloon and Causeway Bay, open until 11 p.m. or later. Some of the night markets are open until 11 p.m.

Major banks are open 9 a.m. to 4:30 p.m. Monday to Friday and 9 a.m. to 12:30 p.m. on Saturday. Business hours are generally 9 a.m to 5 p.m. Monday to Friday and Saturday mornings.

Government offices open at 9 a.m. and close at 5 p.m. Monday to Friday and at noon or 1 p.m. on Saturday. Some close from 1 to 2 p.m.

Most shops and stores are open on weekends and public holidays, except for a few days at Chinese New Year, but banks, post offices, and government offices close.

Religion
The main religions in Hong Kong are Buddhism and Taoism, but there is also a sizable number of Christians. Muslims count for around 100,000; there are smaller groups of Hindus, Sikhs, and Jews.

Places of Worship
Catholic Cathedral of the Immaculate Conception, 16 Caine Rd., Mid-Levels, Hong Kong Island, tel 2522-8212

Anglican Dioceses of Hong Kong, 1 Lower Albert Rd., Central, tel 2526-5335

Kowloon Mosque, 105 Nathan Rd., Tsim Sha Tsui, tel 2724-0095

Jewish Cultural Center and Synagogue, 1 Robinson Pl., 70 Robinson Rd., Mid-Levels, tel 2589-0095

Time Differences
The difference from Greenwich Mean Time (GMT) is +8 hours in winter and +7 in summer. The time difference is +13 hours from New York and +16 hours from Los Angeles. Hong Kong does not observe daylight saving.

Tipping
Hong Kong is not a tipping town. Most hotels and upscale restaurants add a 10 percent service charge to their bills, so tipping is redundant. In places that don't, a tip of less than 10 percent can be left at your discretion, depending on the level of service given. In small cafés and bars, leaving a few coins in the check tray is normal practice. In taxis, simply round up the fare to the nearest dollar.

Visitor Information
The Hong Kong Tourism Board (HKTB) has several visitor centers, as well as an English-language telephone information service (tel

2508-1234), which operates from 8 a.m. to 6 p.m. daily. The offices have plenty of travel brochures and will arrange tours, or visit www.discoverhongkong.com.

Airport: In the arrival halls and transfer section. Literature available 24 hours; staffed between 7 a.m. and 11 p.m.
Kowloon: At the Star Ferry terminal, 8 a.m. to 8 p.m.
Hong Kong Island: Causeway Bay MTR (near exit F), 8 a.m. to 8 p.m.

Tourist Offices abroad: The HKTB has offices in a number of countries. Some main addresses:

United States, 115 East 54th St., New York, NY 10022, tel 212/421-3382, fax 212/421-8428; 10940 Wilshire Blvd., Suite 2050, Los Angeles, CA 90024, tel 310/208-4582, fax 310/208-1869

United Kingdom, 6 Grafton St., London W1S 4EQ, tel 020/7533-7100, fax 020/7533-7111

EMERGENCIES IN HONG KONG
Consulates
United States: 26 Garden Rd., Hong Kong Island, tel 2523-9011

Canada: 14th floor, One Exchange Sq., Central, Hong Kong Island, tel 3719-4700

United Kingdom: 1 Supreme Court Rd., (opposite the Conrad International Hotel), Hong Kong Island, tel 2901-3000

Australia: 23rd–24th floors, Harbor Center, 25 Harbor Rd., Wan Chai, tel 2827-8881

Emergency Phone Numbers
For police, fire, or ambulance services, tel 999

Medical Services
On Hong Kong Island: Queen Mary Hospital, Pokfulam Rd., tel 2855-3838
In Kowloon: Queen Elizabeth Hospital, 30 Gascoigne Rd., tel 2958-8888
Hospitals with 24-hour services:
Caritas Medical Center, 111 Wing Hung St., Sham Shui Po, Kowloon, tel 3408-7911
Prince of Wales Hospital, 30–32 Ngan Shing St., Sha Tin, New Territories, tel 2632-2211

Lost or Stolen Credit Cards & Travelers' Checks
American Express, tel 2811-6122
Diners Card, tel 2860-1888
MasterCard, tel 800-966677
Visa, tel 800-900 782

Travelers with Disabilities
Many modern buildings provide wheelchair access, but older buildings can be challenging. Though most of the top hotels have facilities for people with disabilities, check in advance. Navigating Hong Kong's crowded streets in a wheelchair can be a nightmare. The MTR is perhaps the best equipped for wheelchairs, with most stations offering access; elsewhere, assistance is available. About half of Hong Kong's buses offer wheelchair access, with dedicated ramps and parking spaces. The Star Ferry has wheelchair access, as do most ferries departing from Central piers; elsewhere, access is patchy. Trams have no wheelchair access (except the Peak Tram). People with visual disabilities will find tactile guide paths and audio announcements on most public transportation. Detailed information is at www .td.gov.hk.

Health
No special precautions or inoculations are necessary before visiting. Tap water should generally be avoided. Bottled water is easily and cheaply available.

Visitors are not covered by the government health service and are advised to obtain medical insurance before traveling. Most government hospitals provide 24-hour emergency outpatient treatment services for a modest charge, but they can be crowded. Most large hotels can summon a doctor at short notice.

If you need to take quantities of prescribed drugs for medical reasons you should carry a letter from your doctor at home to verify that they are for your own use only. This can be presented to customs or immigration authorities if necessary.

Hong Kong's outlying islands and nature trails are plagued with mosquitoes, especially during the hot, humid summer. They are most active at dusk, and although nonmalarial, can cause severe itching to sensitive skin. It's advisable to cover up as much as possible or use a roll-on or spray repellent.

In hot, humid weather, drink plenty of bottled water if you are walking or hiking. Also wear a sunscreen (SPF 15 and above), as the subtropical sun can burn skin very quickly, even in cloudy conditions.

Safety
Hong Kong is a very safe city. There is usually no problem walking in most parts of the city at any time of night or day—even for women. Violent crime against visitors is virtually nonexistent. Because of its small size and large police force, beat cops are seen regularly. If you get into trouble, it should not be difficult to find one. As anywhere, don't leave bags or luggage unattended in public places. Pickpockets sometimes haunt the MTR and crowded night markets.

Hotels & Restaurants

Hong Kong hotels used to be among the most expensive in the world and although prices have come down, the city still isn't cheap. Famed for being home to some of the finest hotels anywhere, the city still defines hotel luxury, however competition in the mid-range and budget spectrum is vibrant, and quality has increased.

Hong Kong is famed throughout Asia for its restaurants, notably its Cantonese cuisine. Being a cosmopolitan place, there are also hundreds of other excellent dining options from around the world. But don't expect to find too many bargains—when it comes to restaurants, Hong Kong is expensive.

Hotels

After a substantial downturn during the 2003 SARS crisis (when room rates were slashed), Hong Kong hotels have slowly recovered, with both occupancy and prices creeping back up. Fueling this demand is an ever increasing number of Chinese mainland tourists, who fill up the city's mid-range hotels, and a booming convention industry, which can occasionally result in hotels in the city becoming full.

Quality has always been high in the city's premium hotels, but has also increased substantially in both the mid-range and budget range, with better service, more amenities, and simply better rooms. Prices, while not cheap, have remained affordable and the increasing number of business oriented hotels and 3-stars aimed at mainland tourists has kept rates in check. Recent years have also seen a spate of boutique openings, which lack the facilities of the major chains, but match them for service, room quality, and price, while offering a more intimate experience.

Expect exceptional service and quality in the best hotels, but be prepared to pay for it. These are often found in the Central and Admiralty Districts on Hong Kong Island, and along the waterfront across the harbor in Tsim Sha Tsui.

Less expensive and budget-priced hotels—many with excellent service and accommodations—tend to be in districts such as Tsim Sha Tsui, Causeway Bay, and farther up the Kowloon Peninsula. Because of Hong Kong's excellent transportation system, all are within easy reach of the main tourist areas.

As a general rule, don't expect big guest rooms in mid-range and budget hotels. Like Hong Kong apartments, they are often small and some are downright poky.

Start your search for a hotel before you visit. The Hong Kong Hotel Association has a comprehensive website (www.hkha.org) that lists all its member hotels and provides links to their websites. Making reservations online will bring substantial savings with some hotels and many give big discounts for stays of seven days or longer, but you will need to ask for them. Booking ahead, while not essential, is advisable, particularly during the peak seasons from March to May and September to November.

There are some excellent value accommodations in neighboring Macau, where prices for food and lodging are cheaper than in Hong Kong, although prices are increasing.

Most big hotels have decent restaurants; ones that are worth a special trip (and their own entry) have been noted with a restaurant icon beneath the hotel icon.

All hotels offer dedicated nonsmoking rooms and usually floors, at the very least. In line with Hong Kong's new indoor smoking laws, many have banned smoking all together.

Restaurants

Hong Kong has the highest per capita ratio of restaurants in the world. Many visitors come to Hong Kong primarily to savor Chinese cuisine, which is overwhelmingly Cantonese, but they will also find a wealth of other cooking styles—from within Southeast and East Asia and from other parts of the world.

Hong Kong is not a particularly cheap place to eat out. Food is of a consistently high standard, but don't expect bargain prices, although many have daily lunch and dinner specials that can cut a decent slice off your bill. The mark-up on wine can be astounding, especially in the upscale places.

Macau is a special treat, offering not only Portuguese dishes but also the unique Macanese style—a fusion of cuisines evolved over the past 400 years from Portugal's colonial empire. It incorporates elements of Cantonese, Portuguese, Indian, Malaccan, and African.

Cantonese cuisine emphasizes freshness, and menus often reflect what was bought that day from the numerous markets. Fish and other seafood is often kept alive and on view in the restaurants to be cooked to order.

Restaurants typically open for lunch about 11:30 a.m. and close about 3 p.m. They reopen again around 6 p.m. for dinner and close about 11 p.m. A 10 percent service charge added to the bill means you don't need to leave a tip.

Many of the restaurants on the following pages are busy, especially during lunch from 1–2 p.m. and in the evening, so make reservations. Hong Kong has introduced a smoking ban, meaning the majority of restaurants and bars are smoke free, however a number of establishments have exemptions until 2009.

Additional Information

Many hotels and restaurants accept all major credit cards. Smaller ones may accept only some, as indicated in each entry. Abbreviations used are: AE American Express, DC Diners Club, D Discover, MC MasterCard, and V Visa.

L = lunch
D = dinner

The hotels and restaurants have been arranged alphabetically by price range within each district.

■ HONG KONG ISLAND NORTH

CENTRAL

🏨 FOUR SEASONS
$$$$$

8 FINANCE ST.
TEL 3196-8888   FAX 3196-8899
www.fourseasons.com
The clean lines and white spaces can make the Four Seasons seem a little sterile, but what it lacks in character, it makes up for in opulence. Amenities and services are unrivalled, while the luxurious rooms feature some of the best harbor views in the city. The hotel is also home to an award-winning spa.

ⓘ 399 🅿 🚇 🅢 🅢 🏊 🍸
🅢 All major cards

🏨 MANDARIN ORIENTAL
$$$$$

5 CONNAUGHT RD.
TEL 2522-0111   FAX 2810-6190
www.mandarinoriental.com
Service and room quality are what you would expect from one of the very top hotels in Hong Kong. After a recent top-to-bottom renovation, the Mandarin is back to its

best and its central location couldn't be better. The indoor swimming pool resembles Roman baths.

ⓘ 502 🅿 🚇 🅢 🅢 🏊 🍸
🅢 All major cards

🏨🍴 BISHOP LEI INTERNATIONAL
$$

4 ROBINSON RD.
TEL 2868-0828   FAX 2868-1551
www.bishopleihtl.com.hk
Bishop Lei is a quiet hotel in the residential district above Central with excellent views of the downtown skyline and harbor. More than one-third of the accommodations are suites. The Terrace Room restaurant has a large open-air terrace. Free shuttle services run to the main tourist areas.

ⓘ 217 🚇 🅢 🅢 🏊 🍸
🅢 All major cards

🍴 CAPRICE
$$$$$

FOUR SEASONS HOTEL,
8 FINANCE ST.
TEL 3196-8888   FAX 3196-8899
www.fourseasons.com
Stroll down Caprice's glass catwalk into one of the city's most exclusive restaurants. A designer interior, mixing the contemporary and the classic, is the stage for superlative French dishes by master chef Vincent Thiery. Reservations and a large wallet essential.

🪑 100 🅿 🅢 🅢
🅢 All major cards

🍴 MANDARIN GRILL
$$$$$

MANDARIN ORIENTAL HOTEL,
5 CONNAUGHT RD.
TEL 2825-4004
www.mandarinoriental.com
Wholly unrecognizable from the clubby dining room that used to be the Mandarin Grill, the new sleek, bright interior is far more inviting. At tables covered with crisp, white linens, the city's movers and shakers tuck into oysters and

---

crustaceans, as well as freshly cooked slices of prime beef.

🪑 60 🅿 🅢 🅢
🅢 All major cards

🍴 LUMIERE
$$$$

3101, IFC MALL
TEL 2393-3933
Perfect harbor views and a designer interior set the stage for spicy Sichuan dishes cooked with a Latin American twist by Lumiere's award-winning chef. Try the seared crab claw in pickled chili sauce and bean paste for a taste of Lumiere's unique flavors. If your wallet won't stretch to the food, try some of their fusion cocktails.

🪑 80 🅿 🅢 🅢
🅢 All major cards

🍴 M AT THE FRINGE
$$$$

2 LOWER ALBERT RD.
TEL 2813-6262
Michelle Garnaut's restaurant has been delighting Hong Kong patrons for almost 20 years. The gorgeous design complements a delicious European menu—one highlight

---

is the salt-encased leg of lamb with grilled aubergine, roasted pumpkin, beans, and potatoes.
🍴 70 🚭 ❄️ 💳 All major cards

🍴 HUNAN GARDEN
$$$
THE FORUM, 3RD FL., EXCHANGE SQUARE
TEL 2868-2880
It may be in a modern glass-and-concrete tower, but the indoor waterfall, bright marble decor, and musicians playing the traditional pipa and erdu (dinner only) all help to transport diners back to the home province of the late Chairman Mao. Hunan cuisine, which is richer and in some cases spicier than Cantonese, is not so common in Hong Kong. Specialties include Hunan ham with a hint of sweetness, mashed chicken in bamboo soup, eels in garlic sauce, and spicy vegetable rolls. Try the Chinese rice wine.
🍴 80 🚭 ❄️ 💳 All major cards

🍴 JIMMY'S KITCHEN
$$$
SOUTH CHINA BLDG., 1–3 WYNDHAM ST.
TEL 2526-5293
Jimmy's is an essential part of Hong Kong for many residents; it's been around for more than 70 years. Its English pub-like ambience and decor, such as mock Elizabethan beams and gleaming brass, belie the excellent British-oriented cooking, with Chinese touches. Regular dishes include oysters kilpatrick and black pepper steak. The seafood mixed grill is a specialty. Regulars save room for the solidly English bread-and-butter pudding. Good wine selection from Europe and elsewhere. Make reservations, especially at lunch time.
🍴 100 🚭 ❄️
💳 All major cards

🍴 KIKU
$$$
13 BASEMENT, THE LANDMARK
TEL 2521-3344
A business haunt in the heart of Hong Kong's financial district, hence the privacy screens between tables. The problem of attracting service is overcome by the use of call-buttons on each table. Benkay is noted for its fresh and very fishy sushi, beef shabu-shabu, and clear clam soup. Ginseng wine is available.
🍴 120 🚭 ❄️
💳 All major cards

🍴 LE TIRE BOUCHON
$$$
45 GRAHAM ST.
TEL 2523-5459
This stand-alone French restaurant on a steep quiet street away from the line of rival eateries has a spacious yet romantic setting. Specialties include baked goat cheese salad, pan-fried duck liver with apple and calvados, and a tender chateaubriand. Vintage French wines complement the food.
🍴 80 🚭 ❄️
💳 All major cards

SOMETHING SPECIAL

🍴 LUK YU TEA HOUSE
$$$
LUK TEA BLDG., 24 STANLEY ST.
TEL 2523-1970
No modern reproductions here: The early 20th-century art deco, stained glass, wood paneling, and ceiling fans are genuine. The ambience is busy and loud, but customers seeking some privacy can reserve a partitioned booth. Cantonese cuisine includes shark's fin and bird'snest soups, and prawns stir-fried with Chinese mushrooms and bamboo shoots. Dim sum is also served. Wine is very limited, but most customers drink beer or tea.
🍴 76 🚭 ❄️ 💳 All major cards

🍴 ORANGE TREE
$$$
17 SHELLEY ST.
TEL 2838-9352
Dutch owner-chef Pieter Onderwater cooks up an interesting range of European and oriental dishes, served in a small clubby setting alongside Hong Kong Island's Mid-Levels escalator. Most fish and the smoked eel are imported from Onderwater's homeland, while smoked duck with mango suggests a more exotic origin than the Netherlands. Vegetarians are well catered for with dishes such as globe artichoke stuffed with asparagus. In spring or fall, try to reserve one of the two tables on the tiny balcony overlooking the escalator.
🍴 50 🚭 ❄️ 💳 All major cards

🍴 SOHO SOHO
$$$
4–8 ARBUTHNOT RD.
TEL 2147-2618
Soho Soho's owners seek to persuade the world the British can cook more than fish and chips and soggy vegetables. So-called Modern British is offered—a fusion of traditionally solid English dishes with lighter Mediterranean touches, such as roast chicken stuffed with Parma ham, and calfs' liver and bacon with mashed potatoes and onion gravy. British desserts include toffee and bread-and-butter puddings.
🍴 100 🚭 ❄️
💳 All major cards

🍴 YELLOW DOOR KITCHEN
$$$
CHEUNG HING COMMERCIAL BLDG., 37 COCHRANE ST.
TEL 2858-6555
One of Hong Kong's original private kitchens, Yellow Door is now open to the general public but has thankfully lost none of its charm. Sizzling Sichuan dishes, as well as more mellow Shanghainese offerings

---

🚭 Nonsmoking   ❄️ Air-conditioning   🏊 Indoor Pool   🏊 Outdoor Pool   🏋️ Health Club   💳 Credit Cards

keep the loyal clientèle returning to this low-key, no fuss spot. The steamed ribs and sweet potato are excellent; the braised duck in pickled chili will leave even the hardiest diner reaching for water.

⊞ 40 ⊗ ⊗
⊗ No credit cards

🍽 YUNG KEE
$$$
32–40 WELLINGTON ST.
TEL 2522-1624
This boisterous institution in Cantonese cooking was established in the 1940s. Roast goose is such a renowned specialty that the Yung Kee sells 300 birds every day. There's a constantly changing large menu that also caters for vegetarians. Dim sum served in the afternoon.

⊞ 1,000 ⊗ ⊗
⊗ All major cards

🍽 STAUNTON'S WINE BAR & CAFÉ
$$
10–12 STAUNTON ST.
TEL 2973-6611
This hip restaurant and bar nestling beside the Mid-Levels escalator is a perfect place to see Hong Kong and be seen. Popular with expats and trendy local Chinese, expect reasonably priced fine wines and nouveau cuisine—without the small portions.

⊞ 60 ⊗ ⊗ All major cards

ADMIRALTY

SOMETHING SPECIAL

🏨 ISLAND SHANGRI-LA
🍽 $$$$$
PACIFIC PLACE, SUPREME COURT RD.
TEL 2877-3838   FAX 2521-8742
www.shangri-la.com
The Shangri-la is one of Hong Kong's most luxurious hotels, providing stunning views over the city and the harbor while ideally located above

the Pacific Place shopping mall. The rooms are among the largest in Hong Kong and many open onto a dramatic interior atrium rising 17 floors through the heart of the hotel. There are 34 suites and seven bars and restaurants, including a lobster bar. **Petrus** on the 56th floor (see right) offers fine dining with a view.

① 565 🅿 ⊟ ⊗ ⊗ ⊠ 🍸
⊗ All major cards

🏨 CONRAD
🍽 INTERNATIONAL
$$$$
PACIFIC PLACE
TEL 2521-3838   FAX 2521-3888
www.conrad.com.hk
The 61-story Conrad towers above the Pacific Place shopping mall. Rooms are large and tastefully decorated in neutral colors. The hotel has five restaurants, including the highly regarded **Nicholini's** (see below).

① 513 🅿 ⊟ ⊗ ⊗ ⊠ 🍸
⊗ All major cards

🏨 JW MARRIOTT
🍽 $$$$
PACIFIC PLACE
TEL 2810-8366   FAX 2845-0737
www.jwmarriotthk.com
Located above the Pacific Place shopping mall, the Marriott offers views across Victoria Harbour to Kowloon from most of its spacious, well-appointed rooms. Five restaurants, including **Man Ho** (see below), serve everything from Californian-Asian fusion cuisine to sushi.

① 602 🅿 ⊟ ⊗ ⊗ ⊠ 🍸
⊗ All major cards

🍽 NICHOLINI'S
$$$$$
CONRAD INTERNATIONAL, PACIFIC PLACE
TEL 2521-3838
An elegant Italian restaurant with panoramic views across the harbor and Kowloon

Peninsula. The signature dishes are the northern Italian specials, such as the lemon-crusted monkfish with braised orange fennel or roasted pork confit in a smoked apple sauce. Service is impeccable.

⊞ 80 🅿 ⊗ ⊗
⊗ All major cards

🍽 PETRUS
$$$$$
ISLAND SHANGRI-LA, PACIFIC PLACE, SUPREME COURT RD.
TEL 2820-8590
Discerning diners come for the rotating menu of seasonal and superb French and Mediterranean dishes, which is complemented by a stellar wine list. A heavy interior of chandeliers and important looking paintings is relieved by the breathtaking 56th-floor view of the harbor below.

⊞ 100 🅿 ⊗ ⊗
⊗ All major cards

🍽 MAN HO
$$$$
JW MARRIOTT, 1 PACIFIC PLACE
TEL 2841-3853
It's worth visiting just for the renowned tea-smoked pigeon, but the braised duck with lotus roots in a rich sauce equally reflects a high-quality Chinese menu. The restaurant is busy at lunchtime, but good table spacing and a decor dominated by the color gold help create a relaxed atmosphere most of the time.

⊞ 200 ⊗ ⊗
⊗ All major cards

🍽 ZEN
$$$
THE MALL, LOWER GROUND FLOOR, PACIFIC PLACE
TEL 2845-4555
Very much Westernized Cantonese, the Zen is modeled on its namesake founded in London many years ago. It's extremely busy at lunchtime when lines form to buy takeout. Specialties include

sliced pork rolls and deep fried boneless chicken wings stuffed with vegetables and served with a lemon sauce. Dim sum is cooked to order.

🔲 350 🔳 🔳
🔳 All major cards

🍴 CHIU CHOW GARDEN
$$
GROUND FLOOR, LIPPO CENTER
TEL 2845-4151
The best Chinese restaurants are noisy, frenetic places, and here the clatter is accompanied by bright decor and swinging red lanterns. Specialties include poached cold crab, goose with bean curd, and minced pork in olive leaves with fried green beans. Chiu Chow boasts some of the cheapest restaurant wines. Ask for a window table overlooking busy Queensway, where even the old trams seem to be in a hurry.

🔲 140 🔳 🔳
🔳 All major cards

LAN KWAI FONG

🍴 VA BENE
$$$$
58 D'AGUILAR ST.
TEL 2845-5577
One of Hong Kong's very best Italian restaurants, matched by an extensive Italian wine cellar. Fish dishes, such as pan-roasted *garoupa* in white wine and garlic are prominent, but meat lovers and vegetarians are also well catered for. Beef tenderloin carpaccio is a house specialty and one of chef Pino Piano's personal favorites.

🔲 60 🔳 🔳 🔳 All major cards

🍴 YUN FU
$$$$
43-55 WYNDHAM ST.
TEL 2116-8855
Modelled on a traditional Chinese mansion, descend the steps into a basement filled with grand Buddhas and intricately carved benches in what truly is an inspired design.

Serving cuisine from some of China's far-flung regions, including Tibet, both the stir-fried king prawns in melted crab roe and Chinese wine are a taste out of the ordinary. They also offer fantastic cocktails using Chinese spirits.

🔲 120 🔳 🔳
🔳 All major cards

🍴 BEIRUT
$$$
27 D'AGUILAR ST.
TEL 2804-6611
Beirut is a crowded but cheerful Lebanese restaurant specializing in meze (small servings similar to Spanish tapas, including minced eggplant, hummus, and falafel), making it a popular haunt of vegetarians. Try one of the legume-loaded dips as a main course. Meat-eaters can tuck into generous portions of spicy shawarma lamb. There's a Lebanese vintage wine list.

🔲 50 🕐 Closed Sun. from 4 p.m. 🔳 🔳 🔳 All major cards

🍴 INDOCHINE 1929
$$$
CALIFORNIA TOWER,
30-32 D'AGUILAR ST.
TEL 2869-7399
The mock French colonial style belies the top-quality Vietnamese cuisine. Dishes range from the more French-influenced Hanoi style to the spicier offerings of Ho Chi Minh City. Fish is prominent, but the beef noodle soup is highly recommended. Try the house specialty—soft shell crab cooked in garlic. French wines dominate.

🔲 100 🔳 🔳
🔳 All major cards

🍴 OLE SPANISH BAR AND RESTAURANT
$$$
1/F SHUN HO TOWER,
24-30 ICE HOUSE ST.
TEL 2523-8624
With ingredients, the chef, and the owner all hailing from

Spain, the dishes are as authentic as you'll find in Madrid or Valencia. The unpretentious, Iberian interior, relaxed atmosphere, and first-rate tapas, such as garlic prawns and bell peppers stuffed with codfish, make it an easy lunchtime stop.

🔲 60 🔳 🔳 🔳 All major cards

🍴 RED PEPPER
$$$
7 LAN FONG RD.
TEL 2577-3811
Spicy Sichuan cuisine that caters as much to vegetarians as meat-eaters. A popular choice is sizzling fried prawns in chili sauce delivered in a hot pan. Fragrant lychee tea complements the food.

🔲 50 🔳 🔳 🔳 All major cards

🍴 THAI LEMONGRASS
$$$
BASEMENT, 30–32 D'AGUILAR ST.
TEL 2905-1688
More subtle Thai food, less fiery than elsewhere, is served in an elegant, warm atmosphere. The emphasis here is on seafood—whole fish such as mullet gently simmered in ginger and herbs. Other specialties include crayfish coconut salad and steamed prawns with lemon grass.

🔲 46 🔳 🔳 🔳 All major cards

🍴 DUBLIN JACKS
$$
1/F, 17 LAN KWAI FONG
TEL 2543-0081   FAX 2543-0839
A slice of modern Dublin, with publican and raconteur Nile darting between diners and drinkers making sure everyone is happy. Enjoy pub-grub classics, including fish and chips, on the refreshing back deck.

🔲 200 🔳 🔳
🔳 All major cards

🍴 POST 97
$$
9 LAN KWAI FONG

TEL 2186-1837
Taking its name from the British handover of Hong Kong to China in 1997, this haunt of trendy youthful Westerners and Chinese serves British-style food enlivened with Mediterranean influences. It's famed for its full English-style fry-up, which is served day and night.
🛗 48 Ⓢ Ⓔ Ⓐ All major cards

VICTORIA PEAK

🍴 THE PEAK LOOKOUT
$$$$
121 PEAK RD.
TEL 2849-1000
This restaurant with a view features a seafood and oyster bar as well as an open-air barbecue. Expect regional specialties such as satay and Hainan chicken rice as well as Western fare, like Sunday roast. There is also a children's menu. Expect, however, to pay the price of high-rent realty.
🛗 120 Ⓢ Ⓔ
Ⓐ All major cards

🍴 CAFE DECO
$$$
PEAK GALLERIA, 118 PEAK RD.
TEL 2949-5111
Despite its huge size, the outstanding views from Cafe Deco's floor-to-ceiling windows regularly attract a full-to-bursting crowd during the evening and weekends, although the activity and noise give Deco a real buzz. From the kitchen come a roll-call of European, Asian and other international dishes, including excellent burgers and a tasty Chinese roast duck pizza.
🛗 600 Ⓢ Ⓔ
Ⓐ All major cards

WESTERN DISTRICT

🏨 LAN KWAI FONG HOTEL
$$$$
3 KAU U FONG
TEL 3650-0000   FAX 3650-0088
www.lankwaifonghotel.com.hk

A rare chance to stay in Central leaving the chain hotels behind, but keeping their comfort. This boutique hotel, set just outside the entertainment areas of Lan Kwai Fong and SoHo, has all you'd expect from a 4-star, including Wi-Fi and a modest gym, delivered with a little more panache. Generous rooms are warmly furnished, with individual touches.
Ⓘ 152 Ⓟ Ⓔ Ⓢ Ⓔ
Ⓐ All major cards

🍴 GAIA RISTORANTE
$$$$
GRAND MILLENNIUM PLAZA,
181 QUEEN'S RD. CENTRAL,
SHEUNG WAN
TEL 2167-8200
Alfresco seating on a modest piazza, complete with a spouting fountain, makes Gaia Hong Kong's very own slice of the Mediterranean. Popular with would-be Romeos and Juliets, the wood-oven fired pizzas are highly recommended.
🛗 80 Ⓢ Ⓔ Ⓐ All major cards

🍴 THE PRESS ROOM
$$–$$$
108 HOLLYWOOD RD.,
SHEUNG WAN
TEL 2525-3444
Just off the beaten track, the Press Room's open design, floor to ceiling windows, and earthy colors evoke a cutting-edge New York hangout. The bistro menu runs from finely cooked Italian classics to sandwiches, all superbly prepared before your eyes. Though the cooking matches many of Hong Kong's finest restaurants, the prices, thankfully, don't.
🛗 100 Ⓢ Ⓔ
Ⓐ All major cards

WAN CHAI

🏨 🍴 GRAND HYATT
$$$$
1 HARBOR RD.
TEL 2588-1234
FAX 2802-0677

PRICES

HOTELS

An indication of the cost of a double room in the high season is given by $ signs.

$$$$$	Over $240
$$$$	$160-240
$$$	$110-160
$$	$70-110
$	Under $70

RESTAURANTS

An indication of the cost of a three-course meal without drinks is given by $ signs.

$$$$$	Over $65
$$$$	$50-65
$$$	$30-50
$$	$20-30
$	Under $20

---

www.hongkong.grandhyatt.com
The Grand Hyatt lies in a prime location adjoining the harborfront Hong Kong Convention and Exhibition Center. It's worth a visit just for the lobby's art deco opulence. Sumptuous rooms and suites have down duvets covered in Egyptian cotton bed linen. Seven different dining choices range from Grissini's fine Italian cuisine to the Japanese **Kaetsu** (see opposite).
Ⓘ 549 Ⓟ Ⓔ Ⓢ Ⓔ Ⓢ Ⓔ
Ⓐ All major cards

🏨 🍴 RENAISSANCE HARBOR VIEW
$$$$
1 HARBOR RD.
TEL 2802-8888   FAX 2802-8833
www.renaissancehotel.com
This large, nondescript Marriott group hotel stands on the Wan Chai waterfront, linked to the Hong Kong Convention and Exhibition Center. It offers excellent service, modern, well-appointed rooms, and fantastic harbor views, as well as landscaped gardens with rock gardens and waterfalls. Dining choices include Italian

---

🏨 Hotel 🍴 Restaurant Ⓘ No. of guest rooms 🛗 No. of Seats Ⓟ Parking Ⓔ Closed Ⓔ Elevator

at the **Scala** restaurant and Cantonese at the **Dynasty.**

🛈 860 🅿 🔁 🚫 🈂 🏊 📺
🚫 All major cards

EMPIRE HONG KONG
$$$

33 HENNESSEY RD.
TEL 2866-9111   FAX 2861-3121
www.empirehotel.com
In the heart of the vibrant Wan Chai nightlife district and close to shopping and business areas, this well-appointed property is popular, with 36 suites and two restaurants—a steak house and Chinese cuisine at the **King of Dragon** restaurant.

🛈 360 🅿 🔁 🚫 🈂 🏊 📺
🚫 All major cards

NOVOTEL CENTURY HONG KONG
$$$

238 JAFFE RD.
TEL 2598-8888   FAX 2598-8866
www.novotel.com
Recently renovated and upgraded by new owners, Novotel, this business class hotel is close to the main shopping and nightlife areas. It has 22 suites, two bars, and two restaurants, most notably, Pepinos Cucina Italiana. Causeway Bay is only minutes away on foot, while the nightlife scene of Wan Chai is even closer.

🛈 511 🅿 🔁 🚫 🈂 🏊 📺
🚫 All major cards

COSMO
$$

375–377 QUEEN'S RD. EAST
TEL 3552-8388   FAX 3552-8399
www.cosmohotel.com.hk
Cosmo's bold orange and green rooms are a stylish cut above much of the average offerings in the Wan Chai area, and although this boutique hotel's attention to detail is felt in the excellent service, the lack of facilities make prices somewhat heavy.

🛈 142 🅿 🔁 🚫 🈂
🚫 All major cards

WHARNEY
$$

57–73 LOCKHART RD.
TEL 2861-1000   FAX 2865-6023
www.adhhotels.com
If you want to be in the thick of the neon nightlife of Lockhart Road, you can't get much closer. Prices are reasonable, even if rooms are compact. The hotel has a rooftop pool.

🛈 361 🅿 🔁 🚫 🈂 🏊 📺
🚫 All major cards

KAETSU
$$$$$

GRAND HYATT, 1 HARBOR RD.
TEL 2588-1234 EXT. 7088
Hong Kong's most upscale Japanese dining venue. Tables are arranged in private booths around a central sushi bar. The sushi, along with scallop sashimi, is the best you'll find anywhere. Ingredients are specially flown in from Japan and the menu changes with the seasons. The Kaetsu's set course of nine dishes is a good bet. There is a comprehensive sake menu, offering warm or cold varieties.

🔁 60 🅿 🚫 🈂
🚫 All major cards

FOOK LAM MOON
$$$$

35–45 JOHNSTON RD.
TEL 2866-0663
A venerable Hong Kong institution specializing in exotic Cantonese dishes. The menu tends to be rather expensive, but for delicacies such as shark's fin and double boiled bird's nest, both locals and a high-profile clientele swear that Fook Lam Moon is the only place to go.

🚫 🈂 🚫 All major cards

INGREDIENTS
$$$$

23–29 WING FUNG ST.
TEL 2544-5133   FAX 2544-9588
www.ingredients.com.hk
Once Hong Kong's hidden secret, this former private

kitchen has moved to the blossoming dining district around Star Street and drawn back the curtains. Ambitious international dishes, such as poached mussels in white wine sauce and lemongrass marinated pork, are convincingly carried off, and can be enjoyed either inside the intimate interior or on the rooftop garden.

🔁 200 🚫 🈂
🚫 All major cards

AMERICAN PEKING
$$$

20 LOCKHART RD.
TEL 2527-1000
A local institution since 1948, serving Peking cuisine in a bright and boisterous setting on two floors. Beggar's chicken is an old favorite, but has to be ordered a day in advance. It consists of chicken stuffed with vegetables, shredded mushrooms, and a little pork, marinated for two hours then wrapped in lotus leaves and baked. For dessert, try the soufflé balls and red bean stuffing.

🔁 140 🚫 🈂
🚫 All major cards

LIU YUAN
$$$

303 HENNESSY RD.
TEL 2510-0483
The appeal of Liu Yuan's Shanghainese dishes regularly attracts visitors from Shanghai. Crispy eel is a favorite, along with shredded dried bean curd with ham and chicken sauce. The sesame dessert dumplings are extremely popular.

🔁 90 🚫 🈂 🚫 All major cards

QUARTERDECK CLUB
$$$

FLEET ARCADE, 1 LUNG KING ST., FENWICK PIER
TEL 2827-8882
While the food isn't fancy, it's filling, and the weekly all-you-can-eat barbecue buffet is a rare treat in upscale Hong Kong. However, the real draw

is that the Quarterdeck Club is one of the few places on Hong Kong Island, where you can enjoy alfresco dining. It even has views of the harbor, although relentless land reclamation means you may soon need binoculars to see it.

🔱 350 🅢 🅒
🅢 All major cards

🍴 VICEROY
$$
SUN HUNG KAI CENTER,
2ND FL., 30 HARBOR RD.
TEL 2827-7777
A rich mix of south and Southeast Asian dishes, ranging from India to Indonesia. The emphasis is on spice, but the tandoori specialties are tasty without being explosively hot. Indian vegetarian dishes are plentiful. Once a month they host a comedy night, featuring both local and big-name international stars.

🔱 200 🅢 🅒
🅢 All major cards

🍴 SHAKE EM BUNS
$
2D STAR ST.
TEL 2866-2060
Opened by a Chinese-American, North Carolina transplant, Shake em Buns offers up gourmet burgers at bargain prices. With just a few stools inside, it's best to carry food out. With Hong Kong park just a few minutes away, it's perfect picnic fare.

🔱 8 🅢 🅒 🅢 No credit cards

CAUSEWAY BAY

🏨 EXCELSIOR
🍴 $$$
281 GLOUCESTER RD.
TEL 2894-8888   FAX 2895-6459
www.excelsiorhongkong.com
The Excelsior overlooks Victoria Harbour but fronts an extremely busy six-lane highway. The best harbor views are from the 21 spacious suites on the top floor. The rear entrance

leads straight into the heart of Causeway Bay's shop-till-you-drop scene. Excelsior's **Talk of the Town** grill is a popular nightspot with wide views of the night skyline, live entertainment, and dancing. Its basement sports bar is popular for its big-screen shows of major sporting events.

🛈 886 🅿 🅴 🅢 🅒 🅦
🅢 All major cards

🏨 JIA
$$$
1–5 IRVING ST.
TEL 3196-9000
Jia's fabulous design, conjured up by John Hitchcox and Philippe Starck, draws rave reviews. This award-winning interior is complemented by superior service and in-room gadgets such as a full-blown home entertainment service. As with many boutique hotels in the city, rooms are somewhat cramped.

🛈 54 🅴 🅢 🅒 🅦
🅢 All major cards

🏨 PARK LANE
$$$
310 GLOUCESTER RD.
TEL 2293-8888   FAX 2576-7853
www.parklane.com.hk
The Park Lane borders Causeway Bay shopping center, overlooking the harbor and one of the area's few oases of green, Victoria Park. Rooms are spacious compared to many other hotels in the area.

🛈 810 🅿 🅴 🅢 🅒 🅦
🅢 All major cards

🏨 REGAL HONGKONG
$$$
88 YEE WO ST.
TEL 2890-6633, FAX 2881-0777
www.regalhotel.com
The Regal lies in the heart of Causeway Bay's frenetic shopping, eating, and entertainment scene, close to Victoria Park and both the subway and bus systems. Rooms have a stylish mixture of European

and Asian furnishings.

🛈 425 🅿 🅴 🅢 🅒 🅰 🅦
🅢 All major cards

🏨 ROSEDALE ON THE
🍴 PARK
$$
8 SHELTER ST.
TEL 2127-8888   FAX 2127-3333
www.rosedale.com.hk
Located close to Causeway Bay's entertainment district, the Rosedale offers a peaceful haven from the hustle and bustle. The hotel's 43 suites have kitchenettes and sofa beds, and its restaurant, **Sonata Bistro,** offers a mix of international and Asian dishes.

🛈 274 🅿 🅴 🅢 🅒 🅦
🅢 All major cards

🏨 EMPEROR
$
1A WANG TAK ST.,
HAPPY VALLEY
TEL 2893-3693   FAX 2834-6700
www.emperorhotel.com.hk
A small hotel in the relatively quiet residential Happy Valley District, close to the Happy Valley racetrack and Hong Kong Stadium. Tastefully furnished rooms.

🛈 150 🅿 🅴 🅢 🅒
🅢 All major cards

🍴 COVA
$$$
THE LEE GARDENS,
33 HYSAN AVE.
TEL 2907-3399
Cova features dishes from all over the Italian peninsula, such as fresh mozzarella flown in from Italy. Specialties include grilled steak tagliata and pan-fried codfish with buffalo mozzarella in a basil cream sauce.

🔱 60 🅢 🅒 🅢 All major cards

🍴 FORUM
$$$
485 LOCKHART RD.
TEL 2891-2516
The large Cantonese menu ranges from simple dishes to

the expensively exotic. Aim for the latter—it's a good place to try much talked-about dishes such as abalone, shark's fin soup, and bird'snest soup, all specialties of chief chef Ah Yat.

🔟 100 🅿 📵 🄲
📇 All major cards

🍴 WASABISABI
$$$
SHOP 130 TIMES SQUARE,
1 MATHESON ST.
TEL 2506-0009

The stunningly stylish design of lipstick-red seating and soft lighting has retained its edge over the years. The restaurant attracts a young crowd for excellent sushi and other Japanese dishes. The C-shape cubicles swivel to face the bar, or, for a more romantic evening, the dining room.

🔟 200 📵 🄲
📇 All major cards

🍴 W'S ENTRECOTE
$$$
33 SHARP ST., EAST
TEL 2506-0133

A French steak-house pure and simple. Charbroiled rib-eye in herb butter sauce is a favorite. Serves exclusively French wine.

🔟 120 📵 🄲
📇 All major cards

🍴 BANANA LEAF
$$
440 JAFFE RD.
TEL 2573-8187

Most dishes are eaten off banana leaves in this large, noisy, college canteen-style setting. The cuisine is dubbed Malaysian, but it's really a spicy mix of Indian, Malay, Thai, and Indonesian. Worth trying are the fried chicken in pandanus leaf, crab curry, and the non-alcoholic exotic fruit drinks.

🔟 140 📵 🄲
📇 All major cards

🍴 DIM SUM
$$
63 SING WOO RD.,
HAPPY VALLEY
TEL 2834-8893

A huge dim sum selection, including the noteworthy steamed lobster and shrimp dumplings, brings lines of loyal customers, awaiting the latest dishes. Another specialty, more Sichuan than Cantonese, is pan-fried scallops and prawns with chili sauce and asparagus.

🔟 60 📵 🄲 📇 All major cards

🍴 KUNG TAK LAM
$$
280 GLOUCESTER RD.
TEL 2890-3127

This rare Chinese vegetarian eatery does a great job of imitating meat dishes with its vegetarian Shanghainese deep-fried eel, goose, and chicken. Try the eggplant in Sichuan sauce, Shanghai cold noodles with seven sauces, and, for dessert, rice flour dumplings with black sesame.

🔟 180 📵 🄲
📇 All major card

◼ HONG KONG ISLAND SOUTH

STANLEY

SOMETHING SPECIAL

🍴 THE VERANDAH
$$$$
REPULSE BAY, THE ARCADE,
109 REPULSE BAY
TEL 2812-2722

Overlooking the sea, The Verandah is a delightful open-air spot to take afternoon tea (3:30–5:30 p.m.). It's also popular for Sunday brunch (11 a.m.–2:30 p.m.) when a huge buffet ranges from sushi and salmon to eggs Benedict with caviar, roast lamb and beef, and salads. In the evening it becomes a more sophisticated venue for quiet dining, with

piano accompaniment.

🔟 80 📵 🄲 📇 All major cards

🍴 BAYSIDE BRASSERIE
$$
25 STANLEY MARKET RD.
TEL 2899-0818

This casual brasserie is a great place to soak up Stanley's seaside atmosphere, thanks to its wide, sea-facing windows. An eclectic menu includes curries, seafood, and pastas; the pizzas are recommended.

🔟 110 📵 🄲
📇 All major cards

🍴 LUCY'S
$$
64 MAIN ST.
TEL 2813-9055

This Mediterranean-style café matches the seaside setting. The menu is limited, but offers an ever changing selection of seasonal dishes.

🔟 40 📵 🄲 📇 All major cards

◼ KOWLOON

🏨 🍴 INTERCONTINENTAL HONG KONG
$$$$$
18 SALISBURY RD., TSIM SHA TSUI
TEL 2721-1211   FAX 2739-4546
www.hongkong-ic-.inter
continental.com

This harborfront hotel offers spacious rooms and lavish suites with marble bathrooms, and some of the best views of the harbor and Hong Kong Island. It has 92 suites, two bars, and six restaurants, including **Nobu** (see p. 254) and **Spoon**, serving first-class French and Japanese cuisine.

🛏 495 🅿 📶 📵 🄲 🏊 🏋
📇 All major cards

SOMETHING SPECIAL

🏨 🍴 THE PENINSULA
$$$$$
SALISBURY RD., TSIM SHA TSUI
TEL 2920-2888   FAX 2722-4170

www.peninsula.com
The famous Peninsula is a towering tribute to opulence. It still overlooks Victoria Harbour, but due to development and land reclamation it is no longer on the waterfront. The hotel caters to every whim, including a rooftop heliport to bring guests directly from the airport. The large rooms have marble bathrooms with built-in TVs. There are 54 suites, three bar-lounges, and six restaurants, including the renowned Philippe Starck creation, **Felix,** serving Pacific Rim fare, **Gaddi's,** and **Chesa** (see pp. 254 & 255). Afternoon tea in the lobby is a must, even if you are not staying here.

🛈 300 P ⮃ 🅢 🅒 🎿 📺
🅢 All major cards

🏨 LANGHAM PLACE
$$$$
20 SHANGHAI ST., MONG KOK
TEL 3552-3388   FAX 3552-3322
www.langhamhotels.com
The perfect location, towering over Mong Kok, for those who would like to explore Hong Kong's more traditional side with the city's best markets on your doorstep. Yet despite the surroundings, both the hotel and its rooms are some of the most technologically advanced in the city, including iPod docks, DVD players, and a state-of-the-art Cisco phone, which allows you to get the weather forecast and send free SMs. Their Chuan Spa also comes highly recommended.

🛈 652 P ⮃ 🅢 🅒 🎿 📺
🅢 All major cards

🏨 ROYAL GARDEN
🍽 $$$$
69 MODY RD., TSIM SHA
TSUI EAST
TEL 2721-5215   FAX 2369-9976
www.rghk.com
The Royal Garden provides a refuge from Tsim Sha Tsui's frenetic pace, close to most Kowloon-side attractions.

Rooms tend to be a little garish and overfurnished for their small size. It has 48 suites and five restaurants, both Western and Cantonese.

🛈 422 P ⮃ 🅢 🅒 🎿 📺
🅢 All major cards

🏨 SHERATON HONG KONG
$$$$
20 NATHAN RD., TSIM SHA TSUI
TEL 2369-1111   FAX 2739-8707
www.starwoodhotels.com
Right in the heart of Tsim Sha Tsui, surrounded by shopping streets that bustle all day and half the night, this hotel has good-size rooms which are soundproofed to protect guests from the constant noise from Nathan Road below. The Oyster & Wine Bar is popular with Hong Kong's Chinese yuppies.

🛈 782 P ⮃ 🅢 🅒 🎿 📺
🅢 All major cards

🏨 HOLIDAY INN GOLD
🍽 MILE
$$$
50 NATHAN RD., TSIM SHA TSUI
TEL 2369-3111   FAX 2369-8016
www.holidayinn.com
A standard Holiday Inn tower in downtown Kowloon with its own shopping arcade, five restaurants, and lounges. Light timber furnishings, neutral color schemes, and floor-to-ceiling windows give a spacious feel to the moderately sized rooms. **Café Vienna's** changing buffet attracts lunchtime crowds and evening shoppers.

🛈 600 P ⮃ 🅢 🅒 🎿
📺 🅢 All major cards

🏨 INTERCONTINENTAL
🍽 GRAND STANFORD
$$$
70 MODY RD., TSIM SHA
TSUI EAST
TEL 2721-5161   FAX 2732-2233
www.hongkong.inter
continental.com
The Grand Stanford lies on the Victoria Harbour waterfront and there are great views

to the Hong Kong Island skyline from most of the rooms, as well as from the 18th-floor swimming pool. The renowned **Hoi King Heen** restaurant serves some of the finest Cantonese cuisine around.

🛈 534 P ⮃ 🅢 🅒 🎿 📺
🅢 All major cards

🏨 KOWLOON SHANGRI-LA
$$$
64 MODY RD., TSIM SHA
TSUI EAST
TEL 2721-2111   FAX 2723-8686
WWW.SHANGRI-LA.COM
A recent renovation has brought this Hong Kong institution up-to-date with its newer rivals, and the spacious rooms are as luxurious as any in town. The expansive and warm interiors offer a character missing at other locations, while staff are exemplary.

🛈 700 P ⮃ 🅢 🅒 🎿 📺
🅢 All major cards

🏨 LANGHAM HOTEL HK
🍽 $$$
8 PEKING RD., TSIM SHA TSUI

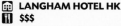

🏨 Hotel 🍽 Restaurant 🛈 No. of guest rooms ⬒ No. of Seats P Parking 🕐 Closed ⮃ Elevator

TEL 2375-1133   FAX 2375-6611
www.langhamhotels.com
The lobby boasts glittering
chandeliers, domed ceiling, and
marble floors, while the rooms
are light and airy. This friendly
hotel has three restaurants
which serve both Cantonese
and American-style cuisine.
🛈 487 P 🔁 🚳 🚫 🏊 🍴
🚫 All major cards

🏨 THE LUXE MANOR
🍴 **$$$**

39 KIMBERLEY RD.,
TSIM SHA TSUI
TEL 3763-8888   FAX 3763 8899
www.theluxemanor.com
A Salvador Dali–inspired
design attracts international
trendsetters to this boutique
hotel. No expense has been
spared on the exquisite
rooms, which include Wi-Fi
access and Hi-Def TV, and
service that is discreet but
friendly. Facilities are limited,
however, with only a small
fitness room and no pool. The
Italian **Asapia** restaurant is
recommended, though.
🛈 159 P 🔁 🚳 🚫 🍴
🚫 All major cards

🏨 MARCO POLO
🍴 **HONG KONG**
$$$

HARBOR CITY, CANTON RD.,
TSIM SHA TSUI
TEL 2113-0088   FAX 2113-0011
www.marcopolohotels.com
The pick of the three Marco
Polos, the Hong Kong has a
higher standard of style and
comfort and bigger rooms
than its sister hostelries.
This one has 44 suites, and
a tempting range of cuisines
in its five restaurants, from
Chinese Chiu Chow to Italian.
🛈 665 P 🔁 🚳 🚫 🏊 🍴
🚫 All major cards

🏨 MIRAMAR
$$$

118–130 NATHAN RD., TSIM
SHA TSUI
TEL 2368-1111   FAX 2369-1788

www.miramarhk.com
A great place to escape the
ubiquitous chain hotels, while
still enjoying all their luxuries,
the Miramar's rooms have had
a full renovation, unveiling sleek
and contemporary rooms with
a selection of technological
gadgets worthy of James Bond.
The heart of the city location
overlooking Kowloon Park is
well placed for transportation,
shopping, and the bars and res-
taurants of Knutsford Terrace.
🛈 494 P 🔁 🚳 🚫 🏊 🍴
🚫 All major cards

🏨 NIKKO HONG KONG
🍴 **$$$**

72 MODY RD., TSIM SHA
TSUI EAST
TEL 2739-1111   FAX 2311-3122
www.hotelnikko.com.hk
The Nikko is a favorite with
Japanese visitors, so expect
discreet but excellent service.
The uncluttered rooms are
decorated in soft neutral
colors, with full-length windows overlooking the harbor.
With comprehensive business
facilities, two bars, and four
restaurants, it is within walking
distance of the main Tsim Sha
Tsui shopping district.
🛈 463 P 🔁 🚳 🚫 🏊 🍴
🚫 All major cards

🏨 EATON
$$

380 NATHAN RD.
TEL 2782-1818   FAX 2782-5563
www.eaton-hotel.com
This modern, well-appointed
hotel lies in downtown
Kowloon, in the heart of the
Nathan Road Golden Mile
shopping mecca. It's well
equipped for kids, and the
front desk has X-boxes avail-
able on demand.
🛈 468 P 🔁 🚳 🚫 🏊 🍴
🚫 All major cards

🏨 HARBOUR PLAZA
HONG KONG
$$

20 TAK FUNG ST., HUNG HOM

TEL 2621-3188   FAX 2621-3311
www.harbour-plaza.com
The Harbour Plaza is on the
Hung Hom waterfront, only
five minutes from the main
Tsim Sha Tsui tourist area and
connecting transportation. It
has 101 roomy serviced suites
with kitchens and maid service
for longer stays.
🛈 534 P 🔁 🚳 🚫 🏊 🍴
🚫 All major cards

🏨 KIMBERLEY
$$

28 KIMBERLEY RD., TSIM SHA
TSUI
TEL 2723-3888   FAX 2723-1318
The deluxe rooms and suites
are large and comfortable; stan-
dard rooms tend to be small.
In addition to the modest gym,
they have golf driving nets.
🛈 546 P 🔁 🚳 🚫 🍴
🚫 All major cards

🏨 KOWLOON
$$

19–21 NATHAN RD., TSIM SHA
TSUI
TEL 2929-2888   FAX 2739-9811
www.harbour-plaza.com
This budget hotel offers excellent bargains for stays of seven
days or longer. The rooms are
a bit small but well appointed.
Guests can enjoy the facilities
at the nearby YMCA, including
a swimming pool and gym.
🛈 736 P 🔁 🚳 🚫
🚫 All major cards

🏨 MARCO POLO
🍴 **GATEWAY**
$$

HARBOR CITY, CANTON RD.,
TSIM SHA TSUI
TEL 2113-0088   FAX 2113-0022
www.marcopolohotels.com
The Marco Polo Gateway
offers a combination of effi-
ciency and comfort. Rooms are
tastefully decorated in subdued
tones and are a decent size.
The **Parisian Brasseries** is the
pick of its three restaurants.
🛈 433 P 🔁 🚳 🚫
🚫 All major cards

🚫 Nonsmoking 🚳 Air-conditioning 🏊 Indoor Pool 🏊 Outdoor Pool 🍴 Health Club 🚫 Credit Cards

🏨 MARCO POLO PRINCE
🍴 $$

HARBOR CITY, CANTON RD.,
TSIM SHA TSUI
TEL 2113-1888   FAX 2113-0066
www.marcopolohotels.com
Superbly located, this hotel
is ideal for both business and
leisure travelers. Room rates,
decor, and service compare well
with the Gateway. It has more
than 50 suites, a lounge, and
two restaurants, including the
Spice Market, which specializes in Southeast Asian dishes.

🛏 394 🅿 😊 😊 😊
😊 All major cards

🏨 REGAL KOWLOON
🍴 $$

71 MODY RD., TSIM SHA
TSUI EAST
TEL 2722-1818   FAX 2369-6950
www.regalhotel.com
The Regal Kowloon offers
elegance and comfort, with 34
suites, a bar-lounge, and four
restaurants. It has a small art
gallery on the first floor and
a playroom for the kids. The
recommended **Zeffirinos** offers quality Italian cuisine.

🛏 593 🅿 😊 😊 😊 😊
😊 All major cards

🏨 RENAISSANCE
🍴 KOWLOON HOTEL
$$

22 SALISBURY RD., TSIM SHA TSUI
TEL 2369-4111   FAX 2369-9387
www.marriott.com
The Renaissance is perfectly
positioned on the harborfront.
Tastefully decorated rooms
have floor-to-ceiling windows.
The **Panorama Restaurant**
has great nighttime views
across to Hong Kong Island's
brightly illuminated skyscrapers.

🛏 546 🅿 😊 😊 😊 😊 😊
😊 All major cards

🏨 SALISBURY
🍴 $$

41 SALISBURY RD., TSIM SHA TSUI
TEL 2268-7888   FAX 2739-9315
www.ymcahk.org.hk
While it may say YMCA on

the door, the prime waterfront
location, bright and well-
maintained rooms, plus amenities like in-room cable, make
this a cut above your average Y
experience. The rooms are the
equal of any three-star hotel in
town, only cheaper, and there
is a bargain canteen, as well as
recreation facilities on-site.

🛏 356 🅿 😊 😊 😊 😊 😊 😊
😊 All major cards

🏨 PARK
$

61–65 CHATHAM RD. SOUTH,
TSIM SHA TSUI
TEL 2731-2100   FAX 2739-7259
www.parkhotel.com.hk
A recent renovation has given
the Park's rooms a needed
face-lift. The contemporary, basic rooms are a decent bargain.
The large number of rooms
make it a good standby when
other hotels are fully booked.

🛏 1,026 🅿 😊 😊 😊
😊 All major cards

🍴 FELIX
$$$$

THE PENINSULA, SALISBURY RD.,
TSIM SHA TSUI
TEL 2315-3188
The renowned Felix is well
known for its dramatic views
across Hong Kong from the
28th floor. The continental
cuisine is exceptional, including
prawn cracker-crusted sea bass
and pancetta-wrapped lamb in
mint juice.

🪑 100 🅿 🕐 Closed L 😊
😊 😊 All major cards

🍴 GADDI'S
$$$$$

THE PENINSULA, SALISBURY RD.,
TSIM SHA TSUI
TEL 2315-3171
One of Hong Kong's most
exclusive and elegant French
restaurants, visited mostly by
the rich and famous. It boasts
its own entrance, separate
from the exclusivity of the
Peninsula. Try the braised veal
cheek in Madeira sauce or the

roasted duck with white bean
casserole. The wine list, pre-
dominantly but not exclusively
French, equals the quality of
the cuisine.

🪑 80 🅿 😊 😊
😊 All major cards

🍴 NOBU
$$$$$

INTERCONTINENTAL HOTEL,
18 SALISBURY RD., TSIM SHA TSUI
TEL 2313-2323
This Hong Kong station of
master chef Nobu's Japanese
eateries, which spread from
Malibu to Melbourne, is a fine
addition to a city that's littered
with Japanese restaurants.
Many dishes are specific to
the Hong Kong location, such
as sashimi with jalapeño and
toro tartar with caviar, both
of which are excellent. Nobu
has an endless selection of
Hollywood friends, who, when
in town, can usually be spotted
amongst the bamboo walls.

🪑 131 🅿 😊 😊
😊 All major cards

🍴 AQUA
$$$$–$$$$$

29/30F, 1 PEKING RD., TSIM
SHA TSUI
TEL 3427-2288
While the excellent Japanese
and Italian dishes don't quite
justify their generous price
tags, the 29th-floor location,
with two-story windows facing
back across Victoria Harbour
onto Central's skyscrapers,
may well be the best in the
city. For those whose budgets
don't stretch to dinner, the
Aqua Spirit bar offers expertly
mixed cocktails, although
these also don't come cheap.

🪑 170 😊 😊
😊 All major cards

🍴 CHESA
$$$$

THE PENINSULA, 1ST FLOOR,
SALISBURY RD., TSIM SHA TSUI
TEL 2315-3169
Well worth exploring for its

---

excellent representation of Switzerland's Italian, German, and French influences. The fondue is a speciality, such as an excellent fondue à la Saviesanne: gruyère and raclette cheese with leeks, bacon, and new potatoes.

🛏 50 🚭 ❄ 🏊 All major cards

🍴 SABATINI
$$$$
THE ROYAL GARDEN HOTEL, 69 MODY RD., TSIM SHA TSUI
TEL 2733-2000
First opened by the Sabatini brothers in Rome back in the 1950s, Hong Kong and Tokyo are the international Sabatini outposts, both lovingly over-seen by the brothers. A warm and cozy trattoria interior is host to masterful Roman classics, including excellent homemade pasta.

🛏 80 🚭 ❄ 🏊 All major cards

🍴 YAN TOH HEEN
$$$$
INTERCONTINENTAL HONG KONG, 18 SALISBURY RD., TSIM SHA TSUI
TEL 2313-2323
Fascinating and sometimes un-usual Cantonese dishes can be found in this classy harborside restaurant, such as salty frog legs. More conventional dishes include barbecued suckling pig.

🛏 90 🚭 ❄ 🏊 All major cards

🍴 HOI KING HEEN
$$$
70 MODY RD., TSIM SHA TSUI
TEL 2731-2883
Excellent Cantonese cuisine with some unusual vegetarian dishes, such as braised black moss with mushrooms and bamboo. The killed-to-order steamed *garoupa* fish is a delightful delicacy, as is the braised bean curd. An interest-ing collection of wines from countries such as Austria, Germany, and Switzerland.

🛏 290 🅿 🚭 ❄ 🏊 All major cards

🍴 WU KONG
$$$
27 NATHAN RD., TSIM SHA TSUI
TEL 2366-7244
Popular basement Shanghai-nese restaurant with friendly, attentive staff. Sautéed fresh shrimp and steamed pork dumplings are two old established favorites, as is the pigeon in wine.

🛏 140 🚭 ❄ All major cards

🍴 LITTLE SHEEP
$$
26 KIMBERLEY RD., TSIM SHA TSUI
TEL 2722-7633
Now with several bright and breezy branches around Hong Kong, Little Sheep built its reputation on its famed Mongolian lamb hot pot, which you cook in your very own personal pot. Aside from the excellent hot pot, they also offer meatball platters and delicious potato noodles.

🛏 50 🚭 ❄ 🏊 All major cards

■ NEW TERRITORIES

🏨 GOLD COAST
$$$
1 CASTLE PEAK RD.
TEL 2452-8888   FAX 2440-7368
www.sino-hotels.com
A beach resort hotel in the far western reaches of the Kow-loon peninsula, the Gold Coast offers leisure facilities set in palm-tree-covered gardens, and there's a marina and private beach. Spacious rooms come with sea views and private balconies. They also offer a dedicated kids' club, tennis courts, and huge swimming pool. Reasonable road and train connections to Tsim Sha Tsui.

🛏 450 🅿 🚭 ❄ 🏊 🏊 📺 All major cards

🏨 REGAL RIVERSIDE
$$
34–36 TAI CHUNG KIU RD.,

SHA TIN
TEL 2649-7878   FAX 2637-4748
www.regalhotel.com
One of the few Hong Kong hotels set amid the greenery of a semirural environment, the Regal Riverside lies close to the MTR for easy access to downtown and the border with mainland China.

🛏 858 🅿 🚭 ❄ 🏊 🏊 📺 All major cards

🏨 ROYAL PARK
🍴 $$
8 PAK HOK TING ST., SHA TIN
TEL 2601-2111   FAX 2601-3666
www.royalpark.com.hk
Renowned for its attentive service, and for its business and recreational facilities, the Royal Park is located on the MTR line with easy access to downtown and the Chinese border. Rooms are large, light, and airy, and its **Sakurada** Japanese restaurant is popular with businesspeople.

🛏 448 🅿 🚭 ❄ 🏊 🏊 📺 All major cards

🏨 PANDA
$
3 TSUEN WAH ST., TSUEN WAN
TEL 2409-1111   FAX 2409-1818
www.pandahotel.com.hk
This monolithic building is set off by a curious piece of mod-ern art illuminated at night down one side of its 30 stories. Its out-of-the-way location means you can get good deals on rooms rates. The restaurant serves Cantonese cuisine, and the bright and breezy café serves a decent buffet.

🛏 1,026 🅿 🚭 ❄ 🏊 🏊 📺 All major cards

■ OUTLYING ISLANDS

LAMMA

🍴 RAINBOW SEAFOOD RESTAURANT
$$$
23–24 FIRST ST., SOK KWU WAN

🚭 Nonsmoking ❄ Air-conditioning 🏊 Indoor Pool 🏊 Outdoor Pool 📺 Health Club 🏊 Credit Cards

TEL 2982-8100
Set on the seafront in Sok Kwu Wan, you pick your meal from the tanks at the front of the restaurant housing a huge variety of creatures plucked from the sea hours earlier. The restaurant is now running free ferries from Central Pier 9, although you'll have to splash out on a minimum spend if you want to catch a ride.

🚇 800 🅂 🅒
🅂 All major cards

LANTAU ISLAND

🏨 HONG KONG DISNEYLAND HOTEL
$$$$
TEL 1-830-830   FAX 3510-6333
www.hongkongdisney
land.com
With typical Disney flair, the Disneyland Hotel presents a sumptuous Victorian fantasy with modern-day luxuries throughout. Rooms feature high-speed Internet and flat-screen TVs, while a Victorian spa and afternoon tea help maintain an old-world sense of charm. The Disneyland features five restaurants and provides transportation to the theme park.

ⓘ 400 🅿 🅂 🅂 🅒 🅂
🅂 🅂 All major cards

🏨 DISNEY'S HOLLYWOOD HOTEL
$$$
TEL 1-830-830   FAX 3510-5333
www.hongkongdisney
land.com
The Hollywood Hotel is a good option for those wishing to extend their Disney experience beyond the standard theme-park visit. With its bright blue exterior and colorful, lively décor, the hotel is Disney's exuberant take on 1930s Hollywood glamour. Four restaurants are located within the hotel and transportation to Disneyland is provided.

ⓘ 600 🅿 🅂 🅂 🅒 🅂 🅂
🅂 All major cards

🏨 REGAL AIRPORT
$$$
9 CHEONG TAT RD., CHEK LAP KOK
TEL 2286-8888   FAX 2286-8686
www.regalhotel.com
One of the largest airport hotels in the world, the Regal is a superbly equipped resort property at Hong Kong International Airport. Landscaped, fully soundproofed, and with a covered sky bridge to the terminal, it offers 26 suites, two bar-lounges and five restaurants serving Beijing, Shanghai, Sichuan, Japanese, Western, and many other specialties.

ⓘ 1,171 🅿 🅂 🅂 🅂 🅒 🅂
🅂 🅂 All major cards

■ EXCURSIONS

MACAU

SOMETHING SPECIAL

🏨 POUSADA DE SAO TIAGO
$$$$$
AVE. DA REPUBLICA, FORTALEZA DE SAO TIAGO DA BARRA
TEL 853/2837-8111
A www.saotiago.com.mo
A converted fortress built by the Portuguese in the 17th century to defend their colonial possession, this charmingly romantic hotel drips with history. The old fortress's chapel has been preserved within the complex, and renovated hand-hewn sandstones form much of the conversion. Guests enter via a cobblestone passage through the old fortress battlements. Rooms, swimming pool, and dining terrace look out over the sea and the entrance to the harbor.

ⓘ 23 🅿 🅂 🅂 🅒 🅂
🅂 All major cards

PRICES

HOTELS
An indication of the cost of double room in the high season is given by $ signs.

$$$$$	Over $240
$$$$	$160-240
$$$	$110-160
$$	$70-110
$	Under $70

RESTAURANTS
An indication of the cost of a three-course meal without drinks is given by $ signs.

$$$$$	Over $65
$$$$	$50-65
$$$	$30-50
$$	$20-30
$	Under $20

🏨 🍴 MANDARIN ORIENTAL
$$$$
956–1110 AVE. DA AMIZADE
TEL 853/2856-7888
FAX 853/2851-5303
www.mandarinoriental.com
Portuguese architectural and design influences can be seen throughout the hotel. Rooms make good use of Portuguese fabrics and teak furnishings. There are 28 suites, and eight restaurants and cafés, notably Café Bela Vista, serving Macanese cuisine. Close to the waterfront, within walking distance of the ferry terminal from Hong Kong and the main shopping district.

ⓘ 435 🅿 🅂 🅂 🅒 🅂 🅂
🅂 All major cards

🏨 🍴 WESTIN RESORT MACAU
$$$$
1918 ESTRADA DE HAC SA, COLOANE
TEL 853/2887-1111
www.starwoodhotels.com
Popular with Hong Kong families looking to escape the rat race, the Westin is set in isolation at the very end of Hac

---

Sa beach. While the building looks like a fortified bunker, rooms are well appointed and spacious, with wide, open terraces, usually with views of the South China Sea. The complex also offers a recreation center, spa, and its own 18-hole golf course, as well as a dedicated children's club.

🛈 208 🅿 🖿 🅂 🅂 🏊
🟦 🟥 🔲 All major cards

VENETIAN
$$$
COTAI STRIP, TAIPA ISLAND
TEL 853/2882-8877
www.venetianmacao.com
There's nothing subtle about the Venetian's grandly styled Italian rooms, which feature king-size beds, their own living rooms, and exquisite marble bathrooms. The location out on Taipa isn't ideal for those who want to explore Macau, although the Venetian runs regular free buses to the center. However, with a host of restaurants and bars onsite, including the excellent Portuguese **Madeira,** as well as spas, swimming pools, and a mini putting course, gamblers need never leave the building.

🛈 2,905 🅿 🖿 🅂 🅂 🟥 🔲
🔲 All major cards

LISBOA
$$
2–4 AVE. DE LISBOS
TEL 853/2888-3888
FAX 853/567-193
www.hotelisboa.com
Along with the attached casino, the Lisboa was once the cream of the crop in Macau, but in recent years its rooms have been surpassed by those at the surge of newcomers to Macau. While recently renovated and made marginally more modern, the rooms here are still full of gold splashes and over-the-top flourishes. However, for the price, the quality is high.

🛈 1,017 🅿 🖿 🅂 🅂 🟥 🔲
🔲 All major cards

SINTRA
$$
AVE. D. JOAO IV MACAU
TEL 853/2871-0111
FAX 853/2851-0527
www.hotelsintra.com
Conveniently located in the heart of Macau overlooking Praia Grande Bay, the Sintra has comfortable, albeit small and somewhat dated, rooms. The **Sintra** restaurant is a 24-hour steak house. The menu also has Macanese and Portuguese dishes.

🛈 220 🅿 🖿 🅂 🅂
🔲 All major cards

TUNG YEE HEEN
$$$$
MANDARIN ORIENTAL,
956 AVE. DA AMIZADE
TEL 853/8793-3821
Unusual flavors and an experimental Cantonese style are hallmarks of this upscale hotel restaurant. Specialties include Macau shrimp paste blended with shellfish dishes, pigeon in tofu sauce, yellow beans, and steamed seafood with ginger sauce. Tung Yee Heen also offers a large selection of exotic Chinese teas.

🔲 160 🅿 🅂
🔲 All major cards

A LORCHA
$$$
289A RUA DO ALMIRANTE
SERGIO, INNER HARBOR
TEL 853/2831-3193
Owner Adriano Neves catches his own fish, thus ensuring freshness. But equally good in this longtime popular Portuguese restaurant are the *feijoada* (pork and bean stew) and *arroz de marisco* (stuffed squid). Try the chocolate mousse in Portuguese brandy to finish.

🔲 70 🕐 Closed Tues. 🅂 🅂
🔲 All major cards

CLUBE MILITAR DE MACAU
$$$
975 AVE. DA PRAIA GRANDE
TEL 853/2871-4000
A delightful and airy dining room in a renovated 19th-century colonial building that used to be the Portuguese military club. Although it's still a private members' club, the restaurant is public. The menu is Portuguese, although some Macanese dishes creep in. Look for *bacalhau a bras,* cod cooked with julienne potatoes and onions. Clube Militar has one of Macau's best Portuguese wine lists, and serves wonderfully rich, thick coffee.

🔲 70 🅂 🅂 🔲 All major cards

SAI NAM
$$$
36 RUA DA FELICIDADE
TEL 853/2857-4072
Aficionados of shark's fin soup gladly travel here from Hong Kong for the delicacy's lower price. Other Cantonese favorites in this restaurant founded in the 1960s, are fried chicken, steamed fish, and an unusual fried rice with pungent lotus leaves. Sai Nam also panders to Macau's taste for star-fruit juice.

🔲 120 🅂 🅂
🔲 All major cards

LITORAL
$$
261A RUA DO ALMIRANTE
SERGIO, INNER HARBOR
TEL 853/2896-7878
Sophisticated Macanese cuisine—a blend of cuisine evolved over the past 400 years from Portugal's colonial empire—is served in a fanciful setting that is much liked and visited by the well-heeled fashion setters of both Macau and Hong Kong. They come not only to be seen, but also to eat crab curry with quail eggs,

chili-spiced diablo stews, and tacho beef stews.

🚹 76 🅿 🇸 🇸
🇸 All major cards

🍴 LORD STOW'S BAKERY
$$
1 RUA DA TASSARA, COLOANE
TOWN SQUARE
TEL 853/2888-2534
This petite bakery is well worth a visit to try the world famous *pasteis de nata*. These soft custard egg tarts have a loyal following, both here and in Hong Kong. Despite many imitators, Lord Stow's version of them is considered the best.

🇸 🇸 🇸 All major cards

🍴 POUSADA DE COLOANE
$$
PRAIA DE CHEOC VAN
COLOANE ISLAND
TEL 853/2888-2143
The Portuguese–Macanese food may not be the best in Macau, but people flock here to sip Portuguese wine and watch night fall across the South China Sea. The restaurant is part of a small hotel built into the cliffs above a beach well away from the hustle and bustle of Hong Kong. The Sunday buffet lunch is an excellent value.

🚹 80 🅿 🇸 🇸
🇸 All major cards

SOMETHING SPECIAL
🍴 FERNANDO'S
$
9 HOC SA BEACH, COLOANE
ISLAND
TEL 853/2888-2264
A visit to Macau is not complete without a meal at the legendary Fernando's. Hong Kong's cognoscenti come here on weekends to eat, drink, and laze in the fresh air. Still owned by a Portuguese family, with its ceiling fans and Portuguese clientèle, it has an undoubted colonial air, and the food is both tasty and

authentic. But there are no reservations and you'll have to wait for a table, though this can be done at the backyard bar.

🚹 80 🇸 🇸
🇸 No credit cards

GUANGZHOU

🏨 GARDEN
🍴 $$$
368 HUANSHI DONG LU
TEL 86-20-8333-8989
FAX 86-20-8335-0467
www.thegardenhotel.com
Guests are greeted by spouting fountains at the main entrance to this huge, modern, and sometimes over-the-top hotel. The large gilded mural in the lobby is an attraction in itself. The Garden Hotel boasts eight restaurants, ranging from the European cuisine of the **Connoisseur** to the Cantonese **Peach Blossom,** as well as several bars and a nightclub. Centrally located in the commercial and financial hub of Guangzhou, and situated close to the Trade Fair Center, airport, and rail and ferry terminals.

🛈 828 🅿 🇸 🇸 🇸 🏊 🍷
🇸 All major cards

🏨 MARRIOTT CHINA
$$$
102 LIU HUA LU
TEL 86-20-8666-6888
FAX 86-20-8667-7288
www.marriott.com
This upscale complex includes a hotel tower, an office tower, two apartment buildings, and a shopping arcade. The rooms are well appointed and the lobby is grand. There are 168 luxury suites and five restaurants.

🛈 885 🅿 🇸 🇸 🇸 🏊 🍷
🇸 All major cards

🍴 DATONG
$$
63 YANJIANG XI LU
TEL 86-20-8188-8988
Famed for its tasty dim sum dishes, this place is teeming at lunchtime, but the crowds and the noise all combine to provide diners with a classic dim sum experience. Housed in an old riverside building with views over the water. Arrive early if you want to secure a window seat.

🚹 80 🇸 🇸 All major cards

SHENZHEN

🏨 NAN HAI HOTEL
🍴 $$$
1 GONG YE 1ST RD., NANHAI
BLVD., SHEKOU
TEL 86-755-2669-2888
www.nanhai-hotel.com
Set on the Shenzhen waterfront in the entertainment and leisure district of Shekou, the Nan Hai's uninviting exterior hides modern, well-appointed rooms with sizable balconies. Geared toward the leisure traveler, the hotel's facilities are extensive, including a swimming pool, martial arts lessons, tennis court, and, quite unexpectedly, a war games center where you can refine your paintball game. There's also a spa, flower shop, cake shop, business center, lounge, and restaurant.

🛈 396 🅿 🇸 🇸 🇸 🏊 🍷
🇸 All major cards

Shopping in Hong Kong

As a duty-free port, Hong Kong is a shoppers' paradise, although not quite as cheap as popular myth suggests. You can buy anything from clothes made to measure in 24 hours to a Ming dynasty vase. Government efforts have been made to stamp out counterfeiting, but Hong Kong is still inundated with low-price, copycat goods, usually made in southern China and bearing the expensive brand names and labels of Japanese and Western producers. The street markets are often the source of counterfeit designer-label clothes, watches, CDs, and some electronic equipment.

Guaranteed genuine goods are sold at shops where you see a red junk (that is, Chinese ship) sign supported by the words *Hong Kong Tourism Board.*

If you are looking for genuine Chinese antiques, you can usually find what you want, at a price, in the Hollywood Road district of Hong Kong Island.

Elsewhere, good bargains in jade, gold, pearls, and silk are possible because of Hong Kong's free port status and the large number of retailers. Check several shops before making a final selection.

There are plenty of lively street markets and discount stores where you can pick up cheap clothing, bags, shoes, souvenirs, and knickknacks.

There are two cut-price sales periods each year—July to September and December to February.

Local clothes and jewelry designers and contractors producing for big-name international clothes brands sometimes sell excess production or slightly flawed goods at their factories, with prices much lower than in the stores. Tourist offices issue pamphlets giving details of these factory outlets. In Central, the Peddler Building on Peddler Street offers European fashion bargains.

Bargaining

Goods in department stores and some other retailers have price tags and are fixed, but at markets, electronic outlets, and some smaller stores bargaining is expected. When buying electronics, always visit a few stores to price goods.

Opening Times

Most shops are open seven days, only closed during a few days at Chinese New Year (see p. 50). Big stores open from 10 a.m. until 8 or 9 p.m. Smaller shops, especially in Kowloon, Wan Chai, and Causeway Bay, stay open as late as 11 p.m.

Antiques & Artifacts

A large selection of Chinese and other Asian antiques and artifacts is available in Hong Kong. The biggest concentration of specialist shops is found on and around Hollywood Road, in Central on Hong Kong Island. In addition to rare porcelain, jade, and furnishings, there is a wealth of inexpensive but evocative curios from China, such as opium pipes and old photographs. The Hollywood Road district also has art from Myanmar (Burma), Thailand, Indonesia, and India.

Mainland China-owned department stores such as the Chinese Arts and Crafts stores stock Chinese antiques and art as well as jade, porcelain, and silk.

Chinese and other East Asian antiques are sold by auction in Hong Kong from time to time. Christie's holds auctions from April to May and October to November. The focus is on Chinese art and jewelry, particularly jade.

K.Y Fine Art, 142 Hollywood Rd., Sheung Wan, tel 2540-4772. One of Hong Kong's most respected dealers and a bona fide expert in Chinese antiques, especially ceramics, furniture, and paintings.

Gallery Oi Ling, 52 & 85 Hollywood Rd., Central, Hong Kong Island, tel 2815-9422. Experts in Chinese terra-cotta and other Chinese antiques, Oi Ling has a distinguished history in sourcing some of China's finest pieces.

Auction Houses

Christie's, Alexandra House, 16–20 Chater Rd., Central, Hong Kong Island, tel 2521-5396, fax 2845-2646

Sotheby's, Standard Chartered Bank Building, 5th fl., 4–4A Des Voeux Rd., Central, Hong Kong Island, tel 2524-8121, fax 2810-6238

Arcades & Malls

Shopping malls offer a convenient way to shop in Hong Kong. Most malls have an excellent range of department stores, boutiques, and camera, jewelry, and electronic goods outlets. Prices are fixed and displayed on the goods, so there is no bargaining here.

Shopping malls also have a good selection of restaurants and food courts where you can relax and replenish your energy, and most have cinemas.

Cityplaza, 18 Tai Koo Shing Rd., Quarry Bay, tel 2568-8665, open 10 a.m.–9 p.m. One of Hong Kong's largest shopping centers, with department stores and retail outlets selling clothes, accessories, jewelry, watches, electronic goods, and cameras. There are also plenty of restaurants, as well as a cinema multiplex.

Pacific Place, 88 Queensway, Admiralty, tel 2844-8988, open 10 a.m.–9 p.m. This vast mall is Hong Kong's premier shopping center. Pacific Place was one of the first of its kind in Asia and a benchmark for retail complexes throughout the region. There are floors of boutiques, specialty electronics shops, cafés, bars, and a cinema complex.

The Peak Galleria, 118 Peak Rd., The Peak, tel 2849-4113, open 10 a.m.–11 p.m. Spectacular setting for clothes shops, souvenir outlets, restaurants (some with a view over Hong Kong Harbor), and an enormous Park 'n' Shop supermarket. Be prepared to pay generously for your purchases— the prices here can be as lofty as the view.

Festival Walk, 80 Tat Chee Ave., Kowloon Tong, tel 2844-2200, open 10 a.m.–9 p.m. One of Hong Kong's newer megamalls, with 200 shops, boutiques, department stores, restaurants, and a massive food court. Festival Walk also features an 11-screen cinema multiplex.

Harbor City, Ocean Terminal, 3 Canton Rd., Tsim Sha Tsui, tel 2118-8668, open 10 a.m.–9 p.m. A huge shopping mall with outlets selling upscale fashion, formal wear, bespoke tailoring, electronics, shoes, and artifacts.

Elements, 1 Austin Rd. West, West Kowloon, tel 2735-5234. Set in the massive Union Square development, the mall is equally gargantuan with over one million square feet of shops and restaurants, an ice-skating rink, and 12-screen cinema multiplex.

Arts & Crafts

Hong Kong has a fine selection of traditional crafts, not least porcelain from China, carpets and rugs from Turkey and Iran, silk garments from China and Thailand, Indonesian batik, and teak furniture from Myanmar. Chinese calligraphers work in several of the open-air markets.

Calligraphy: Some of the best craftsmen work at bustling Stanley Market on Hong Kong Island South. Popular items to purchase as souvenirs include book-size name cards drawn to order in Chinese characters.

Carpets: There are numerous carpet shops along Wyndham Street and Hollywood Road in Central, Hong Kong Island.

Rattan and rosewood furniture: Sold in many shops along Queen's Road East, Wan Chai.

Silk: On sale in Chinese Arts and Crafts stores, Western Market, and Stanley Market on Hong Kong Island.

Books & Prints

Bookazine, Basement, Canton House, 54–56 Queen's Rd., Central, Hong Kong Island, tel 2521-1535, open 10 a.m.–7 p.m

Page One Bookshop, 9/F, Times Square, 1 Matheson St., Causeway Bay, tel 2506-0381, open 10:30 a.m.–10 p.m.

Page One Bookshop, Shop 3002, Level 3, Harbor City, Tsim Sha Tsui, Kowloon, tel 2370-6080, open 10:30 a.m.–10 p.m.

Cameras

Hong Kong is a genuine bargain basement for all makes and types of cameras—from compacts and 35mm single lens reflex models to digital and video cameras—so it is worth waiting until you arrive to purchase a new camera to record your visit.

On Hong Kong Island, check the shops on Stanley Street, Central, and in Causeway Bay. On the other side of the harbor, visit Nathan Road in Tsim Sha Tsui and Sai Yeung Choi Street in Mong Kok. Make sure your purchase includes full international warranty documentation and guide booklet.

Clothing & Accessories

Tailoring has always been one of Hong Kong's trademarks. Suits, evening gowns, shirts, and hats are made to measure by small-shop tailors, and your favorite designs can be copied.

Some of the major hotels have tailor services within their own shopping arcades. Other notable locations, especially for the Indian tailoring community, are in Tsim Sha Tsui. Suits can often be prepared in 24 hours, but make sure you have more than one fitting after the initial measuring.

Shoes and other leather goods are also made to measure.

In addition to all the international Western designer brands on sale in the major stores and upscale boutiques in Causeway Bay, Hong Kong has spawned a number of its own fashion designers— notably Vivienne Tam, William Tang, Walter Ma, and Barney Cheng.

Island Beverley, Island Center, 26th floor, 1 Great George St., Causeway Bay, tel 2890-6823. Young fashion.

Marks & Spencer, Ocean Center, 5 Canton Rd., Tsim Sha Tsui, tel 2926-3346, open 10 a.m.– 8:30 p.m. M&S's house-brand clothes and accessories.

Princeton Custom Tailors, Mary Bldg., 71–77 Peking Rd., Tsim Sha Tsui, tel 2721-0082. **Shanghai Tang,** Ground Floor, Pedder Bldg., 12 Pedder St., Central, tel 2525-7333, open

10 a.m.–8 p.m. (11 a.m. –7 p.m. Sat.–Sun.) Fashionable clothes Hong Kong-style.

Vivienne Tam, Shop 2095, ifc Mall, Central, tel 2868-9268. Stylish clothing from Hong Kong's very own designer.

Department Stores
Lane Crawford, Podium 3, ifc, Central, Hong Kong Island, tel 2118-7683, open10 a.m.–9 p.m. and Times Sq., 1 Matheson St., Causeway Bay, tel 2118-3638, open 10 a.m.–9 p.m. Good source of high fashion, featuring labels from the major international and local designers, as well as a good selection of jewelry and perfumes.

Sogo, 555 Hennessy Rd., Causeway Bay, tel 2833-8338, open 10 a.m.–10 p.m. This huge Japanese department store sells clothes, electronic goods, and Japanese food.

Food & Drink
Oliver's Delicatessen, Prince's Bldg., 2nd floor, 10 Chater Rd., Central, Hong Kong Island, tel 2810-7710, open 8:30 a.m.–8 p.m. Probably the biggest selection of Scotch malt whiskey in east Asia, including many single malts. A fine range of wines is also available here.

Great Food Hall, Pacific Place, 88 Queensway, Admiralty, tel 2918-9986. Popular with expats for the wide selection of foods from around the world, the Great Food Hall also has gourmet takeout sandwiches, soups, and ready-made meals.

Jewelry & Gems
Jade holds a special fascination for the Chinese—they believe it has spiritual properties—so it is on sale in many forms. Colors range

from white and dark orange to numerous shades of the familiar jade green.

The quality of jade is judged by its translucence and color consistency. A receipt detailing the stone's type and origin should accompany any more expensive pieces you purchase.

The best selection of jade is found at the Jade Market in Kowloon (see below). Take the subway (MTR) to Yau Ma Tei and follow exit C.

Gold is also highly prized, as are pearls. There are many stores that sell them along Queen's Road Central and Des Voeux Road on Hong Kong Island, as well as along Nathan Road, Tsim Sha Tsui.

DFS Galleria, Sun Plaza, 28 Canton Rd., Tsim Sha Tsui, tel 2302-6600, open 9 a.m.–11 p.m. Electronics, gems, and watches.

Hong Kong Sky Mart, Hong Kong International Airport, tel 2383-1474, open 7 a.m.–11:30 p.m. Offers a large range of wines, spirits, tobacco, jewelry, and perfumes.

Markets
Hong Kong is renowned for its street markets, selling all manner of goods. Bargaining is an essential part of a market visit, whether you are buying clothes, watches, Chinese medicine, or inexpensive jade trinkets.

Beware of pickpockets when shopping in markets, and be cautious when purchasing what appears to be an exceptionally good bargain: The actual music on your chosen CD, for example, may turn out not to have been recorded by the famous performer pictured on the cover.

Stanley Market, Market Rd., Stanley, open 10 a.m.–6 p.m. Packed with Chinese artwork, silk, curios, and casual clothes.

Western Market, 323 Des Voeux Rd., Sheung Wan, open 10 a.m.–7 p.m. A paradise for silk seekers in the setting of an attractive Edwardian building.

Bird Market, Yuen Po St., Mong Kok, open 7 a.m.–8 p.m. Exotic bird song amid the ornate cages and bric-a-brac.

Flower Market, Flower Market Rd., Mong Kok, open 7 a.m.–7 p.m. Huge variety of cut flowers and fortune-bringing houseplants favored by the Chinese. Sweet scents and exotic blossoms.

Jade Market, Corner of Kansu and Battery Sts., Yau Ma Tei, next to Tin Hau temple, open 10 a.m.–3:30 p.m. A lively market for purveyors of jade, selling a wide range from inexpensive trinkets to pieces costing a small fortune. Unless you have an extensive knowledge of jade, it is wise to settle for a trinket.

Temple Street Night Market, Tsim Sha Tsui, open 3 p.m.–midnight. Hong Kong's favorite night market. Everything under the moon is for sale here, including casual clothes, electronics, watches, toys, CDs, and bric-a-brac. There are many Chinese cafés and restaurants along the street.

Entertainment & Activities

Hong Kong's seasons are marked with a variety of cultural and sporting events and festivals, both Chinese and Western. There always seems to be some excuse for a big fireworks display to light up the harbor. The city's moviemaking heritage is enjoying a renaissance with the emergence of quality film producers and directors making their mark internationally. The thousand-year-old art of Chinese opera, which portrays Chinese folklore, is still practiced and forms part of the local cultural heritage.

Ticket Agency
URBTIX, tel 2111-5999

Ballet & Dance
Hong Kong Ballet Company, G/F, 60 Blue Pool Rd., Happy Valley, tel 2573-7398, open 10 a.m.–11 p.m. Focuses on modern Western performances.

Hong Kong Dance Company, 4/F Sheung Wan Municipal Services Bldg., 345 Queen's Rd., Central, Hong Kong Island, tel 3103-1888. Concentrates on traditional Chinese dance.

Chinese Opera
Chinese opera (see p. 42) can last up to three hours, but it's possible to watch for shorter periods to enjoy the mix of extravagant costumes, makeup, singing, and martial arts. The performers' tone and body language help spectators even if the words cannot be understood.

Traveling operatic companies perform on makeshift stages across the territory throughout the year. The Hong Kong Tourism Board, tel 2508-1234, can give details of performances.

Regular performing venues for Chinese opera include:

City Hall, Edinburgh Pl., Central, tel 2921-2840.

Hong Kong Cultural Center, 10 Salisbury Rd., Tsim Sha Tsui, (next to the Star Ferry Pier), tel 2734-2009.

Ko Shan Theater, 77 Ko Shan Rd., Hung Hom, Kowloon, tel 2740-9222.

Cinema
Multiple-screen cinema centers are attached to most shopping centers (see pp. 259–260). The *South China Morning Post* newspaper has daily *What's On* listings.

Golden Harvest Cinemas
The Gateway, 25 Canton Rd., Tsim Sha Tsui, tel 2186-1313, www.goldenharvest.com. Shows mainstream Hollywood movies, as well as locally produced movies.

UA Cinemas
1 Pacific Place, 88 Queensway, or Times Sq., Causeway Bay, tel 22317-6666, www.uacinemas .com.hk. Both multiplex venues show predominately mainstream Hollywood, English-language films.

Entertainment Centers
Convention & Exhibition Center, 1 Expo Dr., Wan Chai, tel 2582-8888, www.hkcec.com. A huge complex on the harbor with its distinctive "butterfly" roof. Numerous exhibitions and fairs are held here throughout the year. The center also has seven cafés and restaurants; some, notably the Harbor Lounge, have tables that offer dramatic views over the harbor.

The Fringe Club, 2 Lower Albert Rd., Central, Hong Kong Island, tel 2521-7251, www.hkfringe.com.

Stage plays, comedy, and lunchtime art exhibitions in a slightly avant-garde setting next door to the Foreign Correspondents' Club. Offers good-value lunches and an excellent rooftop bar.

Hong Kong Arts Center, 2 Harbor Rd., Wan Chai, tel 2582-0200, www.hkac.org.hk. Features locally written and produced plays and specialty films.

Hong Kong Cultural Center, 10 Salisbury Rd., Tsim Sha Tsui, tel 2734-2009, www.lcsd.gov.hk. The Hong Kong Philharmonic Orchestra is in residence here between September and July. The Hong Kong Chinese Orchestra—one of the world's largest using traditional Chinese instruments—also performs regularly at the center.

Ocean Park, Aberdeen, Hong Kong Island, tel 2552-0291. Open 10 a.m.–6 p.m, HK$208 per person, children HK$103. Ocean Park offers a full day of family entertainment, including cable-car rides overlooking Hong Kong Island's spectacular southern coastline, shark aquarium, butterfly house, giant-panda enclosure, and a goldfish pagoda, which is home to 110 species of brilliantly colored fish. There are also daily dolphin, killer whale, and sea lion shows.

Yuen Long Theater, 9 Yuen Long Tai Yuk Rd., New Territories, tel 2477-1462. An arts venue outside the main conurbations, which concentrates on Chinese opera, music, and dance.

Nightlife

Central

Lan Kwai Fong: Hong Kong's main nightlife venue—a concentration of late-night bars, nightclubs, and restaurants on the narrow, steep streets clustered around D'Aguilar Street, Central, Hong Kong Island, (close to the Fringe and Foreign Correspondents' Club).

Club 97, 9 Lan Kwai Fong, ground floor, tel 2186-1837.
A nightclub institution in Hong Kong. DJs play funk, soul, and jazz. Open to the early hours.

Stormies, 46-50 D'Aguilar St., Lan Kwai Fong, tel 2549 4467. This is Lan Kwai Fong's main party place with revellers spilling onto the surrounding streets during weekends.

Soho: Similar to Lan Kwai Fong. This area, in the shadow of the Central-to-Mid-Levels Escalator around Staunton, Elgin, and Shelley Streets, is full of bars and restaurants.

Wan Chai: Made internationally famous by the book and movie *The World of Suzy Wong,* and a haunt of visiting shore-leave sailors for most of the 20th century. Today's neon-lit pubs, discos, and hostess bars, some offering floor shows with scantily clad girls, occupy several small streets around the junction of Lockhart and Luard Roads.

More salubrious bars include:

Delaney's, 1 Capital Pl., 2nd fl., 18 Luard Rd., tel 2804-2880. Irish theme pub with live Irish music and Guinness. Also good for catching sports.

Devil's Advocate, 48 Lockhart Rd., tel 2865-7271. A British-style pub that sells the locally brewed Dragon's Back ale and offers good drink deals. Happy Hour lasts from noon until 9:30 p.m.
Dusk Till Dawn, 76 Jaffe Rd., Wan Chai, tel 2528-4689.
A smart, well-managed late-night bar that attracts a broad mix of people and features live Filipino cover bands.

JJs, M/F, Grand Hyatt, 1 Harbour Rd., tel 2584-7662. One of Hong Kong's most popular nightclubs. It's a cavernous place populated by the young and wealthy, and is as elegant as the hotel it's located in.

Harbor Cruises
Watertours of Hong Kong Ltd., Star House, 3 Salisbury Rd., Tsim Sha Tsui, tel 2926-3868, open daily. Offers a variety of tours, including:

Sunset Drinks Cruise: Price per person for 90 minutes, including drinks is HK$300. Departure points are Central, Hong Kong Island (6 p.m.), or Tsim Sha Tsui (6:30 p.m.).

Dinner Cruise: The daily tour, including dinner at Lei Yue Mun Seafood Village, lasts three hours. Price per person is HK$400.

Aerial Rides
Helicopters can be rented for tours over Hong Kong and adjoining islands and to fly to Macau (a 30-minute ride).

HeliExpress, tel 2108-9898, www.helihongkong.com

Heliservices Limited, Tel 2802-0200

Active Sports
GOLF
Clearwater Bay Golf & Country Club, Sai Kung, tel 2335-3888.
An 18-hole course. The club accepts reservations from overseas visitors three days in advance, on weekdays only.

The Hong Kong Golf Club, Fanling, tel 2670-1211. Perhaps the territory's most exclusive golf club. Overseas visitors are permitted to play on weekdays by prior arrangement.

Jockey Club Golf Course, Kau Sai Chau Island, Sai Kung, tel 2791-3380 (9:30 a.m.–12:30 p.m. only). This 36-hole public golf course is on an island in a spectacular bay setting a short ferry ride from Sai Kung. The club accepts visitor reservations on weekdays if made seven days in advance.

Hiking
Almost 40 percent of Hong Kong territory is protected in 23 country parks with more flora and fauna than some much larger countries. Hiking trails crisscross most of the parks. On Hong Kong Island South, a 30-mile (50 km) hiking trail snakes over several peaks and through lush subtropical valley flora. A good starting point is Victoria Peak.

A general guide, *Exploring Hong Kong's Countryside,* is sold by tourist offices, or contact the Country Parks Management Office, 303 Cheung Sha Wan Rd., Kowloon, tel 2708-8885.

Swimming
Hong Kong has numerous public swimming pools.

Kowloon Park Swimming Pool, Kowloon Park, 22 Austin Rd., Tsim Sha Tsui, tel 2724-3577, open daily 6:30 a.m.–10 p.m., closed noon–1 p.m. and 5–6 p.m. Indoor Olympic-size pool and several interconnected pools set in gardens.

Victoria Park Swimming Pool,
Victoria Park, Hing Fat St., Causeway Bay, tel 2570-4682, open daily 6:30 a.m.–10 p.m., closed noon–1 p.m. and 5–6 p.m. One Olympic-size pool as well as several smaller and shallower ones.

Tai Chi

Garden Plaza, Hong Kong Park, Admiralty, Hong Kong Island. Open Tuesdays, Fridays, and Sundays, 8:15 a.m.–9:15 a.m. Tel 2508-1234 for free lessons.

Tennis

Victoria Park, Causeway Bay, Hong Kong Island, tel 2890-5824, open 6 a.m.–11 p.m., closed noon–1 p.m. and 5–6 p.m. Five public courts that get crowded on weekends, so reserve in advance in person. You will need your passport to do so.

Water Skiing & Sailing

Despite being perceived as a big, crowded city, the territory of Hong Kong has almost 40 beaches. Equipment can be rented from beachside stores. Some beaches are subject to seasonal conditions such as a heavy swell caused by storms elsewhere. Tel 1823 for details of the best equipped and safest beaches during your visit.

Windsurfing

Cheung Chau Windsurfing Center, Cheung Chau Island, tel 2981-2772. The sport has become popular in Hong Kong since Lee Lai Shan won an Olympic gold medal—a first for Hong Kong—in Atlanta in 1996. She trained at the Cheung Chau beach.

Spectator Sports

Dragon Boat Racing: This exciting sporting event is special to Hong Kong. The main races are held in June when more than a hundred boat teams participate at numerous locations around Hong Kong's sheltered coastline.

The 50-foot-long narrow wooden boats have bows shaped like dragons heads. The Tuen Ng Dragon Boat Festival celebrates Qu Yuan, a Chinese hero who died 2,300 years ago.

Training and racing can be seen at Aberdeen and Stanley on Hong Kong Island; at Sai Kung, Sha Tin, Tai Po, and Tuen Mun on the Kowloon side; and around the islands of Lantau and Cheung Chau.

Check with the Hong Kong Tourism Board (tel 2508-1234) for a list of tour operators running dedicated Dragon Boat Festival tours.

Golf: The Hong Kong Open, which takes place in November and December, is a major international sporting event. It is held across several of the territory's best courses and has featured such prominent players as Tiger Woods. Contact tourist offices for competition schedules, tel 2508-1234.

Horse Racing: Hong Kong's biggest spectator sport is horse racing, which was introduced by the British in the mid-19th century. Between mid-September and mid-June, tens of thousands of people flock to the two racecourses, at Happy Valley and at Sha Tin, every Wednesday evening and Saturday afternoon. Race meetings usually last several hours and cause considerable traffic disruption in the vicinity of the courses. Hundreds of thousands more listen on radios or watch TV to follow the races on which tens of millions of Hong Kong dollars are wagered.

The two biggest events of the local racing calendar are the Queen Elizabeth II Cup, in April, in which horses and jockeys from around the world participate, and the Hong Kong International Races in December. The latter is the final leg of the Emirates World Racing Championship.

The Hong Kong Tourism Board organizes tours to the races. The price per person of HK$490 includes hotel pick-up by air-conditioned bus, guided tour, buffet meal, drinks, admission badge, and race card. Tel 2508-1234 to reserve.

Happy Valley Racecourse,
1 Sports Rd., Happy Valley, tel 2966-7974 for admission badge prices. Races start at 7:30 p.m. on Wednesdays. To get there, take the Happy Valley tram, bus 1M from Admiralty, or taxi.

The Hong Kong Racing Museum is also located here. Closed Mondays.

Sha Tin Race Course, Penfold Park, Sha Tin, New Territories, tel 2695-6223 for admission badge prices. Races start at 2:30 p.m. Saturdays (sometimes Sun.). To get there, take bus 891 from Tsim Sha Tsui Star Ferry Pier, or the MTR East Racecourse station (open only during racing days).

Rugby: Hong Kong Stadium, 55 Eastern Hospital Road, Causeway Bay, tel 2895 7926. The annual Hong Kong Rugby Sevens tournament, part of the World Sevens Series, is the biggest sports event in the city, and during the three-day tournament, rugby fever grips the city. Although tickets sell out months in advance, the carnival atmosphere, with fans from the four corners of the earth, can be soaked up in the bars and pubs of Wan Chai and Lan Kwai Fong.

INDEX

ILLUSTRATIONS CREDITS

Abbreviations for terms appearing below: (t) top; (b) bottom;(c) center; (l) left; (r) right:

Cover, Colin Galloway/drr.net; 2-3, Bob Krist/CORBIS; 4, Catherine Karnow; 8, Charles Walker/Topfoto; 10, Imagestate Media; 12, Hong Kong Tourism Board; 13, Superstock Ltd.; 15, Robert Harding Picture Library; 16, Nigel Hicks; 18-19, Gareth Jones/Getty Images; 20, Nigel Hicks; 22-23, Catherine Karnow; 24-25, Travel Ink/Robin Adshead; 26, Imagestate Media; 29, Hulton Archive; 32-33, Roy Miles Fine Paintings/Bridgeman Art Library, London; 34, Royal Geographical Society; 36, Hulton Archive; 39, AP Photo/ Mike Fiala; 41, Nigel Hicks; 42-43, Robert Harding Picture Library; 45, Robert Harding Picture Library; 47, Jodi Cobb/NGS; 48, David Appleby/Buena Vista/Everett Collection; 51, Chris Stowers/Panos Pictures; 52, Travel Ink/Derek Allan; 54, Robert Harding Picture Library; 56-66 (all photos), Nigel Hicks/AA Photo Library; 68, Robert Harding Picture Library; 69, Nigel Hicks/AA Photo Library; 70, Samantha Sin/AFP/Getty Images; 72, Chris Stowers/Panos Pictures; 74, Robert Harding Picture Library; 77, Nigel Hicks/AA Photo Library; 78, Nigel Hicks; 80, Nigel Hicks/AA Photo Library; 82, Sally and Richard Greenhill; 84, Travel Ink/Derek Allan; 86, Nigel Hicks; 89, Nigel Hicks/AA Photo Library; 90, Art Directors and TRIP Photo Library; 92, Travel Ink/Derek Allan; 93, Art Directors and TRIP Photo Library; 95, Travel Ink/Derek Allan; 96, Nigel Hicks/AA Photo Library; 99, Hong Kong Academy for Performing Arts; 101, Catherine Karnow; 102, Terry Duckham/Asiapix; 104, Art Directors and TRIP Photo Library; 106, Gordon Mills/Alamy; 108, Catherine Karnow; 110, Catherine Karnow; 112, Art Directors and TRIP Photo Library; 113-118 (all), Eye Ubiquitous; 119, Travel Ink/Derek Allan; 123, Art Directors and TRIP Photo Library; 124, Nigel Hicks; 126, Charles Bowman/Robert Harding/drr.net; 129-133 (all), Nigel Hicks/AA Photo Library; 134, Hong Kong Museum of History, Leisure and Cultural Services Dept., HKSAR; 137, Nigel Hicks/AA Photo Library; 138, Jake Wyman/Getty Images; 139, Robert Harding Picture Library; 140, Nigel Hicks; 142, Michael S. Yamashita/NGS; 145, Travel Ink/Mark Reeve; 146, Randall van der Woning; 149, Randall van der Woning; 153, Robert Harding Picture Library; 156, Nigel Hicks; 159, Ron Yue/Alamy; 160, Imagestate Media; 161, Robert Harding Picture Library; 163-170 (all photos), Nigel Hicks; 172, Robert Harding Picture Library; 174, Harry How/Getty Images; 176, Nigel Hicks/AA Photo Library; 178, James Davis/Eye Ubiquitous; 180, Charles Walker/Topfoto; 182, Nigel Hicks; 184, Nigel Hicks/AA Photo Library; 186, Robert Harding Picture Library; 188, China Photo; 190, Michael S. Yamashita/CORBIS; 193, Travel Ink/Derek Allan; 194, Hong Kong Tourism Board; 199, Nigel Hicks; 200, Hong Kong Tourism Board; 201, Robert Harding Picture Library; 202, Catherine Karnow; 204, Nigel Hicks; 206, Ken Hoppen/marinethemes.com; 208, Paul Springett/Alamy; 211, Art Directors and TRIP Photo Library; 212, Travel Ink/Derek Allan; 215, Nigel Hicks; 216, Natalie Behring/drr.net; 218, Peter Adams/acestock.com; 222, Stefan Irvine/OnAsia. com; 226, Imagestate Media; 228, Michael S. Yamashita/CORBIS; 231, Bohemian Nomad Picturemakers/CORBIS; 232, Imagestate Media; 235, Nigel Hicks/AA Photo Library.

National Geographic
TRAVELER
Hong Kong

Published by the National Geographic Society
John M. Fahey, Jr., *President
and Chief Executive Officer*
Gilbert M. Grosvenor, *Chairman of the Board*
Tim T. Kelly, *President, Global Media Group*
John Q. Griffin, *President, Publishing*
Nina D. Hoffman, *Executive Vice President;
President, Book Publishing Group*

Prepared by the Book Division
Kevin Mulroy, *Senior Vice President and Publisher*
Leah Bendavid-Val, *Director of Photography Publishing
and Illustrations*
Marianne R. Koszorus, *Director of Design*
Barbara Brownell Grogan, *Executive Editor*
Elizabeth Newhouse, *Director of Travel Publishing*
Carl Mehler, *Director of Maps*
Barbara A. Noe, *Series Editor*
Cinda Rose, *Series Art Director*

Staff for 2009 Edition
Brooke C. Stoddard, *Project Manager*
Kay Kobor Hankins, *Art Director*
Nicole DiPatrizio, *Designer*
Paula Kelly, *Text Editor*
Steven D. Gardner, Michael McNey,
Nicholas P. Rosenbach, and Mapping Specialists,
Map Research & Production
Al Morrow, *Design Assistant*
Richard Wain, *Production Project Manager*
Sam Corum, Meredith Wilcox, *Illustrations Specialists*
Hunter Braithwaite, Bridget A. English, Jane Sunderland,
Maura Walsh, *Contributors*
Bonnie Hanks, *Indexer*

Jennifer A. Thornton, *Managing Editor*
R. Gary Colbert, *Production Director*

Manufacturing and Quality Management
Christopher A. Liedel, *Chief Financial Officer*
Phillip L. Schlosser, *Vice President*
Chris Brown, *Technical Director*
Nicole Elliott, *Manager*
Monika D. Lynde, *Manager*
Rachel Faulise, *Manager*

**National Geographic Traveler: Hong Kong
(3rd edition)
ISBN: 978-1-4262-0397-8**

First edition: Edited and designed by AA Publishing (a
trading name of Automobile Association Developments
Limited, whose registered office is Norfolk House, Priestley
Road, Basingstoke, Hampshire, England RG24 9NY.
Registered number: 1878835).

Area maps drawn by Chris Orr Associates,
Southampton, England

Illustrations drawn by Maltings Partnership, Derby, England

Founded in 1888, the National Geographic Society is
one of the largest nonprofit scientific and educational
organizations in the world. It reaches more than 285
million people worldwide each month through its
official journal, *National Geographic,* and its four other
magazines; the National Geographic Channel; television documentaries; radio programs; films; books; videos and DVDs; maps; and interactive media. National
Geographic has funded more than 8,000 scientific
research projects and supports an education program
combating geographic illiteracy.

For more information, please call 1-800-NGS LINE
(647-5463) or write to the following address:

National Geographic Society
1145 17th Street N.W.
Washington, D.C. 20036-4688 U.S.A.

Visit us online at www.nationalgeographic.com/books.

For information about special discounts for bulk
purchases, please contact National Geographic
Books Special Sales: ngspecsales@ngs.org.

For rights or permissions inquiries, please contact
National Geographic Books Subsidiary Rights:
ngbookrights@ngs.org.

Printed in Hong Kong

The information in this book has been carefully
checked and to the best of our knowledge is accurate.
However, details are subject to change, and the
National Geographic Society cannot be responsible for
such changes, or for errors or omissions. Assessments
of sites, hotels, and restaurants are based on the
author's subjective opinions, which do not necessarily
reflect the publisher's opinion.

NATIONAL GEOGRAPHIC
TRAVELER

AVAILABLE WHEREVER BOOKS ARE SOLD

Dr Mathai and his wife, Mrs Suja Issac, with
His Holiness The Dalai Lama

Dr Mathai, his mother Dr Annamma Mathai, and
Archbishop Desmond Tutu

Dr Mathai with Sri Sri Ravi Shankar

Dr Deepak Chopra at SOUKYA

Dr Deepak Chopra and Dr Mathai

Dr Mathai with Smt. Mrinalini Sarabhai

*Dr Mallika Sarabhai performing at the Dedication Ceremony
in SOUKYA*

Actor Rajnikanth with Dr Mathai and Mrs Suja Issac
during his stay at SOUKYA

Actor Venkatesh at SOUKYA

Dr Mathai and Mrs Suja Issac with actor Vasundhara Das

*Shri H.D. Deve Gowda, former Prime Minister of India,
at SOUKYA*

Dr Andrew Weil, bestselling author and renowned expert on holistic medicine, during his stay at SOUKYA

Dr Mathai, Mrs Suja Issac, and their three children—Anna, Matthew, and John

The SOUKYA premises

The medical building at SOUKYA